Human, All Too Human I
A Book for Free Spirits

Volume Three

*Based on the edition by
Giorgio Colli & Mazzino Montinari
as adapted by Ernst Behler*

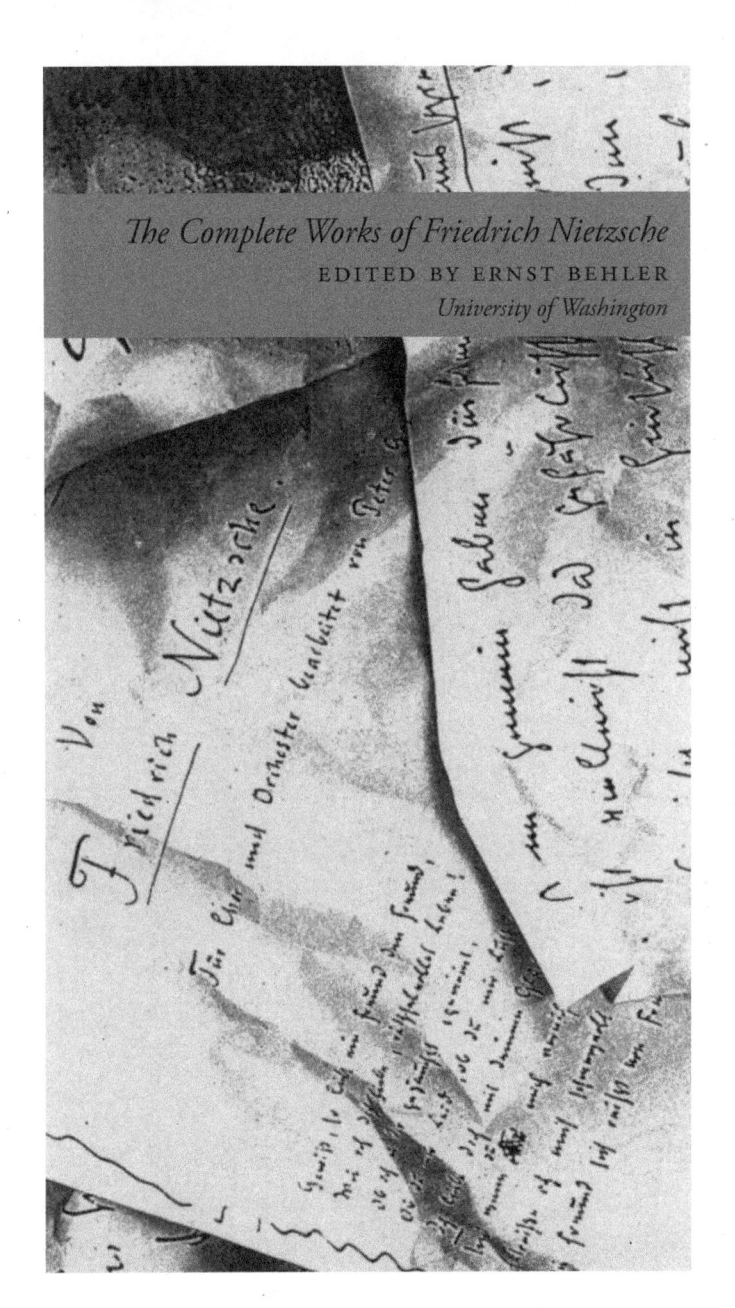

The Complete Works of Friedrich Nietzsche
EDITED BY ERNST BEHLER
University of Washington

Friedrich Nietzsche

Human, All Too Human I

*Translated, with an Afterword,
by Gary Handwerk*

STANFORD UNIVERSITY PRESS

STANFORD, CALIFORNIA

Translated from Friedrich Nietzsche, *Sämtliche Werke, Kritische Studienausgabe*, ed. Giorgio Colli and Mazzino Montinari, in 15 vols. This book corresponds to Vol. 2, pp. 11–363.

Critical edition of Friedrich Nietzsche's *Sämtliche Werke* and unpublished writings based on the original manuscripts. All rights reserved. No part of this publication may be reproduced, stored in a retrieval system, or transmitted in any form or by any means, electronic, mechanical, photocopying, recording, or otherwise, without prior written permission of the Publisher.

© Walter de Gruyter & Co., Berlin and New York, for the
   German Edition
© Adelphi Edizioni, Milan, for the Italian Edition
© Editions Gallimard, Paris, for the French Edition
© Hakusuisha Publishing Comp., Tokyo, for the Japanese Edition
© 1995 by the Board of Trustees of the Leland Stanford Junior
   University for the English edition and associated
   apparatus

Stanford University Press, Stanford, California
Printed in the United States of America

CIP data appear at the end of the book

Contents

A NOTE ON THIS EDITION   ix

Human, All Too Human I

	Preface	5
1	Of the First and Last Things	15
2	On the History of the Moral Sensations	43
3	The Religious Life	85
4	From the Souls of Artists and Writers	114
5	Signs of Higher and Lower Culture	153
6	In Relations with Others	197
7	Woman and Child	219
8	A Glance at the State	236
9	By Oneself Alone	264
	Among Friends: An Epilogue	305

Reference Matter

NOTES 309

TRANSLATOR'S AFTERWORD 361

INDEX OF PERSONS 381

A Note on This Edition

This is the first English translation of all of Nietzsche's writings, including his unpublished fragments, with annotation, afterwords concerning the individual texts, and indexes, in 20 volumes. The aim of this collaborative work is to produce a critical edition for scholarly use. Volume 1 also includes an introduction to the entire edition. While the goal is to establish a readable text in contemporary English, the translation follows the original as closely as possible. All texts have been translated anew by a group of scholars, and particular attention has been given to maintaining a consistent terminology throughout the volumes. The translation is based on *Friedrich Nietzsche: Sämtliche Werke. Kritische Studienausgabe in 15 Bänden* (1980), edited by Giorgio Colli and Mazzino Montinari. The still-progressing *Kritische Gesamtausgabe der Werke*, which Colli and Montinari began in 1963, has also been consulted. The Colli-Montinari edition is of particular importance for the unpublished fragments, comprising more than half of Nietzsche's writings and published there for the first time in their entirety. Besides listing textual variants, the annotation to this English edition provides succinct information on the text and identifies events, names (except those in the Index of Names), titles, quotes, and biographical facts of Nietzsche's own life. The notes do not have numbers in the text but are keyed by line and phrase. The Afterword presents the main facts about the origin of the text, the stages of its composition, and the main events of its reception. The Index of Names includes mythological figures and lists the dates of birth and death as well as prominent personal characteristics.

ERNST BEHLER

Human, All Too Human I
A Book for Free Spirits

This monological book, which came into being during a winter residence in Sorrento (1876 to 1877), would not have been given to the public at this time if the proximity of the 30th of May 1878 had not aroused all too intensely the wish to offer a timely personal tribute to the greatest liberator of the human spirit.

In Place of a Preface

—I decided to review the various occupations that people have in this life, trying to choose the best among them; and without wishing to say anything about those of others, I thought that I could not do better than to continue in the same one in which I found myself, that is to say, to employ my entire life in cultivating my reason and to advance myself as far as I could in the knowledge of the truth, following the Method that I had prescribed to myself. I had felt such deep contentment since having begun to use this Method that I did not believe that anyone could obtain anything sweeter or more innocent in this life; and discovering every day by means of it truths that seemed to me of some importance and of which other people were generally unaware, the satisfaction that I felt filled my mind so fully that nothing else affected me at all.

[1878 EDITION]

Preface

I

It has often enough been said to me, always with great astonishment, that there is something common to and distinctive about all my writings, from *The Birth of Tragedy* through the most recently published one, *Prelude to a Philosophy of the Future*: people have told me that all of them contain snares and nets for unwary birds and an almost constant, yet often unnoticed invitation to overturn our habitual valuations and valued habits. What? *Everything* only—human, all too human? With this sigh, they emerge from my writings, not without a sort of aversion and mistrust even toward morality, indeed sorely tempted and encouraged to make themselves for once advocates of the very worst things: as if they had perhaps only been the most effectually slandered things? My writings have been called a school for suspicion, or even for contempt, but happily, for courage as well, and even for audacity. In fact, I do not myself believe that anyone has ever looked into the world with as deep a suspicion, not only as an occasional devil's advocate, but every bit as much, theologically speaking, as an enemy and challenger of God: and anyone who can guess something of the consequences that lie within every deep suspicion, something of the frosts and fears in the isolation to which every unconditional *difference in views* condemns the one afflicted with it, will also understand how often I sought shelter somewhere to recuperate from myself, as if to forget myself temporarily—in any sort of reverence or enmity or scientism or frivolity or stupidity;

and also why, where I did not find what I *needed*, I had to artificially compel it to appear to me, quite rightly had to forge and to invent it (—and when have poets ever done otherwise? and why else would all the art in the world exist?). But time after time, what I needed most for my cure and self-restoration was the belief that I was *not* the only person made this way, the only one who *saw* things this way—a magical, yet mistrustful intimation of someone else's kinship and likeness in seeing and desiring, a repose within the trust of friendship, a mutual blindness without suspicion and question mark, a pleasure in foregrounds, surfaces, in what is close or closest at hand, in all that has color, skin, and plausibility. In this regard, I could perhaps be charged with having relied upon certain varieties of "art," with having engaged in certain finer kinds of counterfeiting: for example, that I knowingly and willingly closed my eyes to Schopenhauer's blind will to morality at a time when I was already clear-sighted enough about morality; likewise, that I deceived myself about Richard Wagner's incurable Romanticism, as if it were a beginning and not an end; likewise about the Greeks, likewise about the Germans and their future—and might there be a whole long list of such likewises?—yet given that all this were true and could with good reason be charged against me, what do *you* know, what *could* you know about how much cunning in self-preservation, how much reason and higher watchfulness is contained in such self-deception—and how much falsehood I still *require* if I am to continue to allow myself the luxury of *my* truthfulness? . . . Enough, I am still alive; and life has after all not been devised by morality: it *wants* delusion, it *lives* upon delusion . . . but there it is, isn't it? Aren't I already beginning over again and doing what I have always done, old immoralist and bird-catcher that I am—and speaking immorally, extramorally, "beyond good and evil"?—

2

—And so at one time, when I needed to do so, I *invented* for myself the "free spirits" to whom this heavy-hearted, high-spirited book with the title *Human, All Too Human* is dedicated: such "free spirits" do not and did not exist—but at that time I needed their companionship, as I have said, in order to remain in good spirits amid terrible things (sickness, isolation, foreignness, *acedia*, inactivity): as brave companions and ghosts with whom one might chatter and laugh when one wants to chatter and laugh, and whom one can send to the Devil when they become boring—as compensation for a lack of friends. That such free spirits *could* someday exist, that our Europe will have this sort of lively and audacious companion among the sons of its tomorrows, physically and tangibly present, and not only, as in my case, phantoms and a hermit's shadow play: *I* would be the very last person to doubt this. I see them *coming* already, slowly, slowly; and am I perhaps doing something to hasten their coming if I describe in advance the destinies from which I see them arising, the paths on which I see them coming?—

3

One might suppose that the decisive event for a spirit in whom the type "free spirit" is someday to reach a perfect ripeness and sweetness will be a *great liberation*, and that it will previously have been all the more firmly bound and have seemed forever fettered to its corner and column. What binds most securely? what cords are nearly impossible to tear? For human beings of a high and select kind, it will be their duties: that reverence appropriate for youth, that shyness and gentleness in the presence of everything long-venerated and worthy, that gratitude toward the soil from which they grew, toward the hand that led them, toward the holy place where they learned to worship—their highest moments will themselves bind them most securely, obligate them most enduringly. The great liberation for people bound to this extent comes suddenly, like an earthquake: all at once the youthful soul is deeply shaken, torn loose, torn from its place—it does not itself understand what is happening. An impulse and a pressure rule it and master it as if by command; a will and a wish awaken to depart at any cost for somewhere else; an intense, dangerous curiosity about an undisclosed world flames and flickers in all its senses. "Better to die than to live *here*"—thus the imperious voice and temptation rings out: and this "here," this "feeling of being at home" is all that up until now it had loved! A sudden fear and suspicion of what it has loved, a flash of contempt for what was termed its "duty," a rebellious, capricious, volcanically thrusting desire for travel, foreign lands, alienation, coldness, sobriety, freezing, a hatred for love, perhaps a desecrating groping and glancing *behind* at what it has up to now worshipped and loved, perhaps a burning shame at what it has just done, and an exultation as well at *having* done so, a drunken, inner, exultant trembling that betrays that a victory has been won—a victory? over what? over whom? an enigmatic, equivocal, questionable victory, but the *first* victory nonetheless—such awful and painful things are part of the history of the great liberation. It is a sickness as well, which can destroy someone, this first outbreak of strength and of a will to self-determination, to establishing one's own values, this will to *free* will: and how much sickness expresses itself in the wild experiments and peculiar behaviors by which the freed one, the liberated one, henceforth seeks to demonstrate his mastery over things! He roams around ferociously, with an unsatisfied lust; whatever he captures must atone for the dangerous tension of his pride; he tears apart whatever attracts him. With an evil laugh he turns around anything that he finds concealed or protected by some sort of shame: he investigates how these things appear *if* one turns them around. It is willfulness and a pleasure in willfulness if he perhaps directs his favor toward what has up to now had a bad reputation—if he curiously and inquisitively prowls around what is most forbidden. Behind his activity and roaming—for he is on the move restlessly and aimlessly, as if in a desert—stands the question mark of an ever more dangerous curiosity. "Can we not reverse *all* values? and is good perhaps evil? and God only an invention and a subtle ploy of the Devil? Is everything perhaps at bottom false? And if we are deceived, are we not thereby also deceivers? *must* we not also be deceivers?"—such thoughts lead him on and lead him astray, ever farther off, ever farther away. Solitude surrounds and encircles him, ever more threatening, suffocating, heart-constricting, that fearful goddess and *mater saeva cupidinum*—but who today knows what *solitude* is?...

4

From this sickly isolation, from the desert of such years of trial, it is still a long way to the tremendous, overflowing certainty and health that cannot dispense even with sickness as a means and a hook for knowledge, to the *ripened* freedom of spirit that is just as much self-mastery and discipline of the heart and that permits one to take the paths of many varied and opposed ways of thinking—to the inner comprehensiveness and pampered overabundance that exclude the danger that the spirit may somehow lose itself, even upon its own paths, fall in love with them, and remain sitting, intoxicated, somewhere in a corner, to the excess of plastic, healing, imitating, and restoring forces that is the sign of *great* health, the excess that gives to the free spirit the dangerous privilege of living *for experiments* and of being allowed to offer itself to adventure: the master privilege of the free spirit! Long years of convalescence may lie in between, years full of many-hued, painfully magical transformations, controlled and bridled by a stubborn *will to health* that often presumes to take on prematurely the guise or disguise of health. There is a middle state along the way, which someone destined to such a fate cannot recall later without emotion: a pale, subtle light and a sunny happiness are his, a feeling of birdlike freedom, birdlike vision, birdlike exuberance, some third thing in which curiosity and a gentle contempt are united. A "free spirit"—this cool word does one good in that state; it practically warms one up. One lives without being any longer in the fetters of love and hate, without Yes, without No, near or far off by one's own will, preferably slipping away, evading, fluttering off, flying once again upward and away; one is spoiled like anyone who has ever seen a tremendous abundance of things *beneath* him—and one becomes the opposite of those who concern themselves with things that have nothing to do with them. In fact, the free spirit henceforth has to do only with things—and how many things!—that no longer *concern* him...

5

One step further in convalescence: and the free spirit again draws near to life, slowly, to be sure, almost reluctantly, almost mistrustfully. Once again it grows warmer around him, yellower, as it were; feeling and sympathy take on depth, all sorts of thawing winds pass over him. It almost seems to him as if, now for the first time, his eyes were opening upon what lies *near at hand*. He is astonished and sits quietly: where *had* he been? These near and nearest things: how they seem to him to be transformed! what downy texture and magical air they have acquired in the meantime! He glances gratefully backward—grateful for his travels, for his hardness and self-alienation, for his far-reaching vision and birdlike flights upon the cold heights. How good it is that he did not always remain "at home," always "in his own place," like a delicate, stupefied loafer! He has been *beside* himself: there is no doubt of it. Now for the first time he sees himself—and what surprises he finds there! What unprecedented shuddering! What happiness even in the fatigue, the old sickness, the relapses of convalescence. How it pleases him to sit passive and still, to spin out his patience, to lie in the sun! Who understands as he does the happiness of winter or the flecks of sunlight upon the wall! They are the most grateful animals in the world and also the most modest, these convalescents and lizards who have once again turned halfway toward life—there are those among them who do not let a single day pass without hanging a small song of praise on the hem it trails behind. And said in all seriousness: it is a thorough *cure* for all pessimism (the cancerous ill of old idealists and habitual liars, as we know) to become sick as these free spirits do, to remain sick for a good while and then over a longer and longer time to become healthy, by which I mean "healthier." There is wisdom in this, the wisdom of life, in prescribing even health to oneself for a long time only in small doses.

6

At that time, under the sudden illumination caused by a still tumultuous, still variable healthiness, it may happen that the riddle of that great liberation begins to unveil itself to the free, ever freer spirit, a riddle that up until then had been waiting in his memory, dark, questionable, almost untouchable. If for a long time he hardly dared to ask "why so apart? so alone? renouncing all that I once revered? renouncing reverence itself? why this hardness, this suspicion, this hatred for my own virtues?"—now he dares to ask it aloud and even hears something of an answer. "You must become master of yourself and master of your own virtues as well. Previously they were your masters; but they should simply be tools among your other tools. You must acquire power over your For and Against and learn how to take them out and hang them back up according to your higher aim. You must learn how to grasp the perspectival element in every valuation—the displacement, distortion, and seeming teleology of horizons and everything else that pertains to perspectivism; and also how much stupidity there is in opposed values and the whole intellectual loss that must be paid for every For, every Against. You must learn to grasp the *necessary* injustice in every For and Against, injustice as inseparable from life, life itself as *conditioned* by perspective and its injustice. Above all, you must see with your own eyes where injustice is always the greatest: namely, where life has developed in the smallest, narrowest, neediest, most preliminary ways and yet still cannot avoid taking *itself* as the purpose and measure of things and, out of love for its own preservation, secretly and meanly and ceaselessly crumbling away and putting into question all that is higher, greater, richer—you must see with your own eyes the problem of establishing *rank orderings* and how power and right and comprehensiveness of perspective grow up into the heights together. You must"—enough, the free spirit *knows* by now which "you must" he has obeyed and also what he now *can* do, what he now for the first time—*is permitted* to do...

7

In this way, the free spirit gives himself an answer concerning that riddle of liberation and ends by generalizing his own case and thus reaching a decision about his own experience. "What I went through, he tells himself, must be gone through by everyone in whom there is a *task* that wants to be embodied and 'to come into the world.'" The secret power and necessity of this task will rule among and in his particular destinies like an unconscious pregnancy—long before he himself has glimpsed this task and knows its name. Our destined vocation disposes of us, even when we do not yet know it; it is the future that regulates our today. Given that it is *the problem of rank ordering* that we can call *our* problem, we free spirits: only now, at the midday of our lives, do we understand how many preparations, detours, trials, temptations, disguises the problem required before it *was permitted* to rise up before us, and how we first had to experience the most varied and contradictory states of distress and happiness in our souls and bodies, as the adventurers and circumnavigators of that inner world called "man," as the surveyors of every "higher" and "one above the other" that is likewise called "man"—forcing our way in everywhere, almost without fear, despising nothing, losing nothing, savoring everything, purifying everything of its accidental elements and sifting it, as it were—until we are at last permitted to say, we free spirits: "Here—a *new* problem! Here, a long ladder on whose rungs we ourselves have sat and have climbed—which we ourselves *were* at one time! Here lies something higher, deeper, something beneath us, a tremendously long ordering, a rank ordering that we *see*: here—*our* problem!"—

8

—Not for a moment will it remain concealed from any psychologist and soothsayer where the present book belongs (or has been *placed*) in the development just portrayed. But where are there psychologists today? In France, to be sure; perhaps in Russia; certainly not in Germany. There is no lack of reasons for why present-day Germans could take this to be to their credit: bad enough for someone who is in this point German neither by nature nor by tendency! This *German* book has known how to find its readers among a wide circle of countries and peoples—it has been on its way for about ten years—and must know how to perform some sort of music and flute playing that can tempt shy foreign ears to listen—yet it is precisely in Germany that this book has been read most carelessly and *heard* most badly: why is this so?—"It is too demanding," I have heard, "it addresses itself to people who are not overly pressed by coarse obligations, it calls for subtle and indulged senses, it requires excess, an excess of time, of clarity in the heavens and in the heart, of *otium* in the most audacious sense—nothing except those good things that we Germans of today do not have and therefore cannot give either."—After so courteous a response, my philosophy advises me to keep silent and not to ask any more; especially since in certain cases, as the proverb suggests, we only *remain* philosophers by—keeping silent.

NICE, SPRING 1886

Chapter 1

Of the First and Last Things

1

Chemistry of concepts and sensations.—At almost every point, philosophical problems are once again assuming the same form for their questions as they did two thousand years ago: how can something arise from its opposite, for example something rational from something irrational, something sentient from something dead, logic from illogic, disinterested contemplation from willful desire, living for others from egoism, truth from error? Metaphysical philosophy has up to now helped itself get past this difficulty by denying that one emerged from the other and assuming that more highly valued things had a miraculous origin, immediately out of the core and essence of the "thing in itself." Historical philosophy, by contrast, which can no longer be thought of as separate from natural science, the youngest of all philosophical methods, has ascertained in individual cases (and this will presumably be its result in every case) that there are no opposites, except in the habitual exaggeration of popular or metaphysical views, and that an error in reasoning lies at the base of such oppositions: according to its explanation, there are, strictly speaking, neither any unegoistical actions nor any completely disinterested contemplation; both are only sublimations, in which the fundamental element appears to have almost evaporated and reveals its presence only to the keenest observation.—All that we need, and what can be given to us only now, at the present level of the individual sciences, is a *chemistry* of the moral, religious, aesthetic representations and sensations, likewise of all those stimuli that we experience within ourselves amid the wholesale and retail transactions of culture and society, indeed even in solitude: what if this chemistry were to reach the conclusion that in this area, too, the most magnificent colors have been extracted from base, even despised materials? Will many people have the desire to pursue such investigations? Humanity loves to put from its mind questions concerning origins and beginnings: wouldn't we have to be almost dehumanized to find in ourselves traces of the opposite inclination?

2

Original failing of philosophers. — All philosophers have the common failing that they start with present-day human beings and suppose that they will reach their goal by analyzing them. Involuntarily, they allow "man" to hover before their eyes as an *aeterna veritas*, something that remains the same through all turmoil, a secure measure for things. All that the philosopher asserts about humanity, however, is basically nothing more than testimony about the human being of a *very restricted* stretch of time. A lack of historical sensibility is the original failing of all philosophers; many even inadvertently take the most recent shape of human beings, as it emerged under the imprint of specific religious or even specific political events, as the fixed form from which we must proceed. They do not want to learn that humanity has come to be, that even the faculty of cognition has also come to be, while some of them even allow themselves to spin the whole world out of this cognitive faculty. — Now, everything *essential* in human development occurred during primeval times, long before those four thousand years with which we are more or less acquainted; during these years, humanity may well not have changed much more. But the philosopher sees "instincts" in present-day humanity and assumes that these belong to the unchangeable facts of humanity and can therefore provide a key to understanding the world generally; all teleology is built upon speaking of the human being of the last four millennia as something *eternal*, toward which all the things of the world have from their beginning naturally been directed. Everything, however, has come to be; there are *no eternal facts*: just as there are no absolute truths. — From now on therefore, *historical philosophizing* will be necessary, and along with it the virtue of modesty.

3

Estimation of unpretentious truths. — It is the characteristic sign of a higher culture to esteem the small, unpretentious truths found by rigorous methods more highly than the blissful and blinding errors that stem from metaphysical and artistic ages and human beings. At first, people have scorn for the former upon their lips, as though nothing could stand with equal justification against the latter: so modest, simple, sober, apparently even discouraging do the ones stand here, so beautiful, splendid, intoxicating, perhaps even enrapturing do the others stand there. But what has been laboriously acquired, what is certain, enduring, and hence rich in consequences for all further knowledge, is nonetheless something higher; to hold on to it is manly and shows valor, simplicity, temperance. Not only the individual, but all humanity will gradually be raised up to this manliness, when it has finally grown accustomed to esteeming lasting, durable knowledge more highly and has lost all belief in inspiration and the miraculous communication of truths. — Those who worship *forms*, with their measuring stick for the beautiful and the sublime, will admittedly have good reason at first for mocking as the esteem for unpretentious truths and the scientific spirit begin to gain mastery, but only because their eyes have not yet unlocked the charm of the *simplest* form or because people raised in that spirit will for a long time not be fully and inwardly penetrated by it, so that they will still thoughtlessly imitate old forms (and badly besides, like someone who no longer places much importance on it). Formerly the spirit was not under the obligation of thinking rigorously; its earnestness lay in spinning out symbols and forms. That has changed; that earnestness in regard to the symbolic has become a sign of lower culture; as our arts themselves become ever more intellectual, our senses ever more spiritual, and as we now judge what sounds pleasing to our ears quite differently than a hundred years ago, for example, so do the forms of our lives become ever more *spiritual*, though perhaps more *hideous* to the eye of older times, but only because it is unable to see how the realm of inner, spiritual beauty is continually being deepened and widened, and how for all of us a spirited glance can be worth more than the most beautiful structure or the most sublime construction.

4

Astrology and related things.—It is probable that the objects of religious, moral, and aesthetic sensibility likewise belong only to the surface of things, whereas people like to believe that here at least they touch the heart of world; they deceive themselves because those things so deeply enrapture them and make them so deeply unhappy, and they therefore show the same pride here as is the case in astrology. For it believes that the starry heaven revolves around the fate of human beings; the moral person, however, presupposes that whatever lies closest to his heart must also be the essence and heart of things.

5

Misunderstanding of dreams.—In the ages of raw, primordial culture, people believed that in dreams they came to know a *second real world*; here is the origin of all metaphysics. Without dreams, there would have been no reason to divide the world. The separation into soul and body is also connected to the oldest view of dreams, just like the assumption that the soul can appear in bodily form, hence the origin of all belief in ghosts, and probably also the belief in gods. "The dead live on; for they appear to the living in dreams": that was the conclusion one previously drew, throughout many millennia.

6

The spirit of science powerful in the part, not in the whole. — The discrete, *smallest* areas of science are dealt with purely objectively: by contrast, the large, general sciences considered as a whole lead us to pose the question — a quite subjective question, admittedly — what for? where is the utility? Because of this regard for utility, they are dealt with less impersonally as a whole than in their parts. Now in philosophy, as the summit of the whole pyramid of knowledge, the question whether knowledge has any utility at all is automatically raised, and every philosophy unconsciously has the intention of ascribing the *highest* utility to it. Hence there is in all philosophies so much high-flying metaphysics and such dread for the seemingly insignificant solutions of physics; for the significance of knowledge for life *ought* to seem as great as possible. Here lies the antagonism between the individual fields of science and philosophy. The latter wants what art wants, to give to life and action as much depth and meaning as possible; in the former one seeks knowledge and nothing further — whatever may come of it. Up to now there has not been any philosopher in whose hands philosophy has not become an apology for knowledge; in this point, at least, everyone is an optimist, that the highest usefulness must be ascribed to knowledge. They are all tyrannized by logic: and logic is in essence optimism.

7

The disturber of peace in science. — Philosophy divided itself from science when it posed the question: what is that knowledge of the world and of life by which human beings will live most happily? This occurred in the Socratic schools: by keeping their eye upon *happiness*, they tied up the veins of scientific inquiry — and do so to this day.

8

Pneumatic explanation of nature. — Metaphysics explains the script of nature *pneumatically*, as it were, just as the church and its scholars formerly did with the Bible. It requires a great deal of understanding to apply the same sort of more rigorous exegesis to nature that philologists have created for all books: with the intention of simply understanding what the writing means to say, not to scent or in fact to presuppose a *double* meaning. But just as bad exegesis has by no means been fully overcome, even in regard to books, and we still continually stumble upon the leftover traces of allegorical and mystical interpretation in the best-educated society, so it stands in regard to nature — or even far worse.

9

Metaphysical world. — It is true, there could be a metaphysical world; the absolute possibility of it can hardly be contested. We see all things through the human head and cannot cut this head off; and yet the question remains as to what part of the world would still be there if one had in fact cut it off. This is a purely scientific problem and not really a proper concern for human beings; but what has up to now made metaphysical assumptions *valuable, terrible, pleasurable* for them, what engendered such assumptions, is passion, error, and self-deception; the worst of all methods of knowledge, not the best of all, have taught us to believe in them. When we have revealed these methods to be the foundation of all existing religions and metaphysics, we have refuted them. That other possibility still remains, but we cannot even begin to do anything with it, much less to allow happiness, salvation, and life to hang from the spider threads of such a possibility. — For we could assert nothing at all about the metaphysical world except its otherness, an otherness inaccessible to and inconceivable for us; it would be a thing with negative characteristics. — Even if the existence of such a world were to be proven ever so well, any knowledge of it would certainly still be the most irrelevant of all knowledge: even more irrelevant than knowledge of the chemical composition of water must be to a sailor endangered by storm.

10

Harmlessness of metaphysics in the future. — As soon as religion, art, and morality are described in terms of their emergence, so that we can fully explain them to ourselves without taking refuge in the assumption of *metaphysical interventions* at the beginning and in the course of the process, our strongest interest in the purely theoretical problem of the "thing in itself" and "appearance" ceases. For however it may be: with religion, art, and morality we do not get in touch with the "essence of the world in itself"; we are in the realm of representation, no "premonition" can take us further. With complete tranquility we will leave to physiology and the developmental history of organisms and concepts the question of how our image of the world could differ so much from the disclosed essence of the world.

11

Language as a supposed science. — The significance of language for the development of culture lies in the fact that human beings used it to set up a world of their own beside the other one, a place they deemed solid enough that from there they could lift the rest of world from its hinges and make themselves its master. Insofar as people believed for long stretches of time in the concepts for and names of things as if they were *aeternae veritates*, they appropriated for themselves the pride with which they raised themselves above the animals: they really believed that in language they had knowledge of the world. The shapers of language were not so modest as to believe that they only gave designations to things, but fancied instead that they expressed with words the highest knowledge about things; language is in fact the first step of the struggle for science. Here, too, it is *the belief in having found truth* from which the most powerful sources of energy flowed. Long afterward—only just now—is it dawning on people that they have propagated a colossal error with their belief in language. Luckily, it is too late for the development of reason, which rests upon that belief, to be reversed.—*Logic* also rests upon presuppositions to which nothing in the real world corresponds; for example, upon the presupposition of the likeness of things, of the identity of the same thing at different points of time: but this science arose out of the opposite belief (that such things do indeed obtain in the real world). It is the same in *mathematics*, which certainly would not have come into being if one had known that there was in nature no exactly straight line, no real circle, no absolute magnitude.

12

Dreams and culture.—The brain function most impaired by sleep is memory: not that it completely pauses—but it is returned to a state of imperfection, as may have been the case for everyone in the primeval times of humanity, even during the day and while awake. Capricious and confused as it is, it continually mistakes things on the basis of the most fleeting similarities: but with the same caprice and confusion peoples composed their mythologies, and even now travelers typically observe how much the savage inclines to forgetfulness, how his mind begins to stagger this way and that after a short exertion of memory, and he produces lies and nonsense simply due to enervation. But in dreaming we all resemble this savage; failing to recognize things and erroneously equating them are the reasons for the bad inferences that we are guilty of making in dreams: so that whenever we call a dream clearly to mind, we frighten ourselves, because so much folly lies hidden within us.—The perfect clarity of all dream representations, which presupposes an unconditional belief in their reality, reminds us again of the conditions of an earlier humanity, in whom hallucination was exceptionally frequent and sometimes seized upon whole communities, whole peoples at the same time. Therefore: in sleep and dreams we go through the lessons of earlier humanity once again.

13

Logic of dreams.—While we sleep, our nervous system is in a continual state of excitation from multiple inner causes, almost all the organs are secreting and active, the blood circulates tumultuously, the position of the sleeper presses against individual limbs, his bedcovers influence sensation in various ways, the stomach is digesting and unsettles other organs with its movements, the intestines twist themselves around, the position of the head occasions unusual muscular positions, the feet, unshod, without their soles being pressed upon the ground, cause an unfamiliar feeling, as does the different way that the whole body is clothed—all of this through its daily changes and degrees arouses the entire system by being out of the ordinary, reaching even into the functioning of the brain: and so there are a hundred causes for the mind to be astonished and to search for reasons for this excitation: but dreams are the *searching for and representing of the causes* for those aroused sensations, that is, for the supposed causes. For example, anyone who was to bind his feet with two straps might well dream that two snakes are encircling his feet: this is at first a hypothesis, then a belief with an accompanying pictorial representation and elaboration: "these snakes must be the *causa* of the sensation that I, the sleeper, have"—so judges the mind of the sleeper. The immediate past thus inferred becomes present to him by means of the aroused fantasy. Thus, everyone knows from experience how quickly the dreamer weaves into his dream any strongly intrusive sound, for example bells ringing or cannon firing, that is, how he derives an explanation for it *afterward*, so that he *thinks* he experiences the instigating circumstances first, then the sound.—But how does it come about that the mind of the dreamer always guesses wrong, while the same mind when awake tends to be so sober, so careful, and so skeptical in regard to hypotheses? so that the first available hypothesis for explaining a feeling suffices for him to immediately believe in its truth? (for we believe in the dream while dreaming, as if it were reality, that is, we take our hypothesis as fully proven). — In my opinion: just as even today people draw conclusions while dreaming, so for many millennia, humanity drew conclusions *while awake*: the first *causa* that occurred to the spirit explaining anything that needed explanation was sufficient for it and counted as the truth. (According to the tales of travelers, primitive people still behave the same today.) While we are dreaming, this primeval piece of humanity continues to exercise itself in us, for it is the foundation upon which a higher reason was developed and is still developing in every human being: dreams take us back to the distant circumstances of human culture and give us the means for understanding them better. Dream thinking is now so easy for us because during enormous stretches of human development, we have been so thoroughly drilled in precisely this form of fantastic and cut-rate explanation by whatever idea happens to occur to us first. Dreams are therefore recuperation for a brain that during the day has to satisfy the strict demands of thinking, as they have been established by higher culture. — We can directly observe a related process even while our understanding is awake, one that might be considered the gateway and vestibule of dreams. If we close our eyes, the brain produces a host of impressions of lights and colors, probably as a sort of playful afterimage and echo of all those effects of light that press upon it during the day. But the understanding (in combination with the imagination) immediately reworks this play of colors, in itself formless, into distinct figures, forms, landscapes, animated groups. The actual process involved is once again a sort of conclusion from the effect to the cause; by asking where these impressions of light and color come from, the mind presumes that those figures and forms are causes: it considers them as giving rise to those colors and lights, because by day, with eyes open, it is used to finding an instigating cause for every color, every impression of light. Thus, the imagination is continually thrusting images upon the mind by imitating the way that visual impressions are produced during the day, and the dream imagination does precisely the same thing—that is, the ostensible cause is deduced from the effect and conceived *after* the effect: all this occurs with extraordinary rapidity, so that judgment gets confused, just as it might in watching a magician, and something successive can appear to be simultaneous, or even to occur in a reverse order.—We can infer from these processes *how late* a stricter logical thought, a more rigorous perception of cause and effect, came to be developed when *even now* our functions of reason and understanding involuntarily reach back to those primitive forms of deduction and we live roughly half our lives in that state.—The poet and the artist also *foist* causes upon their moods and mental states that are simply not the true ones; to that extent, they remind us of an older humanity and can help us to understand it.

14

Resonances.—All *stronger* moods bring along with them a resonance of related sensations and moods; they churn up our memory, as it were. They bring something to mind, making us conscious of similar states and their origins. In this way habitual, rapid associations of feelings and thoughts are formed, which finally, when they follow after one another with lightning speed, are no longer even sensed as complexes, but rather as *unities*. In this sense, we speak of moral feelings, of religious feelings, as if these were nothing but unities: in truth, they are streams with a hundred sources and tributaries. Here, too, as so often, the unity of the word guarantees nothing about the unity of the thing.

15

No inside and outside in the world.—As Democritus extended the concepts above and below to infinite space, where they do not make any sense, so philosophers in general have extended the concept "inside and outside" to the essence and appearance of the world; they think that with deep feelings we enter deeply into what is within, that we draw near to the heart of nature. But these feelings are profound only insofar as, almost unnoticeably, certain complicated groups of ideas that we call profound are regularly aroused along with them; a feeling is profound because we take the accompanying thought for profound. But a profound thought can nevertheless be very far from the truth, as is for example every metaphysical one; if we subtract from the profound feeling the intermingled elements of thought, what remains is the *strength* of feeling, and this guarantees nothing with respect to knowledge except its own strength, just as a strong belief demonstrates only its strength, not the truth of what is believed.

16

Appearance and thing in itself. — Philosophers are given to placing themselves in front of life and experience — in front of what they call the world of appearance — as in front of a painting that has been unrolled once and for all and shows the same incidents unalterably fixed: they think that one has to interpret these incidents correctly in order to draw any conclusion about the entity that produced the painting and therefore about the thing in itself, which tends always to be regarded as the sufficient reason for the world of appearance. More rigorous logicians, by contrast, after they have rigorously established the concept of the metaphysical as what is unconditioned, hence also unconditioning, have denied every connection between the unconditioned (the metaphysical world) and the world known to us: so that in the actual appearance the thing in itself does *not* appear at all, and any conclusion about the latter drawn from the former is to be rejected. Both sides, however, have overlooked the possibility that the painting — what we human beings now call life and experience — has gradually *come to be*, indeed, is still wholly *becoming*, and therefore should not be considered as a fixed quantity from which we are allowed to draw or even simply to reject any conclusion about the creator (the sufficient reason). Because we have for millennia looked upon the world with moral, aesthetic, and religious demands, with blind inclination, passion, or fear, and have actually reveled in the bad habits of illogical thinking, this world has gradually *become* so wonderfully bright, terrible, profoundly meaningful, soulful, and has taken on color—but we have been the colorists: the human intellect has made appearances appear and carried its erroneous views over into things. Late, very late—it comes to its senses: and now the world of experience and the thing in itself seem to it so extraordinarily different and separate that it rejects drawing any conclusions about the latter from the former—or else in a terribly mysterious way demands that we *surrender* our intellect, our personal will: in order to *thereby* come to what is essential, that we *become something essential*. On the other hand, others have gathered together all the characteristic traits of our world of appearance—that is, of the representation of the world that has been spun out of intellectual errors and handed down to us—and *instead of indicting the intellect as the guilty party*, have accused the essence of things of being the cause of the extremely uncanny character that the world actually has and have preached salvation from being. The steady and laborious process of science, which will someday finally celebrate its highest triumph in a *genetic history of thought*, will make an end of all these conceptions in a decisive way, and its result might perhaps wind up with this sentence: What we now call the world is the result of a host of errors and fantasies, which emerged gradually during the overall development of organic beings, merged together as they grew, and are now passed on to us as the accumulated treasure of the entire past— as treasure: for the *value* of our humanity rests upon it. Rigorous science can really free us only to a small extent from this world of representation—which would not be all that desirable, anyway—insofar as it essentially cannot break the force of age-old habits of sensation: but it can quite gradually, step by step, elucidate the history of the genesis of that world as representation—and lift us at least momentarily above the whole process. Perhaps then we will recognize that the thing in itself is worth a Homeric laugh: that it *appeared* to be so much, in fact everything, and is actually empty, namely, empty of meaning.

17

Metaphysical explanations.—A young person esteems metaphysical explanations because they point out to him something highly meaningful in things that he found unpleasant or contemptible: and if he is dissatisfied with himself, this feeling is relieved if he recognizes the innermost riddle or misery of the world in what he disapproved of so much in itself. To feel oneself more irresponsible and at the same time to find things more interesting—that counts for him as the double benefit that he owes to metaphysics. Admittedly, he will later acquire mistrust for the whole metaphysical way of explaining things, and then he will perhaps perceive that those results can be reached just as well and as scientifically in a different way: that physical and historical explanations induce at least as much of a feeling of irresponsibility, and that the interest in life and its problems is perhaps kindled even more strongly in this way.

18

Basic questions of metaphysics.—When someday the genetic history of thinking has been written, the following sentence of a distinguished logician will stand illuminated in a new light: "The original, general law of the knowing subject consists in the inner necessity of apprehending every object in itself, in its own essence, as something identical with itself, therefore self-existent and always remaining basically the same and unalterable, in short, as a substance." This law, too, that is here called "original," has come to be: it will some day be shown how this propensity gradually emerges in lower organisms, how the weak-sighted mole eyes of these organized entities at first see nothing except the same thing all the time, then how, when the various stimuli of pleasure and displeasure become more noticeable, various substances are gradually differentiated, but each with *one* attribute, that is, a single relationship to this organism. —The first step of logic is judgment, whose essence consists, according to the determination of the best logicians, in belief. At the base of all belief lies the *sensation of pleasure or pain* with respect to the subject experiencing the sensation. A new, third sensation as the result of two prior, single sensations is judgment in its lowest form. —Nothing originally interests us organic beings about anything except its relationship to us with respect to pleasure and pain. Between the moments in which we become conscious of this relation, the states of sensation, lie those of peace, of nonsensation: then the world and everything are without interest for us, we notice no change in them (as even now an intensely preoccupied person does not notice that someone is going past him). For plants, all things are normally peaceful, eternal, everything identical to itself. The belief that *identical things* exist has been handed down to human beings from the period of lower organisms (experience trained in the highest science is what first contradicts this proposition). From the very beginning, the primal belief of everything organic has perhaps even been that all the rest of the world is single and immobile. —What lies farthest away for that primal stage of logic is the thought of *causality*: even now we still basically think that all sensations and actions are acts of free will; when the sensate individual observes itself, it takes every sensation, every change for something *isolated*, that is, unconditioned, without connection: it rises up from within us without any tie to earlier or later things. We are hungry, yet do not originally think that the organism wishes to be sustained; instead, that feeling seems to assert itself *without any ground and purpose*, it isolates itself and takes itself as *arbitrary*. Therefore: the belief in the freedom of will is an original error of everything organic, as old as the stirrings of logic that exist within it; the belief in unconditioned substances and identical things is likewise an original, equally old error of everything organic. But insofar as all metaphysics has concerned itself primarily with substance and freedom of will, we can describe it as the science that deals with the fundamental errors of human beings, but does so as if they were fundamental truths.

19

Number. — The discovery of the laws of numbers was made on the basis of an error already predominant in the earliest times, that several things might be identical (but actually there are no identical things), or that there are at least things (but there is no "thing"). The assumption of multiplicity always presupposes that there is *something* that occurs multiple times: but here is precisely where error already holds sway, already we invent beings, unities, that do not exist. — Our sensations of space and time are false, for they lead, consistently examined, to logical contradictions. In all scientific determinations we are always unavoidably calculating with some false quantities: but because these quantities are at least *constant*, as is our sensation of time and space, for example, the results of science nonetheless acquire a perfect rigor and certainty in their connection with one another; we can build further upon them — up to that final end where the erroneous basic assumptions and the constant mistakes come into contradiction with the results, for example in atomic theory. There, we still feel ourselves forced to assume the existence of a "thing" or a material "substratum" that is moved, whereas all scientific procedures have pursued the task of dissolving everything thinglike (material) into movements: here, too, we still divide in our sensation the moving and the moved and do not escape this circle, because the belief in things has been knotted up with our essence since ancient times. — When Kant says, "the understanding does not derive its laws from nature, but prescribes them to nature," this is completely true in regard to the *concept of nature* that we are required to associate with nature (nature = world as representation, that is, as error), but it sums up a multitude of errors of the understanding. — The laws of numbers are completely inapplicable in a world that is *not* our representation: these have validity only in the human world.

20

A few rungs back.—One stage of cultivation, certainly a very high one, has been reached when human beings get beyond superstitious and religious concepts and fears and no longer believe, for example, in dear little angels or original sin, and have also forgotten how to speak about the salvation of souls: if someone is at this stage of liberation, he still has to overcome metaphysics, which requires the greatest possible exertion of his presence of mind. *Then*, however, a *reverse movement* is necessary: he must grasp the historical justification as well as the psychological one for such conceptions, he must recognize how the greatest advancements of humanity came from them and how he would rob himself of the best results that humanity has thus far produced without such a reverse movement.—With respect to philosophical metaphysics, I now see more and more people who have reached the negative goal (that every positive metaphysics is an error), but still only a few who are climbing a few rungs back; one should, of course, look out over the final rung of the ladder, but not wish to stand upon it. Even the most enlightened people get only far enough to free themselves from metaphysics and to look back on it with superiority: while here, too, as in the hippodrome, it is still necessary to bend back around the end of the track.

21

Presumed triumph of skepticism.—Let us concede for once the skeptical starting point: supposing there were no other, metaphysical world and all of the explanations taken from metaphysics for the only world we know were unusable for us, with what sort of look would we then gaze upon human beings and things? We can think this through for ourselves, and it is useful to do so, even if the question whether Kant and Schopenhauer have scientifically proven anything about metaphysics were to be denied. For it is, according to historical probability, quite possible that in this respect humanity as a whole and in general will someday become *skeptical*; so therefore the question goes: how will human society take shape then under the influence of such a conviction? Perhaps the *scientific proof* that any metaphysical world exists is already so *difficult* that humanity will never again get rid of a mistrust for it. And if we mistrust metaphysics, this has by and large the same consequences as if it had been directly refuted and we were no longer *allowed* to believe in it. The historical question with respect to an unmetaphysical disposition on the part of humanity remains in both cases the same.

22

Disbelief in the "monumentum aere perennius."—A real disadvantage that the cessation of metaphysical views brings with it lies in the fact that the individual keeps his eye too strictly upon his short lifespan and receives no stronger impulses to build durable institutions designed to last for centuries; he wants to pick the fruit himself from the tree that he plants, and he therefore no longer cares to plant those trees that require centuries of constant cultivation and that are intended to shade a long series of generations. For metaphysical views lead us to believe that the final, definitive foundation has been given in them on which henceforth all future generations of humanity will have to settle and to build; the individual promotes his salvation, for example, if he endows a church or a convent; he believes that it will be credited to his account and repaid to him in the eternal life of the soul, it involves working for the eternal salvation of his soul.—Can science also awaken such faith in its results? In fact, it needs doubt and mistrust as its closest confederates; nevertheless, the sum of incontestable truths, that is, truths that have outlasted all the storms of skepticism and all disintegration, can in time become so great (in the dietetics of health, for example) that it prompts people to undertake "eternal" works. In the meantime, our agitated and ephemeral existence still *contrasts* too strongly with the deeply breathing repose of metaphysical ages because both times are still placed too close together; the individual human being himself goes through too many inner and outer developments now for him even to dare orienting himself permanently, once and for all, toward his own lifetime. A completely modern person who wants to build himself a house, for example, feels as if this would be the same as wanting to entomb his living body in a mausoleum.

23

Age of comparison.—The less that people are constrained by tradition, the greater the inner agitation of their motives becomes, and the greater in turn the outward restlessness, the intermingling of peoples, the polyphony of their exertions. Who still feels any strict compulsion to tie himself and his descendants to his particular place? Who feels anything at all to be strictly constraining? Just as all the styles of art are reproduced one beside the other, so, too, are all the stages and forms of morality, of customs, of cultures.—Such an age acquires its meaning from the fact that in it the various worldviews, customs, cultures can be compared and experienced side by side; this was not possible earlier, when the dominance of every culture was always localized and all artistic styles were correspondingly restricted to a particular place and time. An increase in aesthetic feeling will finally decide among so many forms offering themselves for comparison: it will let most of them—namely, all those that it turns away—die off. Likewise, a selection of the forms and habits of a higher morality is now taking place whose goal can be nothing other than the destruction of the lower moralities. It is the age of comparison! That is its pride—but rightfully also its pain. Let us not be afraid of this pain! We should instead understand the task that the age sets for us in the largest terms that we can: for which posterity will bless us—a posterity that knows itself to be as far beyond the isolated, original cultures of individual peoples as beyond the culture of comparison, but glances back with gratitude at both types of culture as at antiquities worth revering.

24

Possibility of progress.—When a scholar of ancient culture swears to no longer associate with people who believe in progress, he is right. For ancient culture has its greatness and excellence behind it, and a historical education forces one to concede that it can never become fresh again; it requires an intolerable stupidity or an equally insufferable fancifulness to deny this. But people can *consciously* decide to develop themselves further in the direction of a new culture, whereas they had previously developed unconsciously and randomly: they can now create better conditions for the emergence of people, for their nourishment, upbringing, instruction, can manage the earth in economic terms as a whole, weigh the powers of humanity generally against one another and put them to work. This new, conscious culture kills the old one that, seen as a whole, has led an unconscious animal and plant life; it also kills the mistrust against progress—progress is *possible*. I mean to say: it is premature and almost nonsensical to believe that progress must *necessarily* result; but how could one deny that it is possible? By contrast, progress in the sense and by the route of ancient culture is not even conceivable. If romantic fantasy has nevertheless also used the word "progress" for its goals (for the self-contained, original culture of an individual people, for instance): it borrows the image for this in any case from the past; its thinking and imagining are without any originality in this area.

25

Private and world morality.—Since people have ceased to believe that a god largely directs the destinies of the world and, despite all the apparent bendings in the path of humanity, is leading them along in splendid fashion, they must now set for themselves ecumenical goals spanning the entire earth. The older morality, notably Kant's, demands from the individual those actions that one desires from all people: that was a beautiful, naive thing; as if everyone would immediately know which modes of action would benefit the whole of humanity, hence which actions would generally be desirable; it is a theory, like free trade, presupposing that a general harmony *must* result of itself according to innate laws of improvement. Perhaps a future survey of the needs of humanity will make it appear not at all desirable for all people to behave in the same way, and instead, in the interest of ecumenical goals, special and perhaps in certain circumstances even evil tasks ought to be given to whole stretches of humanity.—In any case, if humanity is not to destroy itself through such conscious, total regulation, a *knowledge of the conditions of culture* exceeding all previous degrees of such knowledge must be discovered beforehand, as a scientific measure for ecumenical goals. Herein lies the enormous task for the great spirits of the next century.

26

Reaction as progress.—Now and then there appear brusque, powerful, and impassioned, but nonetheless backward spirits who conjure up once again a bygone phase of humanity: they serve as proof that the new tendencies against which they work are not yet powerful enough, that something is lacking in them: otherwise they would offer better resistance to these conjurors. Luther's Reformation, for example, testifies to the fact that in his century, all stirrings of the freedom of spirit were still uncertain, delicate, youthful; science could not yet raise its head. Indeed, the entire Renaissance appears like an early spring that almost gets snowed under again. But in our century, too, Schopenhauer's metaphysics proved that even now the scientific spirit is not yet strong enough: thus, the whole medieval Christian way of viewing the world and perceiving humanity could once again celebrate its resurrection in Schopenhauer's teaching, despite the long-since achieved annihilation of all Christian dogmas. There is a strong ring of science in his teaching, but this does not master it; instead, the old, well-known "metaphysical need" does so. It is surely one of the greatest and quite inestimable advantages we gain from Schopenhauer that he sometimes forces our sensations back into older, powerful ways of viewing the world and people to which no path would otherwise so easily lead us. The gain for history and justice is very great: I believe that without Schopenhauer's assistance, nobody now could easily manage to do justice to Christianity and its Asiatic relatives: to do so on the basis of present-day Christianity is impossible. Only after this great *success of justice*, only after we have corrected in so essential a point the way of viewing history that the Age of Enlightenment brought with it, can we once more bear the flag of the Enlightenment farther —the flag with the three names: Petrarch, Erasmus, Voltaire. We have made reaction into progress.

27

Substitute for religion.—We believe we are saying something good about a philosophy if we present it as a substitute for religion for the common people. In fact, transitional zones of thought are occasionally necessary in the spiritual economy; thus, the transition from religion to a scientific view is a violent, dangerous leap, something to be advised against. To that extent, one is right in making the above commendation. And yet we should finally also learn that the needs that religion satisfied and that philosophy is now supposed to satisfy are not unalterable; we can *weaken* and *exterminate* even them. Think, for instance, of the anguish of the Christian soul, the sighing over inner depravity, the concern about salvation—all are conceptions that derive only from errors of reason and deserve not satisfaction, but annihilation. A philosophy can be useful either by *satisfying* those needs or by *eliminating* them; for they are acquired, temporary needs that rest upon presuppositions contradicting those of science. In order to make a transition here, it is much better to use *art* to relieve a heart overburdened with feelings; for those conceptions will be given much less sustenance by art than by a metaphysical philosophy. Starting from art, we can then more easily make the transition to a truly liberating philosophical science.

28

Discredited words.—Away with those tediously overused words, optimism and pessimism! For there is less and less reason to use them from one day to the next: only babblers still find them so unavoidably necessary. For why in the world should anyone want to be an optimist if he does not have to defend a god who *must* have created the best of all worlds, presuming that he is himself goodness and perfection—but what thinking person still requires the hypothesis of a god?—Yet there is also no reason for a pessimistic creed if we do not have an interest in annoying the advocates of god, the theologians or the theologizing philosophers, and in forcefully advancing the opposite claim: that evil rules, that displeasure is greater than pleasure, that the world is botched work, the manifestation of an evil will for life. But who still troubles himself nowadays about the theologians—except the theologians?—Apart from all theology and the struggle against it, it is obvious that the world is not good and not evil, let alone the best or the worst, and that these concepts "good" and "evil" only make sense in regard to human beings, and perhaps even here are not justified in the way in which they generally get used: we must in any case renounce both the view that curses the world and the one that extols it.

29

Intoxicated by the scent of blossoms.—The ship of humanity, we think, has an ever deeper draught the more it is loaded down; we believe that the more deeply a person thinks, the more delicately he feels, the more highly he values himself, the farther his distance from the other animals becomes—the more he appears as the genius among the animals—the nearer he will come to the real essence of the world and to knowledge about it: and he does in fact do this through science, but he *thinks* he does it even more so through his religions and arts. These are, to be sure, among the world's blossoms, but by no means nearer to *the root of the world* than the stem is: they do not at all enable us to understand the essence of things better, although almost everyone believes that they do. *Error* has made human beings deep, delicate, inventive enough to put forth such blossoms as the religions and arts. Pure knowledge would not be in a position to do so. Anyone who disclosed to us the essence of the world would cause us all the most unpleasant disillusionment. It is not the world as thing in itself, but the world as representation (as error), that is so rich in meaning, deep, and wonderful, bearing happiness and unhappiness in its lap. This result leads to a philosophy that *logically denies the world*: that can moreover itself be combined just as easily with a practical affirmation of the world as with its opposite.

30

Bad habits in drawing conclusions.—The most common erroneous conclusions drawn by human beings are these: a thing exists, therefore it has a right to do so. The purposiveness of a thing is here deduced from its viability, its legitimacy from its purposiveness. And so: an opinion makes us happy, therefore it is the true one; its effect is good, therefore it is itself good and true. Here we attach the predicate pleasing, good, in the sense of useful, to the effect and then equip the cause with the same predicate, good, but here in the sense of logically valid. And the reverse of these propositions goes: a thing cannot establish, maintain itself, therefore it is wrong; an opinion torments, agitates, therefore it is false. The free spirit, who all too frequently comes to know the erroneousness of this way of drawing conclusions and suffers from its consequences, often succumbs to the temptation to draw the contrary conclusions, which are naturally just as erroneous in general: a thing cannot establish itself, therefore it is good; an opinion causes distress, disturbs, therefore it is true.

31

Being illogical necessary. — Among the things that can bring a thinker to despair is the knowledge that being illogical is necessary for human beings, and that from being illogical arises much that is good. It is so firmly fixed in the passions, in language, in art, in religion, and generally in everything that lends value to life that we cannot remove it without thereby doing irremediable damage to these beautiful things. Only people who are all too naive can believe that human nature could be transformed into something purely logical; but if there were degrees of approximation to this goal, how very much would have to be lost along the way! From time to time, even the most rational person requires nature again, that is, his *fundamentally illogical attitude toward all things*.

32

Being unjust necessary. — All judgments concerning the value of life are illogically developed and are therefore unjust. The impurity of judgment lies first in the way that the material is available, namely, very incompletely, second, in the way that the sum is made out of it, and third, in the fact that every individual piece of the material is once again the result of impure knowing and, to be sure, in a wholly necessary way. For example, no amount of experience with a person, however near to us he may be, can be complete enough that we would have a logical right to reach a total appraisal of him; all assessments are premature and have to be so. And finally, the standard with which we measure, our own being, is not of an unchanging size, we have moods and waverings, and yet we would have to know ourselves as a fixed standard in order to justly appraise the relation of anything whatsoever to ourselves. Perhaps it follows from all this that we should not judge at all; if we could only *live* without appraising, without aversion and attraction! — for all aversion is connected to an assessment, just as all attraction is. A drive toward something or away from something, without a feeling that we want what is beneficial and are avoiding what is harmful, a drive without a sort of knowing appraisal about the value of the goal, does not exist among human beings. We are from the beginning illogical and therefore unjust beings, *and can recognize this*: this is one of the greatest and most inexplicable disharmonies of existence.

33

Error about life necessary for life. — Every belief about the value and worth of life rests upon impure thinking; it is possible only because sympathy for the common life and the suffering of humanity is very weakly developed in the individual. Even the rarer people who generally do think beyond themselves do not keep their eye on this common life, but on delimited parts of it. If we understand how to direct our attention primarily to exceptions, I mean to the higher talents and the pure souls, if we take their emergence as the goal of the whole development of the world and rejoice in their activity, then we may believe in the value of life, because we are *overlooking* the other people: therefore thinking impurely. And likewise, if we do indeed keep our eye on all human beings, but take account of only one class of drives in them, the less egotistical ones, and justify these with respect to the other drives: then we can in turn hope for something from humanity as a whole and to that extent believe in the value of life: in this case as well, therefore, by impurity of thought. But whether we behave in one way or the other, we are by this behavior an *exception* among people. Most people, however, endure life without a great deal of complaining and thus *believe* in the value of existence, but precisely because each of them wills and affirms only his own life and does not step outside himself like those exceptions do: everything outside themselves is either not noticeable at all for them or at most a faint shadow. Thus, for the ordinary, everyday person, the value of life rests solely upon him taking himself to be more important than the world. The great lack of imagination from which he suffers makes him unable to empathize with other beings, and hence he participates in their fate and suffering as little as possible. By contrast, *anyone* who really could participate in such things would have to despair of the value of life; if he did manage to conceive and to feel the total consciousness of humanity within himself, he would collapse with a curse against existence—for humanity as a whole has *no* goal, and consequently the individual cannot find anything to comfort and sustain him by considering the whole process, but only despair. If in all that he does he is looking at the ultimate purposelessness of humanity, his own activity takes on the character of squandering in his eyes. But to feel oneself as humanity (and not only as an individual) just as much *squandered* as we see the individual blooms of nature squandered, is a feeling beyond all feelings.—But who is capable of that? Certainly only a poet: and poets always know how to comfort themselves.

34

For reassurance.—But won't our philosophy thus turn into tragedy? Won't truth become inimical to life, to better things? A question seems to lie heavily upon our tongue and yet not to want to become audible: whether we *could* consciously remain in untruth? or, if we *must* do this, whether death would not then be preferable? For there is no longer a Thou Shalt; morality, insofar as it was a Thou Shalt, has been as thoroughly destroyed by our way of viewing things as religion. Knowledge can allow only pleasure and displeasure, utility and harm to persist as motives: but how will these motives come to terms with the sense for truth? They, too, are touched by error (insofar as attraction and aversion and their very unjust measurements essentially determine, as I have said, our pleasure and displeasure). All of human life is sunk deeply into untruth; the individual cannot pull it forth from this well without thereby becoming profoundly angry with his past, without finding his present motives, such as honor, absurd, and without opposing his scorn and contempt to the passions that are pushing on toward the future and toward some happiness there. Is it true, would there remain only a single way of thinking that yields despair as the personal result and a philosophy of destruction as the theoretical result?—I believe that the decisive factor in determining what aftereffect knowledge will have is the *temperament* of a person: I could just as easily imagine an aftereffect for individual natures different from the one that has been described, one that would give rise to a much simpler life, more purified of affects than at present: so that even though the old motives produced by more intense desire would at first still have the strength of old, inherited habits, they would gradually become weaker under the influence of a purifying knowledge. We would finally live among human beings and with ourselves as if in *nature*, without praise, reproaches, or excessive zeal, or as if at a play, feasting upon the sight of many things that had previously only made us afraid. We would be rid of *emphasis* and would no longer feel the pricking of the thought that we are not only nature or are something more than nature. Admittedly, as I said, a good temperament would be required for this, a stable, mild, and basically cheerful soul, a mood that would not need to be on guard against pranks and sudden outbursts and whose expressions would have no grumbling in their tone, nor any sullenness—those familiar, burdensome traits of old dogs and people who have been on a chain for a long time. Instead, someone from whom the ordinary chains of life have fallen so far away that he continues to live only in order to know better, must be able to renounce without envy and irritation many things, indeed almost everything that has value for other people; for him, that free, fearless hovering above people, customs, laws, and traditional appraisals of things must *suffice* as the most desirable state. He is glad to share the joy of this state and he *has* perhaps nothing else to share—in which, admittedly, lies one more privation, one more renunciation. But if we nonetheless want more from him, he will point with a well-meaning nod of his head toward his brother, the free man of action, and perhaps not conceal a bit of mockery: for his "freedom" is quite a different thing.

Chapter 2

On the History of the Moral Sensations

35

Advantages of psychological observation.—That reflection upon what is human, all too human—or as the learned phrase goes: psychological observation—is among the means by which we can lighten the burden of life, that the practice of this art lends us presence of mind in difficult situations and amusement in tedious surroundings, that we can even gather maxims from the thorniest and least gratifying stretches of our own lives and thus make ourselves feel somewhat better: people believed that, knew that—in earlier centuries. Why has this century forgotten it, when at least in Germany, and indeed throughout Europe, the poverty of psychological observation makes itself known by many signs? Not precisely in the novel, the novella, or in philosophical reflections—these are the work of exceptional human beings; but more so in the judgment of public events and personalities: above all, the art of psychological dissection and combination is lacking in all ranks of society, where people speak about human beings, to be sure, but not at all *about humanity*. Yet why do people allow the richest and most innocuous material for amusement to escape them? Why do they no longer read the great masters of the psychological maxim?—for, said without any exaggeration: cultivated people in Europe who have read La Rochefoucauld and his spiritual and artistic relatives can rarely be found; and much more rarely anyone who knows them and does not belittle them. But probably even this uncommon reader will take much less pleasure in them than the form adopted by those artists ought to give him; for even the subtlest mind is not capable of properly appreciating the art of polishing maxims if he has not himself been brought up for it and competed at it. Without such practical instruction, we take this creating and forming to be easier than it is; we do not have a sharp enough feel for what is successful and attractive. Hence, the present-day readers of maxims get a relatively paltry satisfaction from them, hardly any pleasure in tasting them, so that they respond just like people generally do in looking at cameos: they praise them because they cannot love them, and are quick to admire, but even quicker to run away.

36

Objection. — Or should there perhaps be an account contrary to the proposition that psychological observation is one of the means for stimulating, remedying, and relieving existence? Could it be that we have convinced ourselves sufficiently of the unpleasant consequences of this art in order to intentionally divert the gaze of those who are educating themselves away from it? In fact, a certain blind faith in the goodness of human nature, an ingrained antipathy to the dissection of human actions, a sort of shamefulness in regard to the nakedness of the soul, may really be more desirable for the overall happiness of a human being than some quality of psychological perspicacity that helps us only on certain cases; and perhaps the faith in the good, in virtuous people and actions, in an abundance of impersonal benevolence in the world, has made human beings better, insofar as it made them less mistrustful. When we imitate Plutarch's heroes with enthusiasm and feel averse to suspiciously tracing the motives of their actions, it is certainly not the truth, but the welfare of human society that benefits from this: psychological error and a general obtuseness in this area help humanity move forward, whereas the knowledge of truth perhaps gains more from the stimulating force of a hypothesis such as La Rochefoucauld set forth at the start of the first edition of his *Sentences et maximes morales*: "Ce que le monde nomme vertu n'est d'ordinaire qu'un fantôme formé par nos passions, à qui on donne un nom honnête pour faire impunément ce qu'on veut." La Rochefoucauld and those other French masters in examining the soul (joined recently as well by a German, the author of the *Psychological Observations*) resemble sharpshooting marksmen who hit the black bull's-eye again and again — but the black bull's-eye of human nature. Their skill arouses amazement, but a spectator who is governed not by the spirit of science, but by humanitarianism, finally curses an art that seems to plant a sense of diminishment and suspicion in the souls of human beings.

37

Nevertheless. — However the balance between the pro and con may be drawn here: given the present state of this specific individual science, the reanimation of moral observation has become necessary, and humanity cannot continue to be spared the gruesome sight of the psychological dissecting table and its knives and forceps. For what rules here is the science that inquires about the origin and history of the so-called moral sensations and that as it advances has to pose and to solve complicated sociological problems — the older philosophy is not at all familiar with these problems and has always had paltry excuses for evading the investigation of the origin and history of moral sensations. With what consequences: that has now made itself quite clearly visible after many examples have demonstrated how the errors of the greatest philosophers generally have their starting point in a false explanation of particular human actions and sensations, how a false ethics is constructed on the basis of an erroneous analysis of the so-called unegotistical actions, for example, which in turn leads one to make use of religion and mythological confusion, and finally the shadows of these dismal spirits fall even upon physics and our entire worldview. But if it is certain that the superficiality of psychological observation has laid the most dangerous snares for human judgment and inference and will continue to do so, what is now required is a persistent laboring that does not tire of piling stone upon stone, pebble upon pebble, what is required is the moderate courage not to be ashamed of such humble work and to defy all contempt for it. It is true: countless individual remarks about human and all too human things have been uncovered and expressed first within those circles of society accustomed to offering every sort of sacrifice, not to scientific knowledge, but to a witty coquettishness; and the scent of that former home of the moralistic maxim—a very seductive scent—has hung almost ineradicably over the entire genre: so that because of it a scientific person involuntarily betrays a certain mistrust of the genre and its seriousness. But it suffices to refer to the consequences: for it is already beginning to be clear that results of the most serious kind are growing from the ground of psychological observation. Yet what is the central proposition at which one of the boldest and coldest thinkers, the author of the book *On the Origin of Moral Sensations*, arrives, thanks to his incisive and decisive analyses of human action? "The moral person," he says, "does not stand any nearer to the intelligible (metaphysical) world than the physical person." This proposition, hardened and sharpened by the hammer blows of historical knowledge, can perhaps someday, at some future time, serve as the ax that gets laid to the root of the "metaphysical need" of human beings—whether *more* as blessing than as curse to the general welfare, who could say?—but in any case as a proposition with the most considerable consequences, fruitful and frightful at the same time, and looking into the world with the double visage that all great realizations have.

38

How far useful.—Therefore: whether psychological observation brings more utility or liability for human beings may still remain undecided; what is certain, however, is that it is necessary, because science cannot dispense with it. But science has as little regard for final aims as nature does: instead, as nature occasionally accomplishes things of the highest purposeful-ness without having willed them, so, too, genuine science, *as the imitation of nature in concepts*, occasionally, even frequently, promotes the utility and welfare of human beings and attains something purposeful—but likewise *without having willed it*. Yet anyone whose spirit feels too much winter in the breath of this way of seeing things may simply have too little fire in him: let him look around, however, and he will perceive illnesses that require ice packs and people who are so "kneaded together" from fire and spirit that hardly anywhere do they find air cold and cutting enough for them. Moreover: as individuals and peoples who are all too serious have a need for frivolity, as others who are all too sensitive and changeable sometimes find heavy, oppressive burdens necessary for their health: shouldn't we, the *more spiritual* human beings of an age that is visibly catching fire in more and more places, have to grasp all available means for quenching and cooling, so that we will remain at least as steady, harmless, and moderate as we are now, and will thus perhaps become useful at some point in serving this age as mirror and self-recollection?—

39

The fable of intelligible freedom.—The history of those sensations that we use in order to attribute responsibility to someone, that is, of the so-called moral sensations, proceeds through the following primary phases. At first, we call individual actions good or evil without any concern for their motives, but instead solely on account of their beneficial or harmful consequences. But we soon forget the origin of these designations and imagine that the quality "good" or "evil" inheres in the actions in themselves, without regard to their consequences: making the same error as when language describes the stone itself as hard, the tree itself as green—that is, by conceiving an effect as the cause. Then we locate the good or evil in the motives and consider the acts themselves to be morally ambiguous. We go further and no longer assign the predicate good or evil to the individual motive, but instead to the whole being of a person, from which the motive grows as does a plant from the soil. Thus we make a person successively responsible for his effects, then for his actions, then for his motives, and finally for his being. We finally discover that even this entity cannot be responsible, insofar as it is entirely a necessary consequence, a concretion of the elements and influences of past and present things: hence, that a person cannot be made responsible for anything, neither for his being, nor his motives, nor his actions, nor their effects. With this, we have attained the knowledge that the history of moral sensations is the history of an error, the error of responsibility: as such, it rests upon the error of free will.—Schopenhauer, by contrast, reasoned thus: because certain actions bring with them a sense of *uneasiness* ("a consciousness of guilt"), responsibility must exist; for there would be *no basis* for this uneasiness if it were the case not only that all human action proceeded by necessity—as in reality and also in the view of this philosopher it does proceed—but that human beings themselves attained to their entire *nature* by the same necessity—which Schopenhauer denies. From the fact of that uneasiness, Schopenhauer believes he can prove the existence of a freedom that people must have somehow possessed, not in respect to their actions, of course, but in respect to their nature: freedom, therefore, to *be* this way or that, not to *act* this way or that. From the *esse*, the sphere of freedom and responsibility, follows in his opinion the *operari*, the sphere of strict causality, necessity, and irresponsibility. That uneasiness is apparently related to the *operari*—to that extent it is in error—but in truth to the *esse*, which is the act of a free will, the basic cause of the existence of an individual; a person becomes what he *wills* to become, his willing is prior to his existence.—Here is where the false inference is made, in that from the fact of uneasiness, the justification and the rational *authorization* for this uneasiness is deduced; and from that false inference, Schopenhauer arrives at his fanciful conclusion about a so-called intelligible freedom. But the uneasiness after the act does not need to be at all rational: indeed, it most certainly is not, for it rests upon the erroneous presupposition that the act would *not* necessarily have had to result. Therefore: because human beings take themselves to be free, but not because they are free, they feel regret and pangs of conscience. — Besides, this uneasiness is a habit that we can break; for many people it is not present at all in actions where many other people do feel it. It is a quite variable thing, linked to the development of custom and culture and perhaps present only during a relatively short period of world history. — No one is responsible for his actions, no one for his nature; judging is the same as being unjust. This holds equally true when the individual judges himself. The principle is as clear as daylight, and yet here everyone prefers to go back into the shadows and into untruth: from fear of the consequences.

40

The Ueber-Thier. — The beast in us wants to be deceived; morality is an unavoidable lie to keep it from tearing us to pieces. Without the errors that lie in the assumptions of morality, human beings would have remained animals. But in it they took themselves for something higher and imposed more stringent laws on themselves. Hence, they have a hatred for the stages that have remained closer to bestiality: which explains the disdain formerly felt toward the slave, as someone nonhuman, a thing.

41

Unalterable character. — That character is unalterable is not in the strict sense true; instead, this popular proposition means only so much as to say that during the short lifespan of a human being, the motives influencing him cannot ordinarily scratch deeply enough to destroy the imprinted script of many millennia. But if we were to imagine a human being eighty thousand years old, we would have in him an absolutely alterable character: so that an abundance of different individuals would gradually develop out of him. The brevity of human life misleads us into making many erroneous assertions about the characteristics of human beings.

42

The ordering of good things and morality. — The rank ordering of good things that was once assumed according to whether a low, or higher, or highest egoism wants one thing or another, now decides what is moral and what is immoral. To prefer a lowly good (for example, sensual pleasure) to a more highly esteemed one (for example, health) is considered immoral, just like preferring a comfortable life to freedom. But the rank ordering of good things is not something settled and identical for all time; if someone prefers revenge to justice, he is moral according to the standard of an earlier culture, immoral according to the present one. "Immoral" therefore signifies that someone does not yet feel or does not yet feel strongly enough the higher, more refined, more spiritual motives that the new culture of a given time has brought with it: it designates someone who is backward, but always only to a certain degree. — The rank ordering of good things is not itself set up and adjusted according to the point of view of morality; though to be sure, its prevailing arrangement will determine whether an action is moral or immoral.

43

Cruel people as backward. — We have to consider the people who are cruel nowadays as stages of *earlier cultures* that have remained behind: the mountain ranges of humanity here openly display the deeper formations that otherwise lie concealed. They are backward human beings whose brains have not been very delicately and manifoldly developed due to some sort of accident in the process of heredity. They show us what we all *were* and make us afraid: but they are themselves no more responsible than a piece of granite is for being granite. In our brains there must also be furrows and whorls corresponding to that state of mind, just as reminders of our existence as fishes should be ascertainable in the form of individual human organs. But these furrows and whorls are no longer the bed along which the stream of our sensation now rolls.

44

Gratitude and revenge. — The reason why someone powerful is grateful is this. His benefactor has, by his act of benevolence, violated the sphere of that powerful person and forced his way into it: now, in retaliation, he violates the benefactor's sphere by the act of gratitude. It is a milder form of revenge. Lacking the satisfaction of gratitude, the powerful person would have shown himself to be powerless and would henceforth be considered so. Hence, every society of good people, which originally meant powerful people, puts gratitude among the first duties. — Swift made the remark that people are grateful to the same extent that they nurture revenge.

45

Dual prehistory of good and evil. — The concept good and evil has a dual prehistory: *first of all*, namely, in the soul of the ruling tribes and castes. Whoever has the power to requite good with good, evil with evil, and who really also engages in requital and is therefore grateful and vengeful, is called good; whoever is powerless and cannot engage in requital is considered bad. As a good person, one belongs to the "good," to a community that has a common feeling because all the individuals are entwined with one another by having a sense that requital is due. As a bad person, one belongs to the "bad," to a mass of submissive, faint-hearted people who have no common feeling. The good are a caste, the bad a mass, like bits of dust. For a long time, good and bad mean the same as noble and base, master and slave. By contrast, one does not regard one's enemy as evil: he can engage in requital. The Trojan and the Greek are both good in Homer. It is not the one who causes us harm, but rather the one who is contemptible, who is considered bad. In the community of the good, goodness is hereditary; it is impossible that a bad person could grow from such good soil. If one of the good nevertheless does something unworthy of them, one resorts to excuses; for instance, one puts the blame on a god by saying: he struck that good person with blindness and madness. — *Secondly then*, in the soul of the oppressed, powerless person. Here every *other* person is considered to be hostile, inconsiderate, exploitative, cruel, crafty, whether he is noble or base; evil is the characterizing word for a human being, indeed, for every living being whose existence one presupposes, like a god, for example: human, divine are considered the same as devilish, evil. The signs of goodness, helpfulness, or sympathy are taken by fear to be a trick, a prelude to some terrible outcome, a narcotic and a deception, in short, as refined evil. When individuals hold such ideas, a communal existence can scarcely arise, or at most the crudest form of one: so that wherever this conception of good and evil rules, the demise of individuals, of their tribes and races, is near. — Our present morality has grown from the ground of the *ruling* tribes and castes.

46

Sympathy stronger than suffering. — There are cases where sympathy is stronger than the actual suffering. We feel it as more painful, for instance, if one of our friends incurs the guilt for something disgraceful than if we ourselves do. First, because we believe more in the purity of his character than he does; and second, because our love for him, probably precisely because of this belief, is stronger than his love for himself. And if his egoism really does suffer more from this than our egoism, insofar as he has to bear more of the bad consequences of his offense, still, the unegotistical element in us — this term is never to be understood too strictly, but only in an attenuated way — is more strongly affected by his guilt than the unegotistical element in him.

47

Hypochondria.—There are people who become hypochondriac out of sympathy and concern for another person; the resulting form of sympathy is nothing other than a sickness. So, too, there is a Christian hypochondria that attacks those solitary, religiously motivated people who constantly keep the suffering and death of Christ before their eyes.

48

Economy of goodness.—Goodness and love, as the most salutary herbs and powers in human affairs, are such precious discoveries that we might well wish to proceed as economically as possible in using these balsamic remedies: yet this is impossible. Economy of goodness is the dream of the rashest utopians.

49

Benevolence.—Benevolence should also be included among the small, but innumerably frequent and hence extremely effective things to which science should pay more attention than it does to large, less frequent things; I mean those expressions of friendly sentiment in social interaction, that smile of the eyes, that shaking of hands, that comfortable pleasure with which almost all human actions are ordinarily entwined. Every teacher, every official, adds this seasoning to what is duty for him; it is the continual activity of human nature, the waves of its light, as it were, in which everything grows; especially in the narrowest circle, within the family, life turns green and blossoms only by means of that benevolence. Goodnaturedness, friendliness, politeness of the heart, are the everflowing streams of the unegotistical drive and have worked more powerfully in building culture than those much more famed expressions of it that we call sympathy, compassion, and sacrifice. But we tend to disparage them, and in fact: there is not actually much that is unegotistical in them. The *sum* of these smaller doses is nonetheless potent, their combined force is among the strongest of forces.—Likewise, we find much more happiness in the world than melancholy eyes see: if we calculate correctly, that is, and do not forget all those moments of comfortable pleasure in which every day of every human life, even the most distressed one, is rich.

50

Wanting to arouse pity.—La Rochefoucauld certainly gets it right in the most notable passage of his self-portrait (first printed in 1658), when he warns all those who are rational against pity, when he advises them to leave that to the common people, who require passions (because they are not governed by reason) in order to bring themselves to help a suffering person and to intervene forcefully in a misfortune; while pity, according to his (and Plato's) judgment, enfeebles the soul. Admittedly, one should *exhibit* pity, but guard against *having* it: for the unfortunate are simply so *stupid* that the display of pity does them the greatest good in the world.—We can perhaps give an even stronger warning against thus having pity if we conceive that need of the unfortunate not exactly as stupidity and intellectual deficiency, as a form of mental disturbance that misfortune brings along with it (and La Rochefoucauld seems to conceive it thus), but understand it instead as something quite different and more questionable. Consider instead children, who cry and scream *so that* they will be pitied, and who therefore await the moment when their condition can catch somebody's eye; live in contact with the sick and mentally depressed and ask yourself whether eloquent complaining and whimpering or making a display of misfortune do not basically pursue the aim of *giving pain* to those who are present: the pity that those people then express is a comfort for the weak and suffering insofar as they recognize by this that they at least still *have one power* despite all their weakness: *the power to give pain*. The unfortunate person gains a sort of pleasure in this feeling of superiority, which the display of pity brings to his awareness; his imagination ascends, he is still important enough to cause pain to the world. Thus, the thirst for pity is a thirst for self-enjoyment, to be earned at the expense of his fellow human beings; it shows the person in complete disregard of his own dear self: but not exactly in his "stupidity," as La Rochefoucauld claims. — In social conversation, three-quarters of all questions are asked and three-quarters of all answers are given in order to give a little bit of pain to the interlocutor; that is why many people thirst so for society: it gives them the feeling of their power. In such countless, but very small doses in which malice makes itself felt, it is a powerful stimulant for life: just as benevolence, spread in the same way throughout the human world, is the ever-ready remedy. — But will there be many honest people who admit that it causes pleasure to give pain? that we not infrequently entertain ourselves in this way — and entertain ourselves well — by vexing other people, at least in their thoughts, and firing the buckshot of a little malice at them? Most people are too dishonest, and a few people are too good, to know anything of this *pudendum*; thus, the latter may still prefer to deny that Prosper Mérimée is right when he says: "Sachez aussi qu'il n'y a rien de plus commun que de faire le mal pour le plaisir de le faire."

51

How seeming becomes being. — Even when in the greatest pain, the actor cannot finally cease to think about the impression made by his person and about the whole scenic effect; even at the burial of his child, for instance, he will weep over his own pain and its expression, as his own spectator. The hypocrite who always plays one and the same role finally ceases to be a hypocrite; priests, for instance, who as young men are generally conscious or unconscious hypocrites, finally become natural and are then really priests, without any affectation; or if the father does not get quite so far, then perhaps the son, who uses the father's head start and inherits his habits. If for a very long time someone stubbornly wants to *seem* to be something, it will finally be difficult for him to *be* anything else. The profession of almost everyone, even of the artist, begins with hypocrisy, with a mimicking from the outside, with a copying of what is effective. Anyone who always wears the mask of a friendly countenance must finally acquire a power over benevolent dispositions without which the expression of friendliness cannot be compelled to appear—and finally they acquire power over him, he *is* benevolent.

52

The point of honesty in deceit.—All great deceivers proceed in a way that is worth noting, for to this they owe their power. In the actual act of deceit, among all the preparations, the awe-inspiring features of their voice, expression, gestures, amid scenery contrived for effect, the *belief in themselves* comes over them: this is the one who then speaks so wondrously and so authoritatively to the surrounding people. The founders of religions differ from those great deceivers in that they do not emerge from this state of self-delusion: or they have only on very rare occasions those clearer moments when doubt overpowers them; but they generally comfort themselves by imputing these clearer moments to the evil antagonist. Self-deception must be present for these individuals, as well as those, to *bring about* their great *effects*. For human beings believe in the truth of what is quite manifestly strongly believed.

53

Supposed stages of truth.—One common false deduction is this: because someone behaves truthfully and frankly toward us, he speaks the truth. Thus, the child believes in the judgments of its parents, the Christian in the assertions of the founder of the church. Likewise, we do not want to concede that all those things that people in earlier centuries defended by sacrificing their happiness and lives were nothing but errors: perhaps we say that they have been stages of truth. But we basically mean that if someone sincerely believed in something and fought and died for his belief, it really would be awfully unfair if it was actually only an error that inspired him. Such a proceeding seems to contradict eternal justice; therefore, sensitive people set their hearts against their heads time after time in decreeing this principle: there absolutely must be a necessary connection between moral action and intellectual insight. Unfortunately, it is otherwise; for there is no eternal justice.

54

The lie. — Why do people almost always tell the truth in everyday life? — Certainly not because a god has forbidden lying. But instead, first: because it is easier; for lies require inventiveness, dissimulation, and memory. (On account of which Swift says: anyone who tells a lie seldom notices the heavy burden that he has taken on; for in order to maintain a lie, he must invent twenty others.) And second: because in simple circumstances it is advantageous to say directly: I want this, I have done this, and the like; and therefore because the way of coercion and authority is surer than that of cunning. — But if a child has been brought up in complicated domestic arrangements, he finds it natural to employ lies and always involuntarily says whatever corresponds to his interest; a sense for truth, an aversion to lies in themselves is completely foreign and inaccessible to him, and so he lies in complete innocence.

55

To suspect morality because of belief. — No power can maintain itself if none but hypocrites represent it; the Catholic church may possess ever so many "worldly" elements, but its strength rests upon those priestly natures, still numerous even today, who make life hard and deeply meaningful for themselves, and whose glances and emaciated bodies speak of night vigils, fasting, fervent prayers, perhaps even of flagellation; they unnerve people and make them afraid: what if it were *necessary* to live thus? — this is the awful question that the sight of them brings to our tongue. In spreading this doubt, they are constantly founding new pillars for their power; even independently minded people do not dare to oppose that sort of selflessness with a hard sense for the truth and to say: "You who are deceived, do not deceive others!"—Only the difference of opinions separates them from him, absolutely no difference of goodness or badness; but whatever we do not like, we generally also tend to treat unjustly. Thus, we speak of the slyness and the notorious artfulness of the Jesuits, but overlook how much self-overcoming every individual Jesuit imposes upon himself and how the easier lifestyle preached by the Jesuit manuals is not at all meant for their benefit, but for the laity. We might in fact ask whether we enlightened ones, using exactly the same tactics and organization, would be equally good tools, equally admirable in our self-vanquishing, tirelessness, devotion.

56

Triumph of knowledge over radical evil.—It produces an abundant yield for anyone who wants to become wise to have had for a time a conception of human beings as fundamentally evil and corrupt: it is false, like the opposite conception; but for long stretches of time it was predominant, and its roots have branched out into us and our world. In order to comprehend ourselves, we must comprehend *it*; but then, in order to climb higher, we must climb beyond it. Then we recognize that there are no sins in the metaphysical sense; but, in the same sense, no virtues either; that this whole field of moral conceptions is continually in flux; that there are higher and lower concepts of good and evil, moral and immoral. Anyone who does not desire much more from things than knowledge of them easily arrives at peace of soul and will err (or sin, as the world calls it) at most out of ignorance, but hardly out of excessive desire. He will no longer want to slander and exterminate the desires; but the single goal that fully governs him, to *know* at all times as well as he possibly can, will make him cool and will calm all the savagery in his disposition. Besides, he is free of a multitude of tormenting conceptions, he feels nothing anymore from such terms as the punishments of Hell, sinfulness, incapacity for the good: he recognizes them as being only the flickering shadow images cast by false views of the world and of life.

57

Morality as self-division of human beings. — A good author who really has his subject at heart wishes that someone would come and annihilate him by representing this subject more clearly and by answering fully the questions contained within it. A girl in love wishes that she could prove the devoted fidelity of her love by measuring it against the unfaithfulness of her beloved. The soldier wishes that he might fall on the battlefield for his victorious fatherland: for in the victory of his fatherland, his highest wishes also triumph. The mother gives to her child what she takes from herself, sleep, the best food, in certain circumstances her health, her property. — But are all these states unegotistical? Are these acts of morality *miracles* because they, according to Schopenhauer's expression, are "impossible and yet real"? Isn't it clear that in all these cases the person loves *some part of himself*, a thought, a desire, an offspring, more than *some other part of himself*, that he therefore *divides* his being and sacrifices one part to the other? Is it something *essentially* different if an obstinate fellow says: "I would rather be shot on the spot than to move one step out of that person's way"? — The *attraction to something* (wish, drive, desire) is present in all the aforementioned cases; to give in to it with all its consequences is in any case not "unegotistical." — In morality, people treat themselves not as *individuum*, but instead as *dividuum*.

58

What we can promise. — We can promise actions, but not feelings; for the latter are involuntary. Anyone who promises to love someone forever or to hate him forever or to be true to him forever promises something that is not in his power; but he can certainly promise such actions as are ordinarily the consequences of love, of hate, of fidelity, but that can also spring from other motives: for there are many paths and motives that lead to an action. The promise to love someone forever therefore means: as long as I love you, I will display toward you the actions of love; if I should no longer love you, you will continue to receive the same actions from me, albeit from other motives: so that the appearance will persist in the eyes of our fellow human beings that the love is unchanged and still the same. — We are therefore promising the persistence of an appearance of love, if, without self-delusion, we pledge everlasting love to someone.

59

Intellect and morality. — We have to have a good memory to be able to keep promises we have made. We have to have a strong power of imagination to be able to feel sympathy. So tightly is morality bound to the excellence of the intellect.

60

Wanting to take revenge and taking revenge. — To have a vengeful thought and to carry it out means suffering an intense attack of fever, but one that passes away: but to have a vengeful thought without the strength and courage to carry it out means carrying around with us a chronic suffering, a poisoning of body and soul. Morality, which looks only at intentions, assesses both cases in the same way; ordinarily, we assess the first case as the worse one (because of the evil consequences that may result from the act of revenge). Both estimations are short-sighted.

61

Being able to wait. — Being able to wait is so difficult that the greatest writers have not disdained making the inability to wait into a motif of their literary works. Thus Shakespeare in *Othello*, Sophocles in *Ajax*: whose suicide, as the oracle implies, would no longer have seemed necessary to him if he had only let his feelings cool off for one more day; he would probably have outwitted the fearful insinuations of his wounded vanity and said to himself: who in my situation has not taken a sheep for a hero? is it then something so dreadful? On the contrary, it is something typically human: Ajax might have spoken some such words of comfort to himself. Passion does not want to wait; the tragic element in the lives of great men frequently lies not in their conflict with their time and the baseness of their fellow human beings, but instead in their incapacity to defer their action for a year or two; they cannot wait. — In all duels, the advising friends have to determine one thing, whether the persons involved can still wait: if this is not the case, a duel is reasonable, insofar as both of them say to themselves: "either I live on, in which case *he* must die immediately, or the reverse." To wait in such a case means continuing to suffer from the fearful torment of feeling one's honor wounded by the offender; and this can involve even more suffering than life is really worth.

62

Reveling in revenge. — Coarse people who feel themselves offended tend to take as great a degree of offense as possible and to relate the cause in greatly exaggerated terms, simply in order to be able to revel thoroughly in the feeling of hate and vengeance that has been aroused.

63

Value of belittling. — It is not merely a few, but perhaps almost all people who, in order to maintain their self-esteem and a certain proficiency in action, find it absolutely necessary to disparage and belittle for themselves all the other people whom they know. But since petty natures are in the majority, and it matters a great deal whether they have or lose that proficiency, then—

64

The irate one. — We should be as careful with someone who becomes irate with us, as we would be with someone who has at some point made an attempt upon our life: for *the fact that* we are still alive is due to the absence of the power to kill; if a look sufficed, we would long since have been done for. It is a piece of unrefined culture to silence someone by visibly manifesting physical savagery or by exciting fear.—Likewise, the cold glance that persons of high rank give their servants is a remnant of the castelike distinction between one person and another, a piece of unrefined antiquity; women, the keepers of the past, have more faithfully preserved this survival as well.

65

Where honesty can lead.—Someone had the bad habit of occasionally expressing quite honestly the motives from which he acted, which were as good and as bad as the motives of everyone else. At first he gave offense, then he aroused suspicion, and was eventually proscribed outright and declared an outlaw from society, until finally the law recalled the existence of such a depraved being on occasions when it otherwise closed or averted its eye. The lack of reticence concerning the general secret and the irresponsible propensity for seeing what no one wants to see—oneself—brought him to prison and a premature death.

66

Punishable, never punished.—Our crime against criminals consists in treating them like scoundrels.

67

Sancta simplicitas of virtue.—Every virtue has its privileges: for example, that of supplying to the pyre of a condemned person its own little bundle of wood.

68

Morality and success.—The witnesses of an action are not the only ones who frequently measure its morality or immorality according to its success: no, the agents themselves do this. For the motives and intentions are seldom clear and simple enough, and sometimes even memory seems to be obscured by the success of the action, so that the person himself ascribes false motives to his action or treats inessential motives as essential. Success often gives an action the fully honorable gloss of good conscience, failure throws the shadow of remorse over the most estimable action. From this follows the well-known practice of the politician, who thinks: "just give me success: with that, I have also drawn all honorable souls to my side—and have made myself honorable in my own eyes."—In a similar way, success supposedly makes up for a better justification. Many educated people still believe that the triumph of Christianity over Greek philosophy is proof of the greater truth of the former—although it was only the case that the coarser and more violent force triumphed over the more spiritual and delicate one. How it stands with respect to the greater truth can be seen from the fact that the awakening sciences have point by point attached themselves to Epicurus's philosophy, but have point by point rejected Christianity.

69

Love and justice.—Why do we overestimate love to the disadvantage of justice and say the most beautiful things about it, as if it were of a much higher nature than the latter? Isn't it obviously more stupid than justice?—Certainly, but for precisely that reason so much more *pleasant* for everyone. Love is stupid and possesses a rich cornucopia; from this, it distributes its gifts to everyone, even if they do not deserve them or even express thanks for them. Love is as impartial as the rain that, according to the Bible and experience, soaks to the skin not only the unjust, but in certain circumstances the just as well.

70

Execution.—How does it happen that every execution offends us more than a murder? It is the coldness of the judge, the painstaking preparation, the insight that here a human being is being used as a means of deterring others. For the guilt is not punished, even if such a thing existed: this lies in teachers, parents, environment, in us, not in the murderer—I mean the instigating circumstances.

71

Hope. — Pandora brought the box filled with evils and opened it up. It was a gift from the gods to humanity, on the outside a beautiful, seductive gift that had been named "the box of happiness." Then all the evils flew forth from it like living, winged beings: from then on, they have been wandering about and doing harm to people by day and by night. One single evil had not yet slipped out of the box: then Pandora, by the will of Zeus, slammed the lid shut and so it remained inside. And now man has the box of happiness in his house forever and thinks that he has some amazing treasure there; it stands at his service, he can reach for it whenever he desires to do so; for he does not realize that the box Pandora brought was the box of evils, and he takes the evil that remained behind for the greatest of worldly possessions—it is hope.—For Zeus did not want human beings, however much tormented by the other evils they might be, to throw away their lives, but instead to continue letting themselves be tormented anew. Hence, he gives hope to humanity: it is in truth the worst of evils because it lengthens their agony.

72

Degree of moral inflammability unknown. — Whether our passions become red hot and direct our entire lives or not depends upon whether we have or have not experienced certain unnerving sights and impressions, such as an unjustly executed, killed, or martyred father, an unfaithful woman, or a cruel surprise attack. No one knows how far circumstances, pity, indignation can drive him; he does not know the degree of his inflammability. Pitiful, petty circumstances make us pitiful; it is generally not the quality of the experiences, but their quantity that determines whether we fall lower or rise higher in regard to good and evil.

73

The martyr against his will.—In a political party there was someone who was too fearful and cowardly ever to contradict his comrades: they used him to perform any service, they obtained anything from him, because he was more afraid of the bad opinion of his associates than of death; he was a pitiful, weak soul. They recognized this and on the basis of it made him a hero and finally even a martyr. Although the coward always said No inside, his lips always said Yes, even on the scaffold as he died for the views of his party: for beside him stood one of his old comrades, whose word and glance tyrannized him so thoroughly that he really did suffer his death in the most respectable way and has since then been celebrated as a martyr of great character.

74

Everyday standard.—We will seldom go wrong if we trace extreme actions back to vanity, middling ones to habit, and petty ones to fear.

75

Misunderstanding concerning virtue.—Anyone who has become acquainted with vice in connection with pleasure, such as someone who has a lascivious youth behind him, imagines that virtue must be connected with displeasure. In contrast, anyone who has been greatly plagued by his passions and vices yearns toward virtue as the source of spiritual peace and happiness. Hence, it is possible that two virtuous persons may not understand each other at all.

76

The ascetic.—The ascetic makes a miserable necessity out of virtue.

77

Transferring honor from the person to the thing. — We generally honor actions of love and self-sacrifice for the benefit of our neighbor, wherever they are displayed. Thus we increase our *esteem for the things* that we love in this way or for which we sacrifice ourselves: although they are perhaps not worth very much in themselves. A valiant army convinces others of the cause for which it fights.

78

Ambition a surrogate for moral feeling. — Moral feeling dare not be lacking in those people who by nature have no ambition. Ambitious people manage even without it, with almost the same success. — Hence, sons from modest, unambitious families, if they ever lose their moral feeling, generally descend very quickly into complete scoundrels.

79

Vanity enriches. — How poor the human spirit would be without vanity! With it, however, it resembles a well-filled and ever newly replenished warehouse that attracts customers of every kind: they can find almost everything, have everything, provided that they bring with them the proper currency (admiration).

80

The old man and death. — Apart from the demands set by religion, we might well ask: why should it be more praiseworthy for a man who has grown old and who senses the decline of his powers to await his slow exhaustion and disintegration, than with full consciousness to set a limit for himself? Suicide is in this case an entirely natural, obvious action, which as a victory for reason ought in justice to arouse respect: and did arouse it, too, in those times when the leaders of Greek philosophy and the bravest Roman patriots were accustomed to dying by suicide. In contrast, the mania for prolonging our lives from day to day, anxiously consulting doctors and living on in the most painstaking way while lacking the strength to come closer to the real goal of life, is much less respectable.—Religions are rich in evasions of the demand for suicide: thus they ingratiate themselves with those who are enamored of life.

81

Errors of the sufferer and the perpetrator.—If someone who is rich takes a possession away from someone who is poor (for example, a prince takes the beloved from some plebeian), an error arises in the poor person; he thinks that the rich person must be completely vile to take from him the little that he has. But the rich person does not feel the value of a *single* possession nearly so deeply because he is accustomed to having many of them: so he cannot put himself in the place of the poor person and does not do nearly so much of an injustice as the latter believes. Both have a false conception of the other. The injustice of the powerful, which infuriates people the most in history, is not nearly so great as it seems. The inherited sense of being a higher being with higher claims already makes a person fairly cold and leaves his conscience in peace: all of us, in fact, when the difference between us and another being is quite large, no longer feel any sense of injustice, and so we kill a gnat, for instance, without any remorse. So it is no sign of wickedness in Xerxes (whom even all the Greeks depict as outstandingly noble), when he takes a son from his father and has him cut to pieces, because the father had expressed an anxious, ominous mistrust of the whole campaign: the individual is in this case done away with like a disagreeable insect; he ranks too low to be permitted to cause a world ruler any further annoying sensations. Indeed, no cruel person is cruel to as *great* an extent as the one whom he mistreats believes; imagining pain is not the same as suffering it. It is precisely the same with the unjust judge, with the journalist who leads public opinion astray by being slightly dishonest. Cause and effect are in all these cases surrounded by completely different clusters of sensations and thoughts; whereas we automatically assume that perpetrator and sufferer think and feel alike, and in accordance with this assumption measure the guilt of the one by the pain of the other.

82

Skin of the soul. — As the bones, flesh, intestines, and blood vessels are enclosed by a skin that makes the sight of a human being bearable, so the movements and passions of the soul are covered over by vanity: it is the skin of the soul.

83

Sleep of virtue. — When virtue has slept, it will arise refreshed.

84

Refinement of shame. — People are not ashamed of thinking something dirty, but are ashamed if they imagine that someone believes them capable of having these dirty thoughts.

85

Malice is rare. — Most people are far too preoccupied with themselves to be malicious.

86

Tipping the scale. — We praise or blame according to whether the one or the other gives us more opportunity for letting our power of judgment shine.

87

Luke 18:14 improved. — He who humbles himself wants to be exalted.

88

Hindering suicide. — There is a right by which we take from a person his life, but none by which we take from him his death: this is mere cruelty.

89

Vanity. — The good opinion of other people matters to us first because it is useful for us and second because we want to give pleasure to them (children to parents, students to teachers, and benevolent people to other people generally). Only where the good opinion of other people is important to someone apart from his advantage or from his wish to give pleasure do we speak of vanity. In this case, the person wants to give himself pleasure, but at the expense of his fellow human beings, in that he either seduces them into having a false opinion of him or aims at a degree of "good opinion" that must be painful for everyone else (by exciting envy). The individual ordinarily wants to use the opinion of others to verify and reinforce for himself the opinion that he has of himself; but the powerful habituation to authority — a habituation as old as humanity — also leads many people to support their own belief in themselves upon authority, hence to accept it first from the hand of others: they trust other people's powers of judgment more than their own. — The interest in oneself, the wish to please oneself, reaches such a height in a vain person that he seduces others into having a false, excessively high appraisal of him and yet still relies upon the authority of those other people: thus, he induces an error to which he nonetheless gives credence. — We must therefore concede that vain people not only want to please others, but themselves as well, and that they go so far as to neglect their own advantage here; for they are often willing to make other people unfavorably, inimically, enviously, and therefore harmfully disposed toward them, simply in order to have the pleasure of self-satisfaction.

90

Limit of the love for humanity. — Everyone who has pronounced someone else to be an idiot, a bad fellow, gets annoyed if that person finally shows himself not to be so.

91

Moralité larmoyante.—How much enjoyment morality provides! Just think what a sea of pleasant tears has already flowed from tales of noble, magnanimous actions.—This charm of life would fade if the belief in complete irresponsibility were to gain the upper hand.

92

Origin of justice.—Justice (fairness) has its origin among people of approximately *equal power*, as Thucydides correctly understood (in the terrible dialogues of the Athenian and Melian ambassadors); where there is no clearly discernible superiority and a struggle would lead to ineffectual damages on both sides, the thought arises of coming to an understanding and negotiating the claims of both sides: the character of *exchange* is the original character of justice. Each satisfies the other, in that each receives what he values more than the other. We give the other person what he wants, as henceforth belonging to him, and receive in return what we wanted. Justice is therefore requital and exchange under the assumption of an approximately equal position of power: thus, revenge originally belongs in the domain of justice; it is an exchange. Likewise gratitude.—Justice naturally goes back to the point of view of judicious self-preservation, hence to the egoism of this reflection: "why should I uselessly harm myself and still perhaps not attain my goal?"—So much for the *origin* of justice. Since people, in accordance with their intellectual habits, have *forgotten* the original purpose of so-called just or fair actions, and especially because children have been trained for millennia to admire and imitate such actions, the appearance has gradually arisen that a just action is an unegotistical one: the high estimation given to that action, however, is based upon that appearance, and moreover, like all estimations, it is still increasing all the time: for people will sacrifice and strive for what they esteem highly, imitate and reproduce it, so that it grows in size by adding the value of the applied effort and zeal of every individual to the value of what is esteemed. — How scarcely moral the world would seem without forgetfulness! A poet could say that God posted forgetfulness as the doorkeeper at the threshold to the temple of human worth.

93

Of the right of the weaker. — If someone submits under certain conditions to someone stronger, as for example a besieged city does, the reciprocal condition is that he can destroy himself, burn the city, and thus cause a great loss to the stronger foe. Hence, a sort of *equivalence* arises here, on the basis of which rights can be stipulated. The enemy gains an advantage from one's preservation. — To this extent, there are even rights between slaves and masters, that is, precisely to the extent that the possession of the slave is useful and important for his master. One's *rights* originally extend *only as far* as the one person *seems* valuable, essential, indispensable, unconquerable, and the like to another. In this regard, even the weaker person still has rights, but lesser ones. Hence, the famed *unusquisque tantum juris habet, quantum potentia valet* (or more exactly: *quantum potentia valere creditur*).

94

The three phases of morality up to the present. — It is the first sign that the animal has become a human being when its actions no longer relate to a momentary, but instead to an enduring sense of well-being, that is, when a human being becomes *useful, purposeful*: there, for the first time, the free rule of reason breaks forth. A still higher stage is reached when he acts according to the principle of *honor*; by means of which he aligns himself with others, subordinates himself to common sensations, and that raises him high above the phase in which only a sense of usefulness understood in personal terms directed him: he respects and wants to be respected, that is: he understands utility as depending upon what he thinks of others, what others think of him. Finally, at the highest stage of morality *up to the present*, he acts according to *his own* standard for things and persons, he himself determines for himself and others what is honorable, what useful; he has become the legislator of opinions, according to an ever more highly developed concept of the useful and the honorable. Knowledge enables him to give precedence to what is most useful, that is, to general, enduring utility, over personal utility, and to the respectful acknowledgement of general, enduring worth over momentary worth; he lives and acts as a collective individual.

95

Morality of the mature individual.—Up to now, we have regarded impersonality as the real distinguishing sign of moral action; and it has been proven that in the beginning, the concern for general utility was the reason why people praised and distinguished all impersonal actions. Might a significant transformation of these views not be imminent now, when we perceive more and more clearly that it is precisely the greatest regard for *personal* concerns that has the greatest general utility: so that strictly personal actions correspond exactly to the present concept of morality (as general usefulness)? To make of oneself a whole *person*, and in all that one does, to keep an eye upon one's own *highest welfare*—that gets us further than those sympathetic movements and actions for the sake of others. Admittedly, we all still suffer from having far too little consideration for what is personal in us; it has been badly developed—let's admit that to ourselves: we have instead forcibly diverted our attention from it and offered it up as a sacrifice to the state, to science, to the needy, as if it were something bad that had to be sacrificed. Even now we want to work for our fellow human beings, but only so far as we find our own greatest advantage in this work, no more, no less. It is simply a question of what we understand *our own advantage* to be; the immature, undeveloped, crude individual will also understand it the most crudely.

96

Customary and moral. — To be moral, to follow custom, to be ethical, means showing obedience to long-established law or tradition. Whether we submit to it with difficulty or readily does not matter; it is enough that we do so. We call someone "good" who, as if by nature, after long inheritance, hence easily and readily, does what is customary, whatever this may be (takes revenge, for instance, if taking revenge belongs to good moral behavior, as among the ancient Greeks). He is called good because he is good "for something"; but since benevolence, sympathy and the like were always felt to be "good for something," to be useful amid the shifting of customs, we now refer especially to the benevolent, helpful person as "good." Evil means being "not moral" (immoral), acting against custom, resisting tradition, however reasonable or stupid it may be; but in all the moral codes of various times, harming one's neighbor has been particularly felt to be harmful, so that now the word "evil" makes us think especially of harming our neighbor intentionally. The fundamental opposition that human beings have used for differentiating moral and immoral, good and evil, is not the "egotistical" and the "unegotistical," but instead: attachment to a tradition or law and dissociation from it. How the tradition *originated* does not matter here; it was in any case without regard to good and evil or any immanent categorical imperative, but above all for the purpose of preserving a *community*, a people; every superstitious custom that has arisen out of a falsely interpreted, accidental event compels us to follow a tradition as the basis of what is moral; dissociating oneself from it is dangerous, even more harmful for the *community* than for the individual (because the gods punish the community for sacrilege and for every offense against their prerogatives, and only to that extent the individual as well). Now every tradition becomes continually more venerable the more remote its origin and the more that is forgotten; the reverence paid to it accumulates from generation to generation, the tradition finally becomes sacred and awakens awe; and so in any case the morality of piety is a much older morality than the one that requires unegotistical actions.

97

The pleasure in custom. — An important class of pleasure, and thus an important source of morality, originates in habit. We do habitual things more easily, better, therefore by preference, we feel a pleasure in them and know from experience that what is habitual has proven itself, is therefore useful; a custom with which we can live has been proven to be salutary, beneficial, in contrast to all new, not yet proven experiments. Custom is thus the union of the pleasant and the useful, and moreover, it requires no reflection. As soon as a person has the power to compel others, he exerts it in order to introduce and enforce his *customs*, because for him they are the proven wisdom of life. Likewise, a community of individuals forces every individual to follow the same customs. Here is the false deduction: because someone feels satisfied with a given custom or at least carries on his existence by means of it, this custom is necessary, for he considers it the *sole* possibility by which he can feel satisfied; the satisfaction in life seems to grow from it alone. This conception of the habitual as a condition of existence is realized in even the smallest details of morality: since there is very little insight into genuine causality among peoples and cultures at a lower stage of development, they see to it with superstitious fear that everything goes on in the same old way; even where a custom is difficult, hard, burdensome, it will be preserved because its utility seems to be the greatest. They do not know that the same degree of well-being can also exist under other customs and that even higher degrees of it can be attained. But they do no doubt perceive that all customs, even the hardest ones, become more pleasant and mild over time, and that even the strictest way of life can become habit, and thus pleasure.

98

Pleasure and social instinct.—From our relations with other people, we gain a new class of *pleasures* beyond those sensations of pleasure that we get from ourselves, thereby considerably extending the realm of pleasurable sensations. Much that pertains to this has perhaps come down to us from animals, who obviously feel pleasure when they play with one another, especially mothers with their young. And then consider sexual relations, which make almost every female seem interesting to every male in regard to pleasure, and vice versa. In general, the sensation of pleasure based upon human relations makes human beings better; the joy that is shared, the pleasure that is enjoyed together, is enhanced; it reassures the individual, makes him better-natured, dispels mistrust, envy: for he feels happy himself and sees others feeling happy in the same way. *Similar expressions of pleasure* awaken a fancied sympathy, a feeling of being somewhat alike: common sufferings, the same storms, dangers, enemies do the same thing, too. On this, then, the oldest alliance is built: the import of which is, everyone together turns away and defends against threatened displeasure for the benefit of every individual. And thus the social instinct grows forth from pleasure.

99

What is innocent in so-called evil actions.—All "evil" actions are motivated by the drive for preservation, or more exactly, by the individual's striving for pleasure and avoidance of pain; thus, they are motivated, but are not evil. "Causing pain as such" *does not exist*, except in the brain of philosophers, just as little as "causing pleasure as such" (pity in Schopenhauer's sense). In the condition *prior* to civil society, we kill the creature, be it ape or human, that wants to beat us to the fruit of a tree, if we are ourselves hungry and heading for the tree: as we would still do to an animal if we were traveling in a desolate area.—The evil actions that now infuriate us the most rest upon the error that the one who inflicts them upon us has a free will, that it therefore lay within his *freedom of choice* not to do this terrible thing to us. This belief in free will provokes hatred, vengefulness, malice, an entire degradation of the imagination, whereas we get much less angry with an animal because we do not consider it to be responsible. Harming someone not out of a drive for preservation, but instead for the sake of retaliation — is the consequence of a false judgment, and therefore innocent as well. In the condition that precedes civil society, the individual can treat other beings harshly and cruelly for the sake of *deterrence*: in order to make his existence secure by demonstrating his power of deterrence. This is how violent and powerful people behave, as does the original founder of a state who subjugates weaker individuals. He has the right to do so, the same right as the state still assumes; or rather: there is no right that can hinder this. The basis for all morality can be established only when a greater individual or a collective individual (society or the state, for example) subjugates individuals, hence removes them from their isolation and organizes them into an association. *Coercion* precedes morality, indeed, the latter still is coercion for a long time, something to which we accommodate ourselves to avoid pain. Later it becomes custom, still later free obedience, finally almost instinct: then, like everything that has been habitual and natural for a long time, it is linked to pleasure — and is now called *virtue*.

100

Shame. — Shame exists everywhere that there is a "mystery": but this is a religious concept, which was widely influential in ancient times of human culture. Everywhere there were circumscribed areas to which divine right prohibited access except under specific conditions: at first wholly spatial, insofar as certain places were not to be trod by the foot of the uninitiated, who shuddered and felt fear when near them. This feeling was frequently carried over to other circumstances, for example, to sexual relations, which, as a privilege and *adytum* of a more mature age, were supposed to be kept from the sight of young people for their own benefit: relations for the protection and consecration of which many gods were thought to be active, who were posted as guardians in conjugal chambers. (In Turkish, this chamber is therefore called a harem, "holy place," and is therefore designated by the same word usually used for the forecourt of mosques.) Thus, the kingship, as a center from which power and splendor shine forth, is for its subjects a mystery full of secrecy and shame: numerous after-effects of this can even now be sensed among peoples that would not otherwise be characterized as feeling shame at all. Likewise, the whole world of inward states, the so-called soul, is still a mystery for all nonphilosophers, after endless ages in which it was believed to be of divine origin, worthy of intercourse with the divine: it is therefore an *adytum* and awakens shame.

101

Judge not. — When considering earlier periods, we must take care not to slip into unfair abuse of them. The injustice in slavery, the cruelty in the subjugation of persons and peoples, cannot be measured by our standards. For at that time the instinct of justice had not yet been developed very far. Who dares to reproach the Genevan Calvin for the burning of Doctor Servetus? It was an action following consistently from his convictions, and the Inquisition was equally justified; it was only that the predominant opinions were false and produced a logical result that seems harsh to us because those views have become foreign to us. Besides, what is the burning of an individual in comparison with eternal punishments in Hell for almost everyone! And yet this conception dominated the whole world then, without its much greater awfulness doing any essential damage to the idea of God. Even among us, partisans of political sects are treated harshly and cruelly, but because we have learned to believe in the necessity of the state, we do not feel the cruelty here as much as we do where we repudiate the views behind it. The cruelty to animals among children and Italians goes back to a lack of understanding; in the interests of church doctrines, animals have been placed too far below human beings. — Many horrible and inhuman events in history, things that we can scarcely believe, are also mitigated by the consideration that the one giving orders and the one carrying them out are different individuals: the first does not see what happens and hence does not have a strongly imagined impression of it, the latter obeys a superior and does not feel himself responsible. Due to their lack of imagination, most princes and military leaders seem casually cruel and harsh without really being so. — *Egoism is not evil*, because the conception of our "neighbor" — the word is of Christian origin and does not correspond to the truth — is very weak in us; and we feel ourselves nearly as free and irresponsible toward him as toward plants and stones. That another being suffers must be *learned*: and it can never be fully learned.

102

"People always do what is good." — We do not accuse nature of being immoral if it sends us a thunderstorm and gets us wet: why do we call a harmful human being immoral? Because here we assume a voluntarily controlled free will, there necessity. But this distinction is an error. Then too: we do not even call the intentional doing of harm immoral in all circumstances; for instance, we kill a gnat on purpose and without any scruples simply because its singing displeases us, we intentionally punish a criminal and do him harm in order to protect ourselves and society. In the first case, it is the individual who intentionally does harm in order to preserve himself or just in order not to cause himself any displeasure; in the second, the state. All morality allows us to intentionally do harm in *self-defense*: that is, when it is a matter of *self-preservation*! But these two points of view *are sufficient* to explain all the evil actions committed against one person by another: we want some pleasure for ourselves or want to avoid some displeasure; in one sense or another it is always a matter of self-preservation. Socrates and Plato are right: whatever a person does, he always does what is

good, that is: what seems good (useful) to him, according to the degree of his intellect, the prevailing measure of his rationality.

103

The harmlessness in malice. — Malice does not have as its aim the suffering of others as such, but instead our own gratification, a feeling of revenge for example, or a stronger stimulus to our nerves. All sorts of teasing already show how we delight in unleashing our power on someone else and in bringing about a pleasurable feeling of superiority. Now is the *immoral* element in this the fact that we take *pleasure in the displeasure of others*? Is *Schadenfreude*, the pleasure we take in someone else's misfortune, diabolical, as Schopenhauer says? When out in nature, we give ourselves pleasure by shattering branches, loosening stones, battling with wild animals, clearly in order to become aware of our strength. Should *knowing* that another person suffers on account of us make immoral here something in regard to which we otherwise feel ourselves irresponsible? But if we did not know this, we would also not take any pleasure in our own superiority; this can only *make itself known* in someone else's pain, as in teasing, for instance. All pleasure is in itself neither good nor evil; whence should the stipulation arise that we are not allowed to cause displeasure to others in order to take pleasure in ourselves? Solely from the point of view of utility, that is, out of a concern for the *consequences*, for some eventual displeasure, if the injured party or the state as his representative makes us expect retaliation and revenge: only this can originally have provided a reason for renouncing such actions. — Sympathy aims as little at someone else's pleasure as the malice previously described aims at someone else's pain as such. For it conceals within itself at least two (and perhaps many more) elements of personal pleasure and is thus self-gratification: first, a pleasure in emotion, the sort of pity we find in tragic drama, and second, if it forces us into action, the pleasure of satisfaction in the exercise of power. If a suffering person is, moreover, close to us, we diminish our own pain by exercising sympathetic behavior.—Apart from a few philosophers, people have always placed sympathy fairly low in the ranking of moral sensations: and rightly so.

104

Self-defense.—If we consider self-defense in general to be moral, we must also consider almost all manifestations of a so-called immoral egoism to be moral, too: someone causes suffering, robs, or steals in order to preserve or protect himself, to prevent personal harm; we lie whenever cunning and dissimulation are the right means of self-preservation. *Intentionally doing harm*, if it is a question of our existence or security (preservation of our well-being), is conceded to be moral; the state itself does harm from this point of view when it inflicts punishments. Naturally, there cannot be any immorality in unintentionally doing harm, for chance rules there. Is there then any form of intentionally doing harm where it is *not* a question of our existence, of the preservation of our well-being? Is any harm ever done out of pure *malice*, for example in cruelty? If we do not know how much pain an action causes, then it is not an act of malice; thus, a child is not malicious, not evil, toward an animal: it investigates and destroys it like a toy. But do we ever fully *know* how painful an action is to someone else? As far as our nervous system extends, we guard ourselves against pain: if it extended farther, namely inside our fellow human beings, we would not cause suffering to anyone (except in such cases where we do it to ourselves, that is, where we cut ourselves for the sake of healing, trouble and exert ourselves for the sake of health). We *infer* by analogy that something causes someone pain, and our own recollection and strength of imagination can make us sick ourselves. But what a difference always remains between a toothache and the pain (sympathy) that the sight of a toothache evokes? Therefore: in any harm done out of so-called malice, the *degree* of the pain engendered is unknown to us in any case; but insofar as there is a *pleasure* along with the action (a feeling of our own power, of our own strong stimulation), the action occurs in order to preserve the well-being of the individual and thus falls under a point of view similar to self-defense or unavoidable lying. Without pleasure, no life; the struggle for pleasure is the struggle for life. Whether the individual fights this battle in such a way that people call him *good* or in such a way that they call him *evil*, that is decided by the measure and constitution of his *intellect*.

105

Remunerative justice.—Anyone who has completely grasped the doctrine of full irresponsibility can no longer bring so-called punitive and remunerative justice under the concept of justice: presuming that this consists of giving everyone his due. For the one who is punished does not deserve the punishment: he is merely used as a means to deter people from certain actions in the future; likewise, the one who is rewarded does not deserve this reward: he could not have acted otherwise than he did. Therefore, the only meaning of the reward is to encourage him and others in order to provide a motive for later actions; praise is shouted at the one still running the race, not to him who has reached the end. Neither punishment nor reward is something that comes to anyone as *his due*; they are given to him for reasons of utility, without him being able to lay claim to them in justice. We must say, "the wise person does not give rewards because someone has behaved well," just as readily as we have said, "the wise person does not punish because someone has behaved badly, but so that people will not behave badly." If punishment and reward were to disappear, the strongest motives that impel us away from certain actions and toward certain actions would also disappear; the utility of human beings requires their perpetuation; and insofar as punishment and reward, blame and praise, work most susceptibly upon vanity, the same utility also requires the perpetuation of vanity.

106

At the waterfall.—When we look at a waterfall, we think that we are seeing freedom of will and free choice in the countless bendings, twistings, and breakings of the waves; but all is necessary, every movement mathematically calculable. So it is, too, with human actions; we would certainly be able to calculate every individual action in advance if we were omniscient, likewise every step forward in knowledge, every error, every act of malice. The agent himself is admittedly stuck in the illusion of free will; if at some moment the wheel of the world were to stand still, and an omniscient, calculating understanding were there to make use of this pause, it could tell the future of every creature, on into the most distant times, and describe every track on which that wheel had yet to roll. The agent's delusion about himself, the assumption of free will, is itself a part of this still-to-be-calculated mechanism.

107

Irresponsibility and innocence.—The complete irresponsibility of a human being for his behavior and his nature is the bitterest drop that the man of knowledge must swallow if he has been accustomed to seeing in responsibility and duty the attestation of nobility for his humanity. All his evaluations, distinctions, and aversions are thereby devalued and falsified: his deepest feeling, which he offered up to endurance and heroism, was no more than an error; he is allowed neither to praise nor to blame any longer, for it is absurd to praise and to blame nature and necessity. Just as he loves but does not praise a good work of art because it cannot help being what it is, just as he stands before a plant, so he must stand before the actions of human beings, before his own actions. He can admire the strength, beauty, and fullness of them, but cannot find any merit therein: the chemical process and the strife of elements, the agony of the sick person who thirsts for recovery, have as little merit as those struggles of the soul and states of distress in which we are torn this way and that way by various motives until we finally decide upon the most powerful one—so we say (but in truth, until the most powerful motive decides for us). But all these motives, however lofty the names we give to them, have grown from the same roots in which we think evil poisons reside; there is no difference in kind between good and evil actions, but at most in degree. Good actions are sublimated evil ones; evil actions are good ones made coarse and stupid. The individual's single-minded desire for personal gratification (together with the fear of losing it) satisfies itself in all circumstances, though a person may act in whatever way he can, that is, as he must: be it in deeds of vanity, revenge, pleasure, utility, malice, or cunning, be it in deeds of self-sacrifice, sympathy, or knowledge. The degree of his capacity for judgment determines where someone lets himself be drawn by this desire; a rank ordering of good things is constantly present in every society, every individual, in accordance with which he determines upon his actions and judges those of others. But this standard is constantly changing, many actions are called evil and are only stupid, because the degree of intelligence that decided upon them was very low. Indeed, in a certain sense *all* actions are still stupid even today, for the highest degree of human intelligence that can be reached at present will surely still be surpassed: and then, in retrospect, all *our* actions and judgments will seem as restricted and precipitate as the actions and judgments of backward, savage tribes now appear to us to be.—To perceive all this can cause profound pain, but afterward there is something comforting: such pains are birth pains. The butterfly wants to break through its sheath, it pulls at it, it tears it apart: then the unknown light, the kingdom of freedom, blinds and confuses it. In such people, ones who are *capable* of that sorrow—how few it will be!—the first attempt is being made to see whether humanity *could transform* itself from a *moral* into a *wise humanity*. The sun of a new gospel throws its first beam upon the highest peak in the soul of those individuals: the fog gathers more thickly than ever and the brightest light and the gloomiest twilight lie side by side. All is necessity—so says the new knowledge: and this knowledge itself is necessity. All is innocence: and knowledge is the way to insight into this innocence. If pleasure, egoism, vanity are *necessary* for the engendering of moral phenomena and their loveliest blossoms, the sense for the truth and for justice in knowledge, if error and the errancy of imagination were the sole means by which humanity might gradually raise itself to this degree of self-illumination and self-deliverance—who could belittle those means? Who could be sad, if he became aware of the goal toward which those paths lead? Everything in the field of morality has come to be, is changeable, unsteady; everything is in flux, it is true:—but *everything is also streaming*: toward a single goal. The inherited habit of erroneously evaluating, loving, hating may still hold sway in us, but under the influence of increasing knowledge it will become weaker: the new habit of comprehending, not loving, not hating, overlooking is gradually implanting itself in the same soil within us and will in some thousands of years perhaps be powerful enough to give humanity the strength to bring forth a wise, innocent human being (one conscious of his innocence) as regularly as it now brings forth—*as the necessary, preliminary stage to him, not his opposite*—human beings who are unwise, unjust, conscious of their guilt.

Chapter 3

The Religious Life

108

The double battle against misfortune. — If a misfortune befalls us, we can get over it either by removing its cause or by changing the effect that it has on our sensibility: that is, by reinterpreting the misfortune as something good whose utility will perhaps only later become visible. Religion and art (metaphysical philosophy, too) endeavor to bring about a change in sensibility, in part by changing our judgment about experiences (for example, with the help of the sentence: "whomever God holds dear, He chastises"), in part by awakening a pleasure in pain, in emotion generally (which is where the art of the tragic takes its starting point). The more someone is inclined to reinterpret and to account for things, the less he will keep his eye upon the causes of a misfortune and eliminate them; momentary alleviation and anesthetizing, as is usual with a toothache, for instance, also suffices for him in more serious suffering. The more the dominion of religions and of every anesthetizing art decreases, the more rigorously people keep their eye upon the real elimination of misfortunes, which admittedly turns out badly for the tragic poets—since less and less material for tragedy can be found because the domain of an inexorable, invincible fate is becoming ever narrower—yet even worse for the priests: for up to now they have earned their livelihood by anesthetizing human misfortune.

109

Sorrow is knowledge. — How gladly we would exchange the false assertions of priests that there is a God who demands what is good from us, the watcher and witness of every action, every moment, every thought, who loves us and wants the best for us in every affliction — how gladly we would exchange all this for truths that would be just as salutary, soothing, and beneficial as those errors! Yet such truths do not exist; philosophy can at best set metaphysical probabilities (fundamentally untruths as well) against them. Yet the tragedy is that we cannot *believe* those dogmas of religion and metaphysics if we have the strict method of truth in our hearts and heads, but on the other hand, the development of humanity has made us so delicate, irritable, and sickly that we need remedies and consolations of the highest kind; in consequence of which, therefore, the danger arises that humanity may bleed to death from recognizing truth. Byron expresses this in immortal verses:

> Sorrow is knowledge; they who know the most
> must mourn the deepest o'er the fatal truth,
> the tree of knowledge is not that of life.

Nothing helps more against such cares than conjuring up Horace's festive levity, at least for the worst hours and eclipses of the soul, and saying to oneself along with him:

> quid aeternis minorem
> consiliis animum fatigas?
> cur non sub alta vel platano vel hac
> pinu jacentes —

But certainly any degree of levity or melancholy is better than a romantic turn to the past and desertion, an accommodation with any form of Christianity whatsoever: for in the present state of knowledge, we simply cannot have anything to do with it any more without irredeemably soiling our *intellectual conscience*, surrendering it for ourselves and for others. That suffering may be painful enough: but one cannot become a leader and teacher of humanity without suffering; and woe to him who would like to attempt this and no longer has that pure conscience!

110

Truth in religion. — In the period of the Enlightenment, people did not do justice to the significance of religion; that cannot be doubted: but it is just as certain that in the subsequent reversal of the Enlightenment they went a good way beyond justice, too, in treating religions with love or even with infatuation, and acknowledging, for instance, that they possessed a profounder, indeed the most profound, understanding of the world; this was what science had to divest of its dogmatic garb in order to possess the "truth" in unmythical form. Religions were therefore — this was the claim of every opponent of the Enlightenment — supposed to express *sensu allegorico*, with consideration for the understanding of the masses, the age-old wisdom that is wisdom in itself, toward which, rather than away from which, all true science of recent times has always led: so that a harmony, even an identity of views prevails between the oldest sages of humanity and all later ones, and any progress of knowledge — in case we want to speak of such a thing — relates not to the essence, but instead to the communication of that truth. This entire conception of religion and science is erroneous through and through; and nobody would still dare to profess it, if Schopenhauer's eloquence had not given it protection: this eloquence, ringing loudly and yet first reaching its audience a generation later. As surely as we can gain a great deal for the understanding of Christianity and other religions from Schopenhauer's religious-moral interpretation of human beings and the world, just as surely was he in error concerning the *value of religion for knowledge*. In this, he was himself only too obedient a student of the scientific teachers of his time, all of whom paid homage to Romanticism and had abjured the spirit of the Enlightenment; born into our present time, he would not possibly have been able to speak of the *sensus allegoricus* of religion; he would instead have honored truth, as he generally did, with the words: *never yet has a religion, either indirectly or directly, either as dogma or as allegory, contained a truth.* For every religion has been born out of fear and need; on errant paths of reason it has crawled into existence; perhaps at one time, endangered by science, it may have mendaciously absorbed one philosophical doctrine or another into its system, so that we would find it there later: but this is a theologian's trick from the time when a religion already doubts itself. These tricks of theology, which were admittedly already practiced very early in Christianity, as the religion of a learned age saturated with philosophy, have led to those superstitions about a *sensus allegoricus*, as did to an even greater extent the philosophers' habit (especially in those half-beings, the poetizing philosophers and the philosophizing artists) of treating all the sensations that they found in *themselves* as the basic essence of human beings generally and thus allowing their own religious sensations to have a significant influence on the conceptual structure of their systems. Because philosophers often philosophized under the influence of traditional religious habits, or at least under the ancient hereditary power of that "metaphysical need," they arrived at doctrines that in fact looked very similar to Jewish or Christian or Indian religious beliefs—similar in the way that children tend to look like their mothers, only that in this case the fathers were not very clear about just how that maternity came about—but instead, in their innocent astonishment, they spun fables about a family-resemblance of all religion and science. In fact, there is neither relationship, nor friendship, nor even enmity between religion and real science: they live on different stars. Every philosophy that lets the tail of a religious comet gleam forth from the darkness of its final vistas makes everything that it puts forward as science suspicious in itself: all of this is presumably religion, too, although decked out as science.—Besides, if all peoples were in agreement about certain religious things, for example, the existence of a God (which, by the way, is not the case in respect to this point), this would still be only a *counterargument* against the things thus asserted, for example, the existence of a God: the *consensus gentium* and even *hominum* can in all fairness only be considered foolishness. On the contrary, there is no *consensus omnium sapientium* at all, in regard to anything whatsoever, with that exception of which Goethe's verse speaks:

> All the wisest of all times
> smile and nod and agree:
> Foolish, to await the improvement of fools!
> Children of cleverness, oh make fools
> of the fools, too, as is fitting!

Spoken without verse and rhyme and applied to our case: the *consensus sapientium* consists in taking the *consensus gentium* to be folly.

III

Origin of the religious cult. — If we place ourselves back in the times when religious life flourished most vigorously, we come upon a fundamental conviction that we no longer share, and because of this we see the gates to a religious life closed to us once and for all: it concerns nature and our intercourse with it. In those times, people still know nothing of natural laws; neither for the earth nor for the heavens is there a "must"; a season, the sunshine, the rain can come or stay away. Any concept whatsoever of *natural causality* is lacking. If one rows, it is not the rowing that moves the boat, but the rowing is instead only a magical ceremony by means of which one forces a spirit to move the boat. All sickness, even death itself, is the result of magical influences. Falling ill and dying never come about naturally: the whole conception of a "natural process" is lacking—it dawns first among the ancient Greeks, that is, in a very late phase of humanity, in the conception of the *moira* that reigns over the gods. If someone shoots with a bow, there is still always an irrational hand and strength present; if springs suddenly dry up, one thinks first of subterranean spirits and their tricks; it must be the arrow of a god under whose invisible effect someone suddenly sinks down. In India (according to Lubbock), a carpenter generally makes offerings to his hammer, his hatchet, and his other tools; a Brahmin treats the pen with which he writes in the same way as a soldier does the weapons that he needs in the field, or a mason his trowel, or a worker his plough. In the conception of religious people, all of nature is a sum of the actions of conscious and intentional beings, a colossal complex of *arbitrary actions*. With regard to everything outside us, we are not allowed to conclude that something *will be* this way or that, *must* occur in this way or that; *we* are what is approximately certain, calculable: humanity is the rule, nature the *absence of rules*—this sentence contains the fundamental conviction that dominates raw, religiously productive primitive cultures. We human beings of today feel a completely reverse way: the richer someone feels within himself and the more polyphonic his subjectivity, the more powerfully the regularity of nature affects him; with Goethe, we all recognize in nature the great means for soothing the modern soul, we hear the ticking of this largest of clocks with a yearning for peace, for being at home and in stillness, as if we could drink in this regularity and thereby come to enjoy ourselves for the first time. Formerly it was the reverse: if we think back upon the raw, early conditions of tribal peoples or if we see present-day savages near at hand, we find them to be determined most strongly by the *law*, by *tradition*: the individual is almost automatically bound to those things and moves with the uniformity of a pendulum. To him, nature—uncomprehended, dreadful, mysterious nature—must appear to be the *realm of freedom*, of an ability to do as one pleases, of a higher power, an almost superhuman stage of existence, a god. Yet every individual in such times and conditions feels how his existence, his happiness and that of the family, of the state, as well as the success of all undertakings depend upon those arbitrary acts of nature: some natural events must occur at the right time, others not occur at the right time. How can one exert an influence on these terrible, unknown things, how can one bind the realm of freedom? thus he asks himself, thus he anxiously inquires: is there then no way of using tradition and law to regulate those powers just as you yourself are regulated?—The reflections of human beings who believe in magic and miracles are directed toward *imposing a law on nature*: and succinctly put, the religious cult is the result of these reflections. The problem that those people pose for themselves is related in the closest way to this one: how can the *weaker* stem dictate laws to the *stronger* one, determine it, direct its actions (in its conduct toward the weaker one)? First, one recollects the most inoffensive form of compulsion, the compulsion that one exerts when one has made someone *well disposed* toward oneself. By entreating and praying, by being submissive, by engaging oneself to provide regular tributes and gifts, by exalting them with flattery, it is therefore also possible to compel the powers of nature, insofar as one makes them well disposed toward oneself: love binds and is bound. And next one can make *contracts* by which one reciprocally engages oneself to specific conduct, makes pledges and exchanges oaths. But much more important is a more powerful sort of compulsion, magic, and sorcery. As one even knows how to harm a stronger enemy with the help of a magician and keep him in fear; as love spells work from a distance, so the weaker person believes he can also control the more powerful spirits of nature. The primary technique of all sorcery involves obtaining power over something that belongs to the other person, hair, nails, some food from his table, or even his image, his name. With such instruments one can then do magic, for the basic presupposition is: everything spiritual has some corporeal element, with the help of which one is able to bind, to harm, to destroy the spirit; the corporeal element provides the handle with which one can grasp the spiritual. Now, just as one human being controls another, he also controls any natural spirit, for it, too, has a corporeal aspect by which it can be seized. The tree in comparison with the seed from which it sprang—this mysterious proximity seems to prove that one and the same spirit embodied itself in both forms, at one time small, at another large. A stone that suddenly moves is the body in which a spirit is acting; if a boulder is lying on a solitary heath, it seems impossible to think of the human power that could have brought it here, so the stone must therefore have moved itself, that is: it must shelter a spirit. Everything that has a body is susceptible to magic, hence natural spirits, too. If a god is tied directly to its image, one can also exert pressure on him quite directly (by denying sacrificial nourishment, whipping or chaining it, and the like). In order to extort the absent favor of their god, the common people in China put ropes around a likeness of the one who has forsaken them, pull it down, and drag it in the streets through piles of mud and dung; "you dog of a spirit," they say, "we let you live in a magnificent temple, we gilded you beautifully, we fed you well, we brought you sacrifices, and still you are so ungrateful." Similarly violent measures directed against images of saints and the Virgin Mary, if they refuse to perform their obligations in times of plague or drought, have occurred even in this century in Catholic countries.—Countless ceremonies are called into existence by all these magical connections to nature: and finally, if they become too chaotic, one strives to order, to systematize them, imagining one can guarantee that the whole process of nature, especially of the great annual cycle, will turn out favorably by developing a system of procedures with a corresponding outcome. The point of a religious cult is to control and to constrain nature for human advantage, hence to *imprint* upon it *a lawfulness that it does not initially have*; while at the present time we want to *attain knowledge of* the lawfulness of nature, in order to adapt ourselves to it. In short, the religious cult rests upon conceptions of the magical ties between one person and another, and the magician is older than the priest. But it rests *just as much* upon other and nobler conceptions; it presupposes a sympathetic relation between one person and another, the existence of good will, gratitude, a readiness to hear out petitioners, of contracts between enemies, of giving pledges, of a claim upon protection of property. Even in very primitive stages of culture, human beings do not stand over against nature as impotent slaves; they are *not* necessarily the servants of nature, devoid of will: at the Greek stage of religion, especially in relation to the Olympian gods, one can even conceive of the coexistence of two castes, one more noble and powerful, and one less noble, but both somehow belong together by lineage and are of the same kind; they do not need to be ashamed in each other's presence. That is the noble element in the Greek religious sensibility.

112

On seeing certain antique sacrificial implements. — How many sensations are lost to us can be seen, for example, in the combination of the farcical or even the obscene with religious feeling: the feeling for the possibility of this mixture fades; we conceive of it only in historical terms any more, that it existed in the festivals of Demeter and Dionysus, in the Christian passion and mystery plays: but we are still acquainted with the sublime allied to burlesque and the like, or the pathetic fused with the ridiculous: which a later time will perhaps no longer understand.

113

Christianity as anachronism. — If on a Sunday morning we hear the old bells chiming, we ask ourselves: is it really possible! this is on account of a Jew crucified two thousand years ago who said that he was the son of God. There is no proof for such an assertion. — Surely in our times the Christian religion is an anachronism projecting out of the distant past, and believing that assertion — while we are otherwise so strict in examining claims — is perhaps the oldest piece of this heritage. A god who engenders children with a mortal woman; a sage who calls on us not to work any more, not to pass judgment any more, but to watch for the signs of the imminent destruction of the world; a justice that takes the innocent as a substitute sacrifice; someone who tells his disciples to drink his blood; prayers for divine intervention; sins committed against a god, atoned for by a god; fear of the hereafter to which death is the gate; the shape of the cross as symbol in the midst of a time that no longer knows the purpose and the humiliation of the cross—how horribly all this blows toward us, as if out of the grave of an age-old past! Are we supposed to believe that something like that is still believed?

114

The non-Greek element in Christianity.—The Greeks did not see the Homeric gods above them as masters and themselves beneath as slaves, as did the Jews. They saw, as it were, only the mirror image of the most successful specimens of their own caste, hence an ideal, not an antithesis of their own being. They feel related to each other; there exists an interest on both sides, a sort of *symmachia*. A human being thinks nobly of himself when he gives himself such gods and puts himself in a relationship like that of the lesser nobility to the higher; whereas the Italian peoples have a real peasant religion, continually fearful about evil and ill-humored despots and tormentors. Wherever the Olympian gods stepped back, Greek life was also more dismal and fearful.—By contrast, Christianity crushed and shattered human beings completely and sank them as if into slimy depths: then suddenly, in the feeling of complete depravity, the gleam of a divine pity could shine in, so that someone surprised and stunned by grace let out a cry of rapture and for a moment believed that he bore the whole of Heaven within him. All the psychological discoveries of Christianity work upon this pathological excess of feeling, upon the deep corruption of head and heart necessary for it: it wants to destroy, shatter, stun, intoxicate; there is only one thing it does not want: *measure*, and hence it is, when understood most profoundly, barbaric, Asiatic, ignoble, non-Greek.

115

Where being religious is advantageous.—There are sober and industrious people onto whom religion has been embroidered like a fringe of higher humanity: they do quite well to remain religious; it embellishes them. — All people who are not skilled in some sort of weaponry — including the mouth and the quill as weapons — become servile: the Christian religion is very useful for such people, for in this case, servility takes on the appearance of a Christian virtue and is amazingly embellished. — People who find their daily lives too empty and monotonous easily become religious: this is understandable and excusable, only they have no right to demand religiousness from those whose daily lives do not pass in an empty and monotonous way.

116

The everyday Christian. — If Christianity, with its tenets of a vengeful God, of general sinfulness, of election by grace, and of the danger of eternal damnation were correct, it would be a sign of imbecility and lack of character *not* to become a priest, apostle, or hermit and work with fear and trembling solely on our own salvation; it would be senseless to lose sight of our eternal advantage for the sake of ephemeral worldly ease. Assuming that he really does *believe*, the everyday Christian is a pitiful figure, someone who really cannot count to three, and who, moreover, precisely because of his lack of spiritual accountability, does not deserve to be punished as severely as Christianity promises him he will be.

117

Of the shrewdness of Christianity. — It is a clever ploy for Christianity to teach the complete unworthiness, sinfulness, and contemptibility of humanity so loudly that contempt for our fellow human beings is no longer possible. "Though he may sin as much as he wants, he still does not differ essentially from me: I am the one who is thoroughly unworthy and contemptible"; so says the Christian. But even this feeling has lost its sharpest sting, because the Christian does not believe in his individual contemptibility: he is evil as a human being in general and reassures himself a little with the phrase: we are all of one kind.

118

Change of roles.—As soon as a religion prevails, it has as its opponents all those who would have been its first disciples.

119

The destiny of Christianity.—Christianity came into being in order to unburden the heart; but it first had to burden the heart in order to be able to unburden it afterward. In consequence, it will perish.

120

The proof by pleasure.—The pleasant opinion is taken as true: this is the proof by pleasure (or, as the church says, the proof by strength) of which all religions are so proud, whereas they ought to be ashamed of it. If a belief did not make us happy, it would not be believed: how little, therefore, will it be worth!

121

Dangerous game.—Anyone now who makes room in himself once again for religious sensibility must also let it grow; he cannot do otherwise. But then his nature gradually changes, it gives preference to what adheres to or adjoins the religious element, all the surroundings of judgment and sensation become clouded, shrouded by religious shadows. Sensibility cannot stand still; therefore, beware.

122

The blind disciples.—As long as someone is very well acquainted with the strength and weakness of his teaching, his kind of art, or his religion, their strength is still slight. The disciple and apostle who has no eye for the weakness of the teaching, the religion, and so on, who is blinded by the appearance of the master and by devotion to him, for this reason generally has more power than the master. Never yet has the influence of a man and his work become great without blind disciples. To help a certain knowledge to triumph often means only: to relate it to stupidity in such a way that the weightiness of the latter also enforces the triumph of the former.

123

Pulling down the churches. — There is not even religion enough in the world to destroy its religions.

124

Sinlessness of human beings. — If we have understood "how sin came into the world," namely, through errors of reason, thanks to which people collectively and even individually take themselves to be much darker and more evil than is really the case, then our whole sensibility is greatly relieved, and human beings and world appear now and then in a halo of harmlessness that does us good from the bottom up. Amid nature, human beings are always essentially children. To be sure, these children do sometimes have an oppressive, frightening dream, but when they open their eyes, they see themselves in Paradise once again.

125

Irreligiousness of artists. — Homer is so much at home among his gods, and so at ease with them as a poet, that he, at any rate, must have been deeply irreligious; he dealt as freely with what popular belief offered him — a meager, crude, partially gruesome superstition — as the sculptor with his clay, hence, with the same unaffectedness that Aeschylus and Aristophanes possessed, and that in modern times distinguished the great artists of the Renaissance, as well as Shakespeare and Goethe.

126

The art and force of false interpretation. — All the visions, terrors, exhaustions, raptures of the saint are well-known states of sickness, which, on the basis of deeply rooted religious and psychological errors, are simply *interpreted* by him quite differently, namely, not as sicknesses. — So, too, the daimon of Socrates is perhaps an ailment of the ear that he, according to his predominantly moral way of thinking, simply *interprets* otherwise than we would today. Nor is it any different with the madness and ravings of the prophets and oracular priests; it is always the degree of knowledge, imagination, effort, and morality in the head and heart of the *interpreters* that *makes* so much out of those things. It is among the greatest effects of those whom we call geniuses and saints that they forcibly bring forth interpreters who *misunderstand* them for the good of humanity.

127

Worshipping madness. — Because people noticed that any stimulation often made the head clearer and called forth the most sudden and happy insights, they believed we would gain access to the happiest insights and inspirations by means of the highest stimulations: and so they worshipped the madman as a sage and giver of oracles. A false deduction lies at the base of this.

128

Promises of science. — Modern science has as its goal: as little pain as possible, as long a life as possible — hence, a sort of eternal bliss, admittedly a very modest one in comparison with the promises of religions.

129

Forbidden generosity. — There is not enough love and goodness in the world to allow us to give any of it away to imaginary beings.

130

Affective persistence of the religious cult. — The Catholic Church and every cult of antiquity prior to it commanded a whole range of means for transposing people into uncommon moods and tearing them away from the cold calculation of advantage or from purely rational thought. A church trembling with deeply resounding tones; the muffled, regular, restrained calls of a priestly troop that transmits its excited tension involuntarily to the congregation and makes them listen almost fearfully, as if a miracle were imminent; the breath of an architecture that, as the dwelling place of divinity, stretches out into indefinite space and makes us fearfully anticipate the stirrings of that divinity in all its dark reaches—who would want to restore such proceedings, if people no longer believed the presuppositions behind them? But the results of all this have nevertheless not been lost: the inner world of sublime, moving, portentous, deeply contrite, blissfully expectant moods has been begotten in humanity principally by the cult; what still exists of it in the soul was nurtured at the time that it sprouted, grew, and blossomed.

131

Religious afterpains.—However much we believe we have weaned ourselves from religion, this has still not occurred insofar as we take pleasure in encountering religious sensations and moods without conceptual content, for example, in music; and if a philosophy shows us some justification for metaphysical hopes, for the profound peace of soul attainable therein, and speaks, for example, of "the complete and confident gospel in the gaze of Raphael's Madonnas," we respond to such expressions and statements in an especially heartfelt way: the philosopher has it easier here by way of proof, he corresponds in what he wants to give with a heart ready to accept it. We notice in this how the less reflective free spirits really take offense only at the dogmas, but are very familiar with the magic of religious sensation; it hurts them to let go of the latter on account of the former.—Scientific philosophy must be very careful not to smuggle in errors on the basis of that need—an acquired and consequently also a transitory need: even logicians speak of "presentiments" of truth in morality and art (for instance, of the presentiment "that the essence of things is one"): which really should be forbidden to them. Between carefully inferred truths and such "intuited" things there remains an unbridgeable gulf, since we owe the former to the intellect, the latter to need. Hunger does not prove that the food that would sate it *exists*, yet it wishes for this food. "Having a presentiment" does not mean knowing in any degree that something exists, but instead, taking its existence to be possible insofar as we wish for it or fear it; the "presentiment" does not take us a single step farther into the land of certainty.—We involuntarily believe that the religiously tinged sections of a philosophy are better proven than the others; but it is basically the reverse; we simply have the inner wish that it *might* be so—hence, that what makes us happy might also be true. This longing misleads us into accepting bad reasons as good ones.

132

Of the Christian need for salvation.—Through careful deliberation, it must be possible to acquire an explanation for the process in the soul of a Christian that we call the need for salvation, an explanation free of mythology: hence, a purely psychological one. Up until now, admittedly, psychological explanations of religious states and processes have been rather disreputable, insofar as a theology calling itself free carried on its fruitless activity in this field: for it aimed from the start at maintaining the Christian religion and perpetuating Christian theologians—as the spirit of its founder, Schleiermacher, lets us surmise—who were supposed to obtain a new anchorage and above all a new occupation in the psychological analysis of religious "facts." Not misled by such predecessors, we hazard the following interpretation of the designated phenomenon. A human being is conscious of certain actions that stand low in the usual rank ordering of actions; he even uncovers in himself a propensity for these sorts of acts, which seems to him almost as unalterable as his entire being. How gladly he would experiment with the other class of actions that are generally esteemed as the foremost and highest ones, how glad he would be to feel himself full of the good consciousness that is supposed to follow from unselfish ways of thinking! But unfortunately it gets no further

THE RELIGIOUS LIFE 101

than this wish: the discontent at not being able to satisfy it gets added to all the other sorts of discontent aroused in him by his destiny generally or by the consequences of those actions that are termed evil; so that he comes to feel a profound discontent, and begins to look for a physician who would be able to eliminate this feeling and all its causes. — This condition would not be felt so bitterly if a person would impartially compare himself only with other human beings: for then he would have no reason to be dissatisfied with himself to any special extent, since he is only bearing the common burden of human dissatisfaction and imperfection. But he compares himself with a being who alone is capable of those actions that are called unegotistical and who lives in continual consciousness of an unselfish way of thinking, with God; it is from gazing into this shining mirror that his own nature appears to him so gloomy, so unusually deformed. And then the thought of that same being frightens him, insofar as it hovers before his imagination as punitive justice: in every possible experience, small and large, he thinks that he perceives its wrath, its menace, even that he already feels the lashes of his judge and executioner. Who will help him in this danger, the horror of which exceeds all other conceivable terrors in the prospect it offers of an immeasurable eternity of punishment?

133

Before we consider the further consequences of this condition, we at least want to admit to ourselves that human beings have not gotten into this condition due to their "guilt" and "sin," but instead, due to a series of errors in reasoning, that it was the fault of the mirror if their nature appeared to them so gloomy and hateful, and that mirror was *their* work, the very imperfect work of human imagination and judgment. First of all, a being who would be capable of only purely unegotistical actions is even more fantastic than the phoenix; we cannot even conceive it distinctly, if only because the whole concept of "unegotistical action" gets scattered to the winds when rigorously investigated. Never has any human being done something solely for others and without any personal motive; how should he even *be able* to do something that would be without reference to himself, hence without inner compulsion (which would have to have its reason in a personal need)? How would the ego be capable of acting without ego? — By contrast, a god of the sort that people occasionally imagine, one who is *wholly* love, would not be capable of a single unegotistical action: in which regard we should recall a thought of Lichtenberg's, one admittedly taken from a lower sphere: "We cannot possibly *feel* for others, as we tend to say; we feel only for ourselves. The phrase sounds harsh, but is not if it is only understood correctly. We love neither father, nor mother, nor wife, nor child, but instead the pleasurable sensations that they cause in us," or, as La Rochefoucauld says, "si on croit aimer sa maîtresse pour l'amour d'elle, on est bien trompé." As for why actions motivated by love are *esteemed* more highly than others, namely, not on account of their nature, but on account of their utility, compare the previously mentioned investigation "On the Origin of Moral Sensations." But even if some human being should wish to be just like that god, to be love, to do and to want everything for others, nothing for himself, it would be impossible, if only because he must do *a great deal* for himself just to be able to do some things for the sake of others. And then it presupposes that the other person is enough of an egoist to accept that sacrifice, that living for him, over and over again: so that loving, self-sacrificing people have an interest in the continued existence of egoists who are without love and incapable of self-sacrifice, and in order for the highest morality to be able to persist, it would really have to *force* immorality to exist (whereby it would admittedly negate itself). — Furthermore: the conception of a god disturbs and humiliates us as long as we believe in it, but at our present level of comparative ethnology, we can no longer doubt how it *came into being*, and with the insight into this origin, that belief falls away. The Christian who compares his nature with God is in the same position as Don Quixote, who underestimates his own valor because he has the amazing deeds of the heroes of chivalric romances in his head; in both cases, the standard being used to measure belongs to the realm of fable. If, however, the idea of God falls away, so does the feeling of "sin" as a trespass against divine prescriptions, as a blemish on a creature consecrated to God. Yet there probably still remains the sense of uneasiness that has grown up closely related to the fear of punishment by secular justice or to other people's disdain; the uneasiness of a pricking conscience, the sharpest thorn in the feeling of guilt, is nevertheless broken off if we perceive that we may in our actions indeed have offended against human tradition, human statutes and regulations, but still not thereby endangered the "eternal salvation of the soul" and its relationship with divinity. If anyone does finally succeed in gaining a philosophical conviction of the unconditional necessity of all actions and of their complete irresponsibility and absorbs this conviction into his flesh and blood, those remaining pangs of conscience will also disappear.

134

Now if the Christian, as just said, has fallen into a feeling of self-contempt due to certain errors, that is, due to a false, unscientific interpretation of his actions and sensations, he must notice with the greatest astonishment how that state of contempt, that pricking of conscience, that of displeasure in general, does not persist, how hours occasionally arrive when all of this is blown away from his soul, and he once again feels himself free and courageous. In truth, his pleasure in himself, the satisfaction in his own strength, combined with the necessary diminishing of every profound stimulation, has carried off the victory; he loves himself again, he feels it—but precisely this love, this new self-esteem, seems unbelievable to him; he can see in it only the wholly unmerited radiance upon him of a luminous grace from above. If he previously believed that he saw warnings, threats, punishments, and every sort of sign of divine wrath in every occurrence, he now *reads* divine goodness *into* his experiences: one event seems full of love to him, another like a helpful indication, a third one, especially along with his entirely joyous mood, seems to prove that God is merciful. Just as before, especially in his state of uneasiness, he interpreted his actions falsely, now he does the same with his experiences; he conceives of his consoling mood as an effect of some power ruling outside him, the love with which he basically loves himself appears like divine love; what he calls grace and a prelude to salvation is in truth self-pardoning, self-redemption.

135

Therefore: a certain false psychology, a certain kind of fantasizing in the interpretation of motives and events, is the necessary prerequisite for becoming a Christian and feeling the need for salvation. With the insight into this confusion of reason and imagination, one ceases to be a Christian.

136

Of Christian asceticism and holiness. — However much individual thinkers have exerted themselves to represent the infrequent manifestations of morality that we generally call asceticism and holiness as something miraculous, so that holding the light of a rational explanation up to them is almost sacrilege and profanation: the temptation to this sacrilege is, in turn, just as strong. A powerful drive of *nature* has at all times led to protests against those phenomena as such; science, insofar as it, as previously said, is an imitation of nature, allows itself to raise objections at least against their alleged inexplicability, indeed, inaccessibility. Admittedly, it has not yet succeeded: those phenomena are still unexplained, to the great satisfaction of the aforementioned devotees of the morally miraculous. For generally speaking: the unexplained should be thoroughly inexplicable, the inexplicable thoroughly unnatural, supernatural, miraculous—so goes the demand in the souls of all religious people and metaphysicians (artists, too, should they be thinkers as well);

while the scientific person sees in this demand the "evil principle."—The general probability that turns up first in considering asceticism and holiness is that their nature is a *complicated* one: for almost everywhere within the physical world, as well as in the moral one, supposedly miraculous things have been successfully traced back to something complicated and multiply conditioned. Let us therefore venture first to isolate individual drives in the soul of the saint and the ascetic, and then finally to think about how they have grown up together inside us.

137

There is a *defiance of oneself* that includes many forms of asceticism as its most sublime manifestations. Certain people, that is, have so great a need to exercise their passion for power and domination that, because other objects are lacking or because they have always proven unsuccessful otherwise, they finally hit upon the expedient of tyrannizing certain parts of their own nature, sections or stages of themselves, as it were. Some thinkers thus profess views that obviously do not serve to increase or improve their reputations; some actually call down upon themselves the disdain of others when they could easily, by remaining silent, have retained their esteem; others disavow earlier opinions and do not shy away from henceforth being called inconsistent: on the contrary, they strive for this and behave like arrogant riders who like their horse best when it has become wild, covered with sweat, made skittish. Thus a person climbs on dangerous paths into the highest mountains in order to laugh derisively at his fearfulness and his trembling knees; thus, a philosopher professes views about asceticism, humility, and holiness in light of which his own image becomes absolutely odious. This shattering of oneself, this mockery of one's own nature, this *spernere se sperni* of which religions have made so much is really a very high degree of vanity. The whole morality of the Sermon on the Mount fits in here: people have a genuine pleasure in violating themselves with excessive demands and then idolizing this tyrannically demanding something in their souls afterward. In every ascetic morality people worship a part of themselves as a god and therefore need to diabolize the remaining part. —

138

Human beings are not equally moral at all times; this is well known: if we judge their morality according to their aptitude for great, self-sacrificing resolve and self-renunciation (which, persisting and become a habit, is holiness), they are the most moral in regard to *affect*; a higher level of stimulation presents them with entirely new motives of which they, sober and cold as they otherwise are, would perhaps not even have believed themselves to be capable. How does this come about? Probably due to the proximity of everything great and highly stimulating; once someone has been brought to a state of exceptional tension, he can just as easily resolve to commit an act of frightful revenge as he can resolve to frightfully break his own need for revenge. Under the influence of a powerful emotion, he wants in any case what is great, powerful, terrible, and if by chance he notices that sacrificing himself provides him with as much satisfaction as sacrificing someone else, or even more, he chooses the former. It is therefore really only the discharge of his emotion that matters to him; hence, to relieve his tension he may grab hold of his enemies' spears and bury them in his own breast. The idea that something great lies in self-renunciation and not only in revenge first had to be inculcated in humanity through lengthy habituation; a divine being who sacrifices himself was the strongest and most efficacious symbol of this sort of greatness. Victory over the enemy most difficult to defeat, the sudden mastering of an affect — that is what this renunciation *seems to be*; and to that extent it counts as the pinnacle of morality. In truth, this is a matter of substituting one conception for another, while one's disposition maintains the same height, the same flood level. When sobered and resting from affect, such people no longer understand the morality of these moments, but the admiration of all those who have also lived through them sustains them; pride is their comfort when the affect and an understanding of their deed fade away. Therefore: even these acts of self-denial are basically not moral, insofar as they were not done strictly with regard to others; instead, the other person only provides an occasion for the highly strung disposition to relieve itself by means of that denial.

139

In many respects the ascetic, too, tries to make life easy for himself, most generally by complete subordination to an alien will or to a comprehensive law and ritual, much in the way that the Brahmin leaves absolutely nothing to his own determination and guides himself at every minute according to a holy precept. This subordination is a powerful means for becoming master of oneself; we are occupied, hence not bored, and yet have no willful or passionate impulses; after carrying out an action, the feeling of responsibility and hence the agony of regret are absent. We have relinquished our own will once and for all, and this is easier than only occasionally relinquishing it; just as it is also easier to renounce a desire completely than to keep it within measure. If we recall the present position of a person in relation to the state, we find that here, too, unconditional obedience is more convenient than conditional obedience. The saint therefore makes his life easier by completely giving up his personality, and we deceive ourselves if we admire that phenomenon as the most heroic feat of morality. It is in every case harder to assert our personality without wavering and confusion than to free ourselves from it as described above; moreover, it requires much more spirit and reflection.

140

After having found in many of those actions that are more difficult to explain manifestations of a pleasure in *emotion as such*, I would also perceive in self-contempt, which is one of the characteristic features of holiness, and likewise in actions involving self-torture (by hunger and flagellation, dislocation of limbs, simulation of madness), a means by which those natures combat the general exhaustion of their will to live (of their nerves): they make use of the most painful means of excitation and cruelties in order to emerge at least for a time from that torpor and boredom into which their great spiritual indolence and that previously depicted subordination to an alien will so often lets them fall.

141

The most common means that the ascetic and saint employ to make their lives nonetheless bearable and amusing consists of occasionally waging war and alternating between victory and defeat. For that, he needs an opponent and finds him in the so-called "enemy within." He makes use especially of his proclivity for vanity, ambition, and love of power, and then of his sensual desires, in allowing himself to look upon his life as an ongoing battle and himself as a battlefield on which good and evil spirits struggle with varying success. As we know, the sensual imagination is moderated, indeed almost repressed, by regularity of sexual intercourse, but conversely set free and made dissolute by abstinence from or irregularity of intercourse. Many Christian saints had uncommonly dirty imaginations; thanks to the theory that these desires were real demons raging within them, they did not feel themselves all that responsible for this; to this feeling we owe the quite instructive sincerity of their self-testimonies. It was in their interest to maintain this battle at some level of intensity because through it, as has been said, their empty lives were sustained. But in order for the battle to seem important enough to arouse a continual sense of involvement and admiration among the non-saints, sensuality had to be slandered and stigmatized more and more; indeed, the danger of eternal damnation was so closely attached to these things that throughout entire ages Christians most likely procreated children only with a bad conscience, which has certainly done great harm to humanity. And yet here the truth has been stood completely on its head: a state that is

THE RELIGIOUS LIFE

particularly unbecoming for truth. Of course, Christianity had said: every human being is conceived and born in sin; and in the intolerable, superlative Christianity of Calderón, this thought had once again knotted and entwined itself, so that he hazarded the most twisted paradox that exists in the well-known verse:

> the greatest offense of a human being
> is ever having been born.

In every pessimistic religion, the act of procreation is felt to be bad in itself, but in no way is this feeling a general human one; nor is the judgment of all pessimists even the same on this matter. Empedocles, for example, knows nothing at all shameful, diabolical, sinful about erotic things; instead, he sees a single holy and hopeful figure, Aphrodite, appear upon the great meadows of misfortune; she serves as a guarantee for him that strife will not rule forever, but will someday hand over the scepter to a gentler spirit. As has been said, the practitioners of Christian pessimism had an interest in another opinion remaining sovereign; they needed an ever-active enemy in the solitude and the spiritual barrenness of their lives: and a generally acknowledged enemy, one that let them, by battling and overcoming it, present themselves ever anew to the nonsaint as half-inconceivable, supernatural beings. If this enemy finally, as a result of their way of life and their ravaged health, took flight forever, they immediately understood how to *see* their inner life populated with new demons. The upward and downward fluctuations of the scales of pride and humility entertained their brooding heads just as well as the alternation between desire and tranquility of soul. Back then, psychology served not only to make everything human seem suspicious, but also to slander, to flagellate, to crucify; people *wanted* to consider themselves as bad and evil as possible, they sought out anxiety about the soul's salvation, despair of their own strength. Everything natural to which humanity attaches the idea of badness and sinfulness (as we tend to do even now, for example, in regard to the erotic) troubles and darkens the imagination, renders our glance timid, leads us to quarrel with ourselves, and makes us uncertain and mistrustful; even our dreams assume an aftertaste of the tormented conscience. And yet this suffering from what is natural is wholly ungrounded in the reality of things: it is solely the consequence of opinions *about* things. We easily perceive how people become worse from characterizing what is unavoidably natural as bad and ever afterward feeling it to be so constituted. It is a trick of religion and of those metaphysicians who want people to be evil and sinful by nature to make nature seem suspect for them and thus to *make* them bad themselves: for thus they learn to perceive themselves as bad, since they cannot take off the garb of nature. Living for a long time in what is natural, they gradually feel themselves oppressed by such a burden of sins that supernatural powers become necessary for lifting this burden; and with this, the aforementioned need for salvation enters the scene, corresponding not to any real, but only to an imagined sinfulness. Go through the specific moral statements in the original documents of Christianity and you will find that everywhere the demands are made excessive so that people would not *be able* to satisfy them; the intent is not that they *become* more moral, but instead that they feel themselves to be *as sinful as possible*. If this feeling had not been *pleasant* for them — why would they have begotten such an idea and hung on to it for so long? As in the world of antiquity an immeasurable force of spirit and ingenuity was expended in order to increase the joy in life by means of festive cults: so in the Christian era an immeasurable amount of spirit was likewise sacrificed to another aspiration: people should feel themselves to be sinful in every way, and thereby be stimulated, invigorated, animated. To stimulate, to invigorate, to animate at any cost — isn't that the watchword of an enervated, overripe, overcultivated time? The circle of all natural sensations had been run through a hundred times, the soul had grown tired of them: then the saint and the ascetic discovered a new class of enlivening stimulants. They placed themselves before everyone's eyes, not really for many to imitate, but instead as a dreadful and yet ravishing spectacle that was staged at the borders between the world and what lies beyond, where everyone at that time thought he sometimes glimpsed rays of heavenly light and at other times uncanny tongues of flame blazing up from the depths. The eye of the saint, directed upon the significance, dreadful in every respect, of a brief earthly existence, upon the nearness of the final judgment concerning endless new stretches of life, this scorching eye in a half-destroyed body made the people of the ancient world tremble to their depths; to look, shudderingly to look away, to sense anew the stimulating attraction of the spectacle, to give in to it, to sate oneself with it until the soul trembles with fever and chills—that was the final *pleasure that antiquity discovered* after it had itself grown indifferent to the sight of contests between animals or between men.

142

To summarize what has been said: those states of the soul in which the saint or aspiring saint rejoices are composed of elements with which we are all very well acquainted, only they show themselves in different colors under the influence of conceptions other than religious ones and tend then to suffer a condemnation as intense as the admiration, even worship, they can count upon when trimmed with religion and the ultimate meaning of existence—or at least could count upon in earlier times. At times, the saint practices a defiance of himself that is closely related to the love of domination and that gives even the most solitary person a feeling of power; at other times, his swollen sensation leaps from the desire to give his passions free rein over into the desire to make them buck like wild broncos under the powerful pressure of a proud soul; at times, he wants a complete cessation of all disturbing, tormenting, stimulating sensations, a waking sleep, a lasting repose in the lap of a dulled, animal-like or vegetative indolence; at other times, he seeks out battle and kindles it within him because boredom holds its yawning face toward him: he scourges his self-adoration with self-contempt and cruelty; he rejoices in the wild uproar of his desires, in the sharp pain of sins, even in the idea of being lost; he understands how to set a trap for his affects, for his most extreme love of domination, for example, so that he passes over into a state of the most extreme degradation and his aroused soul is ripped to pieces by this contrast; and finally: if he craves for visions, conversations with the dead or with divine beings, it is basically a rare form of voluptuousness that he desires, but perhaps that voluptuousness where all other types are tied into a single knot. Novalis, one of the authorities in questions of the holiness reached through experience and instinct, expresses the whole secret with a naive joy: "It is amazing enough that the association of voluptuousness, religion, and cruelty has only recently made us aware of their inner kinship and common tendency."

143

Not what the saint is, but what he *means* in the eyes of the nonsaints, gives him his world-historical value. Because people were in error about him, because they interpreted the states of his soul incorrectly and separated him as firmly as possible from themselves, as something absolutely incomparable and strangely suprahuman: thus he attained the exceptional strength with which he could dominate the imagination of entire peoples, entire eras. He himself did not know himself; he himself understood the written characters of his moods, inclinations, and actions according to an art of interpretation that was as extravagant and artificial as the pneumatic interpretation of the Bible. What was perverse and sick in his nature, with its coupling together of spiritual poverty, faulty knowledge, ruined health, and overexcited nerves, remained as hidden from his own glance as from those contemplating him. He was not an especially good person, even less an especially wise person: but he *meant* something that reached beyond human measure in goodness and wisdom. The belief in him supported the belief in divine and miraculous things, in a religious meaning for all existence, in an imminent, final Day of Judgment.

In the twilight gleam of an end-of-the-world sun that shone down upon the Christian peoples, the shadowy form of the saint grew to a colossal size: indeed, to such a height that even in our time, which no longer believes in God, there are still plenty of thinkers who believe in the saint.

144

It goes without saying that this sketch of the saint, drawn according to the mean of the entire species, can be contrasted to many a sketch that might elicit a more pleasing sensation. Individual exceptions to that species are conspicuous, be it by their great gentleness and benevolence, be it by the magic of their unusual energy; others are attractive in the highest degree because certain mad ideas pour streams of light over their entire being: as is the case, for example, with the renowned founder of Christianity, who took himself for the only begotten son of God and therefore felt himself to be without sin; so that by means of a delusion—which one would not want to judge too harshly, because all antiquity teems with the sons of gods—he reached the same goal, a feeling of complete freedom from sin, of complete freedom from responsibility, that anyone at all can now acquire through science.—I have also neglected the Indian saints, who stand on an intermediate step between the Christian saint and the Greek philosopher and accordingly do not represent a pure type: knowledge, science—so far as such a thing existed—an elevation above other human beings through logical discipline and schooling of thought, were as much required among the Buddhists as a mark of holiness as these same characteristics, considered a mark of unholiness, were rejected and disparaged in the Christian world.

Chapter 4

From the Souls of Artists and Writers

145

What is perfect cannot have come to be.—We are accustomed to leave aside the question of becoming in regard to everything that is perfect: instead, we rejoice in its presence as if it had risen from the ground at a single, magical stroke. Here we are probably still influenced by the aftereffects of a primeval mythological sensibility. At a Greek temple like that at Paestum, for example, we still *almost* feel as if a god had playfully built his dwelling one morning from those colossal masses: at other times, as if a soul had been suddenly, magically transformed into a stone and now wants to speak from within it. The artist knows that his work achieves its full effect only if it arouses the belief in an improvisation, in the seemingly miraculous suddenness with which it came into being; and so he helps this illusion along and introduces into art elements of an inspired restlessness, a blindly groping disorder, an attentive dreaming at the beginning of the creative act, as a means of deceiving and thereby attuning the soul of the spectator or listener so that it believes in the sudden springing forth of perfection.—The science of art, as is self-evident, has to contradict this illusion as distinctly as possible and to point out the erroneous reasoning and self-indulgence that lead the intellect into the artist's net.

146

The artist's sense of truth.—In regard to apprehending truths, the artist has a weaker morality than the thinker; under no circumstances will he allow his brilliant, deeply meaningful interpretations of life to be taken from him, and he defends himself against sober, simple methods and results. It seems as if he is struggling for the higher dignity and meaning of humanity; in truth, he does not want to give up those presuppositions that are *most effectual* for his art, hence, what is fantastic, mythical, uncertain, extreme, the sense for the symbolic, the overestimation of his own person, the belief that there is something miraculous in genius: hence, he considers the perpetuation of his form of creation to be more important than the scientific devotion to truth in any shape, however plainly this may appear.

147

Art as conjurer of the dead. — Besides performing the task of conserving effaced and faded ideas, art touches them up a little bit; in fulfilling this task, art twines a band around different ages and makes their spirits return. Admittedly, it is only a semblance of life that arises from this, such as we find around gravesites or like the return of the cherished dead in a dream, but at least for a moment the old feeling comes alive once again and the heart beats in an otherwise forgotten rhythm. Now, because art generally serves this function, we have to excuse the artist himself if he does not stand in the foremost ranks of the enlightenment and the progressive *masculinization* of humanity: he has remained a lifelong child or adolescent, held back at the point where he was first overcome by his aesthetic drive; sensations from the first stages of life, however, are admittedly closer to those of earlier times than to those of the present century. Without it being his intent, it becomes his task to juvenilize humanity; this is his glory and his limitation.

148

Poets as the easers of life. — The poets, insofar as they, too, want to make our lives easier, either turn our gaze away from the toilsome present or help the present acquire new colors by shining light upon it from the past. To be capable of this, they must themselves be turned back toward the past in many respects: so that we can use them as bridges to far away times and ideas, to dying or deceased religions and cultures. They are, in fact, always and necessarily *epigones*. Admittedly, we can say some unfavorable things about the means that they use to make life easier: they soothe and heal only temporarily, only for the moment; they even keep people from working toward genuine improvement of their circumstances, because they suspend and, by palliating it, discharge the passion that impels dissatisfied people toward action.

149

The slow arrow of beauty. — The noblest sort of beauty does not sweep us away all at once, does not make stormy and intoxicating assaults (such beauty easily awakens disgust), but is instead the slowly penetrating sort that we carry around with us almost unnoticed and that we encounter again at times in a dream, but that finally, after it has laid discreetly upon our heart for a long time, takes full possession of us and fills our eyes with tears, our hearts with yearning. — What do we yearn for at the sight of beauty? To be beautiful: we imagine that there must be much happiness bound up in this. — But that is an error.

150

The animation of art. — Art raises its head where religions decline. It takes over a multitude of feelings and moods created by religion, takes them to heart, and becomes itself deeper, more animated, so that it can communicate exaltation and enthusiasm, which it was previously unable to do. The surging, flooding abundance of religious feeling breaks forth again and again and wants to conquer new domains: but increasing enlightenment has shaken the dogmas of religion and instilled a thorough mistrust of them: so the feeling that has been forced out of the religious sphere by enlightenment throws itself into art; in individual cases, also into political life, even directly into science. Everywhere that we perceive a higher, gloomy hue in human striving, we can presume that the dread of spirits, the scent of incense, and the shadows of churches still cling to it.

151

How meter embellishes.—Meter lays a gauze over reality; it brings about a certain artificiality of speech and indistinctness of thought; through the shadow that it casts upon thought, it sometimes conceals, sometimes accentuates. As shadow is necessary to embellish something, so is "obscurity" necessary to make it clear.—Art makes the sight of life bearable by laying the gauze of indistinct thinking over it.

152

Art of the ugly soul.—We set the limits of art far too narrowly if we demand that only the well-ordered, morally balanced soul be allowed expression in it. As in the plastic arts, so, too, in music and literature there is an art of the ugly soul, besides the art of the beautiful soul; and the most powerful effects of art, the breaking of souls, the moving of stones, and the turning of animals into human beings, are perhaps most successfully accomplished by precisely that art.

153

Art weighs down the thinker's heart.—We can infer how strong the metaphysical need is and how difficult nature makes it ever to leave it behind from the way that, even when the free spirit has divested himself of everything metaphysical, the highest effects of art easily bring forth a sympathetic resonance from a metaphysical string, though long silenced or even broken; it may be, for example, that at one place in Beethoven's Ninth Symphony he feels himself hovering above the earth in a starry vault, with the dream of *immortality* in his heart: all the stars seem to glitter around him and the earth to sink farther and farther away.—If he becomes conscious of this state, he no doubt feels a sharp pang deep in his heart and sighs for someone who might lead his lost love, whether we call it religion or metaphysics, back to him. At such moments, his intellectual character is put to the test.

154

Playing with life.—The facility and frivolity of the Homeric imagination was necessary in order to soothe and occasionally to suspend the excessively passionate disposition and the overly sharp intellect of the Greeks. When their intellect speaks, how bitter and cruel life seems to be! They do not deceive themselves, but they intentionally and playfully surround life with lies. Simonides advised his compatriots to take life as a game; they were all too familiar with seriousness as a source of pain (human misery, of course, is the theme of the songs that the gods most gladly hear) and they knew that only art could transform misery itself into pleasure. As punishment for this insight, however, they were so plagued by the pleasure of fabricating fables that it became hard for them to keep themselves free from deceit and deception in everyday life, just as every poetic people takes this sort of pleasure in lies, and furthermore does so quite innocently. This no doubt drove the neighboring peoples to despair at times.

155

Belief in inspiration.—Artists have an interest in our believing in sudden flashes of insight, in what we call inspirations; as if the idea for a work of art, for a poem, for the fundamental thought of a philosophy shone down like a gleam of grace from heaven. In truth, the imagination of a good artist or thinker continually produces good, mediocre, and bad things, but his *power of judgment*, highly sharpened and practiced, rejects, selects, ties together; thus, we now see from Beethoven's notebooks that he gradually gathered together the finest melodies and selected them, as it were, out of multiple beginnings. Someone who sorts things less rigorously and likes to give himself over to imitative recollection can in certain circumstances become a great improviser; but artistic improvisation stands low in relation to seriously and laboriously selected artistic thoughts. All the great artists were great workers, tireless not only in inventing, but also in rejecting, sifting, reshaping, ordering.

156

Inspiration again. — If productive power has been dammed up for a long time and hindered by an obstruction from flowing outward, then it will eventually burst forth as suddenly as if an immediate inspiration, that is, something miraculous, were taking place without any preceding inner labor. This is what constitutes the well-known illusion that artists, as noted, have rather too much interest in perpetuating. The capital has simply been *built up*; it has not fallen all at once from heaven. Moreover, such apparent inspiration exists elsewhere as well, in the field of goodness, for example, or virtue, or vice.

157

The sufferings of genius and their value. — The artistic genius wants to give pleasure, but if he stands at a very high level, there may not be anyone able to enjoy what he does; he offers food, but no one wants it. In certain circumstances, that gives him a ridiculous, touching pathos; for basically he has no right to force pleasure upon people. His pipe sounds, but nobody wants to dance: can that be tragic? — Perhaps it can. But finally, as compensation for this privation, he has more pleasure in creating than other people have in any other kind of activity. We find his sufferings exaggerated because the sound of his lament is louder, his mouth more eloquent; and *occasionally* his sufferings really are quite great, but only because his ambition and his envy are so great. The genius of knowledge, such as Kepler and Spinoza, does not ordinarily crave so much and does not make such a fuss about his genuinely greater sufferings and privations. He can count on posterity with greater certainty and dismiss the present, while an artist who does this is always playing a desperate game that must cost him heartfelt pain. In very rare cases—when in the same individual a genius for doing and for knowing and a moral genius fuse together—yet another class of pains is added to those already mentioned, ones that we must take as the most singular exceptions in the world: those extra- and suprapersonal sensibilities turned toward a people, toward humanity, toward all culture, all suffering existence: these pains attain their value from their connection with an especially difficult and remote knowledge (pity in itself is of little value).—But what measure is there for their genuineness, what scale to weigh it? Isn't it almost imperative to mistrust all who *speak* of having this kind of sensibility?

158

The fate of greatness. — Every manifestation of greatness is succeeded by degeneration, especially in the field of art. The example of greatness stimulates vainer natures to imitate it outwardly or to attempt to outdo it; in addition, all great talents have the fateful tendency to crush many weaker forces and shoots and to lay waste, as it were, to all of nature around them. The most fortunate case in the development of an art is when several geniuses keep one another within limits; their struggle usually leaves air and light for the weaker and more delicate natures, too.

159

Art is dangerous for the artist. — If art takes a powerful hold upon an individual, it draws him back to ways of seeing characteristic of those times when art blossomed most vigorously; art then works retrogressively. The artist more and more comes to worship sudden stimulation, believes in gods and demons, sees spirits throughout nature, hates science, becomes changeable in his moods like the people of antiquity, and desires the overthrow of all circumstances that are not favorable to art with the vehemence and unfairness, in fact, of a child. Now, the artist is himself already a backward being because he lingers in games appropriate for adolescence and childhood: besides which, he gradually retrogresses into past eras. Thus, a vehement antagonism finally arises between him and other people his own age, and a gloomy outcome results; just as, according to the tales of the ancients, Homer and Aeschylus wound up living and dying in melancholy.

160

Created people.—When we say that the dramatist (and the artist generally) really *creates* characters, this is a beautiful deception and exaggeration, in the existence and dissemination of which art celebrates one of its unintentional and, as it were, supplementary triumphs. In fact, we do not understand much about any real, living person and generalize very superficially if we attribute to him this character or that: now the poet conforms to this *very imperfect* attitude of ours toward people in that he makes sketches of human beings that are just as superficial as our knowledge of them is (and in this sense he "creates"). There is much deception involved in these characters created by artists; they are not at all corporeal products of nature, but instead, much like painted figures, a little too thin, so that they cannot bear close scrutiny. If we say that the character of an ordinary living person often contradicts itself and that the one created by the dramatist is the ideal image that nature dimly conceived, this is completely false. A real person is something absolutely and entirely *necessary* (even in those so-called contradictions), but we do not always recognize this necessity. The invented person, the phantasm, is meant to signify something necessary, yet only for those who understand even real people only in crude, unnaturally simplified terms: so that a few strong, oft-repeated traits, brightly illuminated and surrounded by shadows and twilight, completely satisfy their demands. They are therefore quite ready to treat the phantasm as a real, necessary human being because with real people they are accustomed to taking a phantasm, a silhouette, an arbitrary abbreviation for the whole.—The idea that the painter and the sculptor might express the "idea" of humanity is vain fancifulness and sensory deception: we are tyrannized by the eye when we say something like that, because it sees only the surface, the skin of the human body; the inner body, however, is just as much part of the idea. The plastic arts want to make character visible on the skin's surface; the verbal arts use words for the same purpose; they portray character in sound. Art proceeds from our natural *ignorance* about what is inside us (in body and character): it does not exist for natural scientists and philosophers.

161

Overestimation of self in the belief in artists and philosophers. — We all think that the excellence of a work of art or of an artist is proven if it takes hold of us and affects us deeply. Here, though, *our own excellence* in judgment and sensibility would first have to be proven: which is not the case. Who in the domain of the plastic arts has moved and delighted people more than Bernini, who has had a more powerful effect than that post-Demosthenean orator who introduced the Asiatic style and established its dominance for two centuries? This mastery over entire centuries proves nothing about the excellence and lasting validity of a style; therefore, we should not be too certain about our favorable belief in any artist: such a belief is, in fact, not only the belief in the veracity of our sensibility, but also in the infallibility of our judgment, whereas judgment, or sensibility, or both can themselves be too coarsely or too finely constituted, exaggerated, or crude. Even the blessings and bliss produced by a philosophy or a religion prove nothing about their truth: just as little as the happiness that the madman enjoys from his fixed idea proves anything about the rationality of this idea.

162

Cult of the genius, from vanity. — Because we think well of ourselves, and yet do not at all expect that we would ever be capable of drawing the outlines of a Rafaelesque painting or producing a scene like one from a Shakespearean drama, we convince ourselves that the capacity for such things is quite excessively amazing, an extremely rare accident, or, if we still have a religious sensibility, a gift of grace from above. Thus, our vanity, our love of self, demands the cult of genius: for only if we think of genius as being quite far away from us, as a *miraculum*, does it not hurt us (even Goethe, someone without envy, called Shakespeare his star of the farthest height; in connection with which one may remember that verse: "we do not desire the stars"). But apart from those insinuations of our vanity, the activity of the genius does not at all appear to be something fundamentally different from the activity of the inventor in mechanics, of the astronomer or the historical scholar, of the master tactician. All these activities can be explained if we imagine people whose thinking is active in a single direction, who use everything as material, who are always eagerly watching their inner life and that of others, who glimpse models and incitements everywhere, who do not become weary of seeking new combinations of their technical resources. The genius, too, does nothing other than learning first to set stone upon stone, then to build, nothing other than forever searching for material and forever reshaping it. Every human activity is astonishingly complicated, not only that of the genius: but none is a "miracle."—Whence, then, the belief that there is genius only in the artist, orator, and philosopher? that only they have "intuition"? (In believing this, we attribute to them a kind of miraculous eyeglass with which they see directly into "being"!) Clearly, people speak of genius only where the effects of a great intellect are most agreeable for them and where they do not wish to feel envy. To call someone "divine" means "here we do not need to compete." And then: everything finished, perfected, is viewed with amazement, everything in process underestimated. Now, nobody looking at the work of the artist can see how it *came to be*; that is his advantage, for wherever we can see the process of becoming, we grow rather cool. The perfected art of representation turns aside all thought about becoming; it rules tyrannically as perfection, here and now. Hence it is especially the artists of representation who are considered to have genius, but scientists are not. In truth, the former estimation and the latter underestimation are only the childishness of reason.

163

The seriousness of craft.—Just don't talk to me about natural gifts or innate talents! We could name great men of every kind who were only slightly gifted. But they *acquired* greatness, became "geniuses" (as we say), by means of qualities, of which when they are lacking, those who are aware of them do not readily speak: they all had that diligent earnestness of the artisan, which learns first to shape the parts perfectly before it dares to make any great whole; they gave themselves time because they took more pleasure in making small, incidental things well than in the effect of some dazzling whole. The recipe for how someone can become a good novelist can easily be given, for example, but following it presupposes qualities that we tend to overlook when we say, "I do not have enough talent." Just make a hundred or more outlines for novels, none longer than two pages, yet of such clarity that every word in them is necessary; write down anecdotes daily until you learn to find their most pregnant, effective form; be indefatigable in collecting and depicting human types and characters; above all, tell and listen to stories as often as possible, keeping a sharp eye and ear upon how they affect others who are present; travel like a landscape painter and costume designer; excerpt from the individual sciences everything that has an artistic effect when it is well represented; and finally, reflect upon the motives of human actions, scorn no instructive hints about this, and be a collector of such things day and night. Allow some ten years to go by in practicing these various things: what is then created in the workshop can even be permitted out into the light of day.—But how do most people proceed? They begin not with the part, but instead with the whole. At one point, perhaps, they hit the right tone, arouse some attention, and from then on hit worse and worse notes, for good and natural reasons. — Sometimes, if the reason and character to shape this sort of artistic career are lacking, fate and necessity take their place and lead the future master step-by-step through all the requirements of his craft.

164

Danger and gain in the cult of genius. — The belief in great, superior, fertile spirits is not necessarily, and yet very often bound up with that wholly or partially religious superstition that those spirits are of superhuman origin and possess certain miraculous capabilities that enable them to acquire their knowledge in a way completely different from other people. We ascribe to them, in fact, an immediate vision into the essence of the world, through a hole in the cloak of appearance, as it were, and believe that they can communicate something definitive and decisive about the human race and the world by means of this miraculous prophetic vision, without the toil and rigor of science. As long as believers in miracles in the realm of knowledge are still to be found, we can perhaps concede that an advantage might result for the believers themselves, insofar as they obtain the best discipline and schooling for their own spirit in its time of development from their unconditional subordination to these great spirits. On the other hand, it is at least questionable whether the superstition about genius, about its privileges and special capabilities, is advantageous for the genius himself if it takes root in him. It is in any case a dangerous sign when awe of oneself comes over any human being, whether it be the famous awe of Caesar's or the awe of genius under consideration here, or when the sacrificial scent that we bring with propriety only to a god makes its way into the brain of the genius, so that he begins to reel and to take himself for something superhuman. Gradually, the consequences are: a feeling of irresponsibility, of exceptional rights, a belief that mere association with him is a favor granted to others, insane rage at the attempt to compare him with others, much less to rate him lower, and to shed light upon the flaws in his work. Because he ceases to criticize himself, one pinion after another finally falls from his plumage: that superstition digs at the roots of his strength and perhaps even makes him into a hypocrite after his strength has left him. For great spirits themselves, it is therefore probably more useful if they gain insight into their strength and whence it came, if they understand, that is, what purely human qualities have flowed together in them, what fortunate circumstances have supervened: first of all, sustained energy, a resolute attentiveness to individual goals, great personal courage, and second, the good fortune of an education that early offered the best teachers, models, and methods. Admittedly, if their goal is to produce the greatest possible *effect*, confusion about oneself, supplemented by that semi-insanity, has always done a great deal; for people have at all times admired and envied precisely that strength in them that enabled them to deprive other people of their will and to sweep them away with the delusion that supernatural guides were leading the way. Indeed, it exalts and inspires people to believe that someone possesses supernatural powers: to that extent, madness, as Plato says, brought the greatest blessings to humanity. —In rare individual cases, this bit of madness may well also be the means by which a nature that was excessive in all directions was held firmly together: in the lives of individuals, too, hallucinations frequently have the value of remedies that are in themselves poisons: yet the poison does finally manifest itself in every "genius" convinced of his own divinity to the degree that the "genius" grows old: recall Napoleon, for example, whose belief in himself and his star and whose resulting contempt for other human beings were exactly what made his own being grow into the powerful unity that sets him apart from all modern men; until, however, this same belief finally turned into an almost insane fatalism, robbed him of his swift, keen vision and became the cause of his demise.

165

Genius and nothingness. — It is precisely those original artistic types, creating out of themselves, who under certain circumstances can bring forth something completely empty and flat, while those with a more dependent nature, so-called people of talent, are crammed with memories of all sorts of good things and even in a state of weakness produce something tolerable. If those with originality are forsaken by themselves, however, memory gives them no help: they become empty.

166

The public. — The common people really desire nothing more from tragedy than to be deeply moved, so that they can cry themselves out for once; the artist, on the other hand, who sees a new tragedy finds his pleasure in the clever technical inventions and tricks, in the handling and distribution of the material, in the new turns given to old motifs and old ideas. His position is the aesthetic position toward the work of art, that of the creator; the one first described, concerning itself only with the subject matter, that of the common people. Of those in between there is nothing to say; they are neither the people nor the artist and do not know what they want: hence even their pleasure is indistinct and slight.

167

Artistic education of the public. — If the same motif has not been treated a hundred times by various masters, the public does not learn how to get beyond an interest in the subject matter; but it will finally grasp and enjoy even the nuances, the delicate, new inventions in the handling of this motif, if it has long known the motif from numerous reworkings and no longer feels attracted by any novelty or suspense.

168

The artist and his followers must keep in step. — The advance from one level of style to another must be slow enough that not only the artists, but also the audience and spectators participate in this advance and know exactly what is going on. Otherwise, a great gulf emerges all at once between the artist, who creates his works on remote heights, and the public, which can no longer reach that height and finally, disgruntled, descends again to the depths. For if the artist no longer raises his public, it quickly sinks downward, and, indeed, plunges all the more deeply and dangerously the higher some genius has carried it, as with the eagle from whose claws the turtle borne up into the clouds falls to disaster.

169

Origin of the comic. — If we consider that for hundreds of thousands of years human beings were animals susceptible to the greatest degree of fear and that everything sudden and unexpected for them meant being ready for battle, perhaps ready for death, and that even later, in social relationships, all security rested upon what was expected and traditional in opinion and action, we should not be surprised that a person responds extravagantly to every sudden and unexpected word or action, provided it befalls him without actual danger or harm, and that he passes over into the opposite of fear: the creature trembling with fear, crumpled together, suddenly springs up and unfolds itself — a human being laughs. We call this transition from momentary fear into short-lived high spirits the *comic*. In the phenomenon of the tragic, on the other hand, a person passes quickly from great, persistent high spirits into a state of great fear; but since great and persistent high spirits are much rarer among mortals than occasions for fear, there is much more of the comic than of the tragic in the world; we laugh much more often than we are deeply shaken.

170

The artist's ambition.—The Greek artists, for example the tragedians, created poetry in order to gain victory; their entire art is unthinkable without competition: the good Hesiodic *Eris*, ambition, gave wings to their genius. Now this ambition required above all that their work maintain the highest excellence in *their own eyes*, thus, in the way that *they* understood excellence, without regard to any prevailing taste or the general opinion about what was excellent in a work of art; and so Aeschylus and Euripides remained unsuccessful for a long time until they had at last *trained* judges of art who valued their work according to the standards that they themselves applied to it. Consequently, they strive for victory over their rivals on their own evaluative terms, before their own tribunal, they want really to *be* more excellent; then they demand outside assent to their own evaluative terms, confirmation of their judgment. To strive for honor here means "to make oneself superior and to wish that this be publicly attested as well." If the first is lacking and the second nevertheless desired, one speaks of *vanity*. If the latter is lacking and is not missed, one speaks of *pride*.

171

What is necessary in the work of art.—Those who talk so much of what is necessary in a work of art exaggerate, if they are artists, *in majorem artis gloriam*, or if they are lay persons, out of ignorance. The forms of a work of art that give expression to its ideas and that are therefore its manner of speaking, always have something careless about them, like every sort of language. The sculptor can add or leave out numerous small details: likewise the performer, whether an actor or, in regard to music, a virtuoso or a conductor. These numerous small details and refinements satisfy him today, but not tomorrow; they are there more on account of the artist than the art, for amid the rigors and self-vanquishing demanded from him in representing some central idea, he, too, occasionally requires sweets and playthings in order not to become ill-tempered.

172

Making us forget the master.—The pianist who performs the work of a master will have played the best if he makes us forget the master and if it seems as if he is telling a story from his own life or is experiencing something right now. Admittedly: if he *is* nothing significant, everyone will curse the garrulousness with which he narrates to us from his own life. Therefore, he must understand how to captivate the listener's imagination on his own behalf. From this, in turn, all the weaknesses and follies of "virtuosity" can be explained.

173

Corriger la fortune.—There are terrible contingencies in the lives of great artists that compel a painter, for example, to sketch only the merest fleeting idea of his most significant picture or that compelled Beethoven, for example, to bequeath us in many great sonatas (as in the great B-flat Major sonata) only the unsatisfactory piano extracts of a symphony. Here, the artist who comes afterward should seek to correct the life of great artists after the fact: what someone would do, for instance, who as a master of all orchestral effects would awaken for us the symphony that seems there to have fallen into a pianistic trance.

174

Making smaller.—Many things, events, or persons cannot stand being dealt with on a small scale. One cannot reduce the Laocoön group to a knick-knack; it needs a large scale. But it is much rarer that something small by nature can stand being enlarged, which is why biographers are always more likely to succeed at representing a great man in small terms than a small one in great terms.

175

Sensuousness in contemporary art. — Artists often miscalculate at present if they try to achieve their aesthetic effects by working upon the senses; for their spectators or listeners no longer have full use of their senses and, quite contrary to the artist's intention, his work of art induces in them a "sanctified" sort of feeling which is closely related to boredom. — Their sensuousness begins, perhaps, exactly where the artist's ceases; at best, therefore, they meet at a single point.

176

Shakespeare as moralist. — Shakespeare reflected a great deal upon the passions and probably had by temperament quite intimate access to many of them (dramatists are in general rather wicked human beings). But he was not capable, like Montaigne, of speaking about them, and instead placed observations *about* the passions in the mouths of the impassioned figures: which is admittedly contrary to nature, but fills his dramas so full of ideas that they make all others seem empty and easily arouse a general antipathy against them. — Schiller's maxims (which are almost always based upon false or trivial insights) are maxims *for* the theater and as such work to great effect: while Shakespeare's maxims do honor to his model, Montaigne, and contain quite serious thoughts in polished form, but are consequently too far-reaching and too finely wrought for the eyes of the theatrical public and are therefore ineffective.

177

Making oneself heard well. — One must not only understand how to play well, but also how to make oneself heard well. Even in the hands of the greatest master, the violin emits only a chirping sound if the room is too large; we can mistake the master for a mere bungler there.

178

The incomplete as what is effective. — As figures done in relief work so strongly upon the imagination because they seem just about to step forth from the wall, as it were, and then suddenly, somehow hindered, come to a stop: so the relieflike, incomplete representation of a thought or of a whole philosophy sometimes has more effect than working it out thoroughly does: we leave more for the viewer to do, he is roused to continue shaping and to think through to the end what has set itself before him in such strong light and shadow, and to overcome by himself the obstacle that hindered it from fully emerging before.

179

Against originals. — When art clothes itself in the most worn-out materials, we most readily recognize it as art.

180

Collective spirit. — A good writer contains not only his own spirit, but the spirit of his friends besides.

181

Two-fold misapprehension. — The misfortune of astute and clear writers is that we take them to be superficial and therefore bestow no effort upon them: and the good fortune of unclear writers that the reader labors over them and ascribes to them the pleasure derived from his own zeal.

182

Relationship to science. — All those who begin to warm to a science only when they themselves have made discoveries there have no genuine interest in it.

183

The key.—A single thought that someone of significance greatly values, though laughed at and mocked by insignificant people, is for him a key to hidden treasure houses, for those others nothing more than a piece of old iron.

184

Untranslatable.—It is neither the best nor the worst of a book that is untranslatable.

185

Paradoxes of the author.—The so-called paradoxes of an author at which a reader takes offense often stand not in the author's book at all, but in the reader's head.

186

Wit.—The wittiest authors raise the least noticeable smile.

187

Antithesis.—Antithesis is the narrow gate through which error prefers to creep toward truth.

188

Thinkers as stylists.—Most thinkers write badly because they communicate to us not only their thoughts, but also the thinking of their thoughts.

189

Thoughts in poems.—The poet leads his thoughts along festively, upon the chariot of rhythm: usually because they cannot walk on their own feet.

190

Sin against the reader's spirit.—When an author denies his talent simply in order to equate himself with the reader, he commits the only mortal sin for which the reader will never forgive him: provided, of course, that the reader notices it. We can as a rule say all sorts of bad things about someone: but in the *way* we say them, we must know how to restore his vanity.

191

Limit of honesty.—One word too many gets away from even the most honest writer when he wants to round off a phrase.

192

The best author.—The best author will be the one who is ashamed of becoming a writer.

193

Draconian law against writers.—We should consider a writer as a criminal who deserves acquittal or pardon only in the rarest of cases: that would be one remedy against the increase of books.

194

The fools of modern culture.—The fools of medieval courts correspond to our feuilletonists; they are the same species of person, half-rational, witty, exaggerated, silly, only there to temper from time to time an atmosphere of pathos with witticisms or babbling to drown out the all too weighty, solemn clanging of great events with their outcry; formerly in the service of princes and nobility, now in the service of parties (since a good deal of the old submissiveness in the people's intercourse with their prince still lives on in party feeling and party discipline). But the whole modern class of literati stands very close to the feuilletonists; they are the "fools of modern culture," whom we judge more tolerantly if we take them as not completely responsible for their actions. To regard writing as a lifelong profession should in fairness be considered a sort of insanity.

195

After the Greeks. — It stands very much in the way of knowledge that all words have become hazy and inflated due to the fact that feeling has been exaggerated for centuries. The higher stage of culture that puts itself under the dominion (if not under the tyranny) of knowledge requires great sobriety of feeling and strong concentration upon every word, in which respect the Greeks of the age of Demosthenes were ahead of us. All modern writings can be characterized as overstrained; and even when they are written simply, the words in them will still be *felt* too eccentrically. Rigorous deliberation, terseness, coldness, plainness, intentionally sustained to their very limits, the restraint of feeling and taciturnity in general — that alone can help. — Moreover, this cold way of writing and feeling is now, as a contrast, very stimulating: and therein, admittedly, lies a new danger. For brisk coldness is as much of a stimulant as a high degree of warmth.

196

Good narrators, bad explicators. — Good narrators often display an admirable psychological certainty and consistency insofar as these things can be brought out in the actions of their characters, but that stands in outright ludicrous contrast to the ineptitude of their psychological thinking: so that their level of culture seems at one moment to be just as remarkably high as in the next to be deplorably low. It happens all too frequently that they explain their own heroes and their actions in an obviously *false* way — there is no doubt of it, however improbable this sounds. The greatest piano player has perhaps reflected very little upon the technical conditions of his art and the special virtue, vice, utility, and educability of every finger (dactylic ethics), and makes clumsy mistakes when he speaks about such things.

197

The writings of acquaintances and their readers.—We read the writings of people we know (friends and enemies) in a double way, inasmuch as our knowledge of them is continually whispering: "that is his, a sign of his inner being, his experiences, his talent," and at the same time another sort of knowledge is seeking to ascertain what the yield is of that work itself, what estimation it deserves in general, apart from its author, what enrichment of knowledge it brings with it. Each of these ways of reading and deliberating interferes with the other, as is self-evident. A conversation with a friend will likewise ripen into the good fruit of knowledge only if both finally think only of the matter at hand and forget that they are friends.

198

Rhythmic sacrifice.—Good writers change the rhythm of many lines simply because they do not attribute to ordinary readers the capacity to grasp the beat that the lines followed in their first version: therefore, they make it easier for them by giving preference to better-known rhythms.—This consideration for the rhythmical incapacity of the present-day reader has already elicited many a sigh, for much has already been sacrificed to it. —Might not the same thing be happening to good musicians?

199

The incomplete as aesthetic stimulant.—Something incomplete is often more effective than completeness, as is especially the case with the eulogy: for its purposes, we need a stimulating incompleteness as an irrational element that dazzles the listener's imagination with the image of a sea, while concealing the opposite coast, that is, the limitedness of the object to be praised, as if it were in fog. If we mention the known merits of someone in a detailed and extensive way, this always lets the suspicion arise that these are his only merits. Anyone who is complete in his praise puts himself above the one being praised; he seems to *survey* him from above. For that reason, completeness has an attenuating effect.

200

What to beware in writing and teaching. — Anyone who has ever begun writing and feels within himself the passion of writing learns from almost everything that he does and experiences only what is communicable in writing. He no longer thinks of himself, but instead of the writer and his public; he wants insight, but not for his own use. Anyone who is a teacher is usually incapable of doing something on his own for his own benefit; he is always thinking of the benefit for his students, and any knowledge gives him pleasure only insofar as he can teach it. He considers himself finally as a passageway of knowledge and generally as a means, so that he has lost the ability to take himself seriously.

201

Bad writers are necessary. — There will always have to be bad writers, for they suit the taste of the undeveloped, immature age groups; these have their needs, as do more mature ones. If the human lifespan were longer, the number of mature individuals would turn out to be preponderant to or at least as great as that of the immature ones; but as it is, by far the most people die too young, that is, there are always many more undeveloped intellects with bad taste. Moreover, these latter crave, with the greater intensity of youth, satisfaction of their needs, and they *compel* bad writers to appear.

202

Too near and too far. — The reader and the author frequently do not understand each other because the author knows his subject too well and finds it almost boring, so that he spares himself the examples that he knows by the hundred; the reader, however, is not familiar with the subject matter and can easily find it to be badly grounded if the examples are withheld from him.

203

A vanished preparation for art.—Of all that college preparatory schools did, the most worthwhile was requiring practice in Latin style: this was an *aesthetic exercise*, whereas all the other activities had only knowledge as their purpose. To privilege the German essay is barbaric, for we do not have an exemplary German style that grew up amid public eloquence; however, if we do want to use the German essay to encourage practice in thinking, it is certainly better to disregard style for the present, that is, to make a distinction between practice in thinking and in presentation. The latter should be based upon multiple versions of a given content and not upon independent invention of content. The mere presentation of some given content was the task of Latin style, for which the teachers of old possessed an acuteness of hearing that has long since been lost. Formerly, anyone who learned to write well in a modern language owed it to this exercise (now one must necessarily go to school with the older French writers); but even more: he acquired a conception of the majesty and difficulty of form and was prepared for art generally in the only correct way, through practice.

204

Dark and overly bright next to each other.—Writers who in general do not understand how to give clarity to their thoughts will in individual cases choose by preference the strongest, most exaggerated designations and superlatives: there results from this an effect of lighting similar to using torches for illumination along tangled forest paths.

205

Writing as painting.—We can represent a significant object best if we take the colors for the painting from the object itself, as a chemist would, and then use them like an artist: so that we let the design grow out of the boundaries and transitions of the colors. The painting thus acquires something of the enrapturing natural element that makes the object itself meaningful.

206

Books that teach how to dance.—There are writers who, by presenting the impossible as possible and speaking of morality and genius as if both were merely a mood, a caprice, produce a feeling of high-spirited freedom, as if one were to get up on tiptoe and simply had to dance for joy.

207

Incomplete thoughts.—Just as not only manhood, but also adolescence and childhood, have value *in themselves* and are not to be appraised simply as passageways and bridges, so, too, do incomplete thoughts have their own value. We must therefore not torment a poet with subtle exegesis and must take pleasure in the uncertainty of his horizon, as if the way to further thoughts still lay open. We stand at the threshold; we wait as though at the excavation of a treasure: it is as if a fortuitous discovery of profound ideas were about to be made. The poet anticipates something of the pleasure of the thinker in discovering a crucial thought and makes us desire it, so that we snatch at it; but it flutters past our heads, displaying the most beautiful butterfly-wings—and yet it slips away from us.

208

The book become almost human.—It surprises every writer anew how a book lives on with a life of its own as soon as it has been detached from him; he feels as if one part of an insect had been separated and were now going its own way. Perhaps he almost completely forgets it, perhaps he raises himself above the views set down there, perhaps he no longer even understands it and has lost the updraft on which he flew when he devised that book: meanwhile, it seeks out its readers, ignites life, causes happiness or fear, begets new works, becomes the soul of projects and of actions—in short: it lives like a being

provided with spirit and soul and yet is not a human being.—
That author has drawn the happiest lot who as an old man can say that every life-creating, invigorating, elevating, enlightening thought and feeling in him still lives on in his writings and that he himself now signifies only the gray ashes, while the fire has everywhere been saved and carried on.—Now if we reflect that every human action, and not only a book, in some way becomes the cause of other actions, decisions, thoughts, that everything that happens is indissolubly tied up with everything that will happen, then we recognize the real *immortality* that exists, that of movement: anything that has ever moved is included and eternalized in the total union of all that exists, like an insect in amber.

209

Joy in old age.—The thinker, and likewise the artist, whose better self has taken refuge in his works feels an almost malicious joy when he sees how his body and spirit are broken and destroyed by time, as if he were watching from some corner as a thief works on his safe, while knowing that it is empty and that all the valuables have been saved.

210

Tranquil fruitfulness.—The born aristocrats of spirit are not too eager; their creations appear and then fall from the tree on a tranquil autumn evening without being impatiently desired, hurried forward, or supplanted by something new. The ceaseless desire to create is vulgar, a sign of jealousy, envy, ambition. If one is something, one does not really need to make anything—and yet one does a great deal. There is a still higher species above the "productive" human being.

211

Achilles and Homer.—It is always as it was between Achilles and Homer: one person has the experience, the sensation, the other *describes* it. A real writer only gives words to the affects and experiences of others; he is an artist in divining a great deal from the little that he has felt. Artists are by no means people of great passion, but they frequently *present* themselves as such, unconsciously sensing that others give greater credence to the passions they portray if the artist's own life testifies to his experience in this area. We need only let ourselves go, not control ourselves, give free play to our wrath or our desire, and the whole world immediately cries: how passionate he is! But there really is something significant in a deeply gnawing passion that consumes and often swallows up an individual: whoever experiences this surely does not describe it in dramas, music, or novels. Artists are frequently *unbridled* individuals, insofar, that is, as they are not artists: but that is something different.

212

Old doubts about the effect of art. — Can it be that pity and fear, as Aristotle claims, really are purged by tragedy, so that the audience returns home colder and calmer? Can ghost stories really make people less fearful and superstitious? With certain physical processes, for example with sexual pleasure, it is true that the drive is eased and temporarily moderated when the need is satisfied. But fear and pity are not in this sense the needs of specific organs, which have to be relieved. And in the long run, every drive is *intensified* by the practice of satisfying it, despite that periodic easing. It might be that in every individual case pity and fear would be attenuated and purged by tragedy: nevertheless, they could on the whole become greater under the influence of tragedy, and Plato would still be correct in asserting that tragedy on the whole makes people more fearful and susceptible to emotion. The tragic poet himself, then, would necessarily acquire a gloomy, fearful view of the world and a soft, sensitive, lachrymose soul; it would likewise correspond to Plato's opinion if the tragic poets and the entire community that especially delights in them would degenerate into ever greater excess and licentiousness. — But what right at all does our age have to give any answer to Plato's great question concerning the moral influence of art? Even if we had the art—where do we see the influence, any influence *whatsoever*, of art?

213

Pleasure in nonsense.—How can people take pleasure in nonsense? For wherever laughter occurs, this is the case; indeed, one can say that almost everywhere that happiness exists, there is pleasure in nonsense. The turning of experience into its opposite, of the purposeful into the purposeless, of the necessary into the arbitrary, yet in such a way that this process does no harm and is only conceived out of high spirits, delights us, for it momentarily frees us from the pressure of what is necessary, purposeful, and in accordance with experience, wherein we generally see our inexorable masters; we play and laugh whenever something expected (which usually makes us fearful and tense) discharges itself without doing any harm. It is the pleasure of slaves at the Saturnalia.

214

Ennobling reality.—Because people saw a divinity in the aphrodisiac drive and felt it working within them with worshipful gratitude, that affect was in the course of time drawn into more elevated conceptual spheres and thus really became greatly ennobled. By virtue of this art of idealization, some peoples created from illnesses powers that were greatly beneficial for culture: for example the Greeks, who in earlier centuries suffered from great epidemics of nervous disorders (in the form of epilepsy and St. Vitus's dance) and constructed from that the magnificent type of the Bacchante.—For the Greeks possessed nothing close to a sturdy healthiness—their secret was to revere even sickness, provided it had *power*, as a god.

215

Music.—In and of itself, music is not so meaningful for our inner being, so deeply stimulating, that it should pass for the *immediate* language of feeling; but its age-old connection with poetry has put so much symbolism in rhythmical movement, in the loudness and softness of tones, that we now imagine it speaks directly *to our inner being* and comes *from* our inner being. Dramatic music first becomes possible when the musical art has conquered an enormous range of symbolic resources through song, opera, and hundredfold attempts at the painting of tones. "Absolute music" is either form in itself, in the primitive state of music where merely making sounds in tempo and in varying loudness causes pleasure, or else the symbolism of forms that by this time speaks to the understanding without poetry, after both arts have been bound together throughout a long period of development and the musical form has finally been completely interwoven with conceptual and emotional threads. People who remain backward in their musical development can apprehend in a purely formalistic way the same piece of music that more advanced people understand in a completely symbolic way. No music is in itself profound and meaningful, it does not speak of the "will" or of the "thing in itself"; the intellect could come to fancy such things only in an age that had conquered the entire expanse of inner life for musical symbolism. The intellect has itself *placed* this significance in sounds, as it likewise put into the relations of lines and masses in architecture a significance that is in itself, however, completely foreign to the laws of mechanics.

216

Gesture and speech. — Older than speech is the mimicking of gestures, which takes place involuntarily and is even now, despite a general repression of gestural language and a cultivated mastery of the muscles, so strong that we cannot look upon facial movements without innervation of our own face (one can observe that feigned yawning evokes a natural yawning in someone who sees it). The imitated gesture led the person who was imitating back to the sensation that expressed itself in the face or body of the person being imitated. Thus people learned to understand one another; thus the child still learns to understand its mother. In general, painful sensations may well have been expressed by gestures that themselves caused pain (for example, tearing out one's hair, beating one's breast, violent contorting and tensing of the facial muscles). Conversely: gestures of pleasure were themselves pleasurable and hence were easily adapted for the purposes of communicative understanding (laughter as an expression of being tickled, which is pleasurable, served for the expression of other pleasurable sensations besides). — As soon as people understood one another in gestures, a *symbolism* of gestures could arise: I mean that people could agree upon a language of sound signals by first producing sound *and* gesture (the former symbolically joined to the latter) and later only the sound. — It seems as if often in early times the same thing occurred that now takes place before our eyes and ears in the development of music, especially of dramatic music: whereas at first music without explanatory dance and mime (gestural language) is empty noise, through long habituation to the juxtaposition of music and movement the ear has been schooled to immediately interpret the tonal figures, finally reaching a level of rapid understanding where it no longer requires the visible movement and *understands* the tonal poet without this. We speak then of absolute music, that is, of music in which everything is immediately understood symbolically without further assistance.

217

The desensualizing of higher art. — Due to the exceptional exercising of the intellect caused by the aesthetic development of modern music, our ears have become ever more intellectual. Hence we now tolerate much greater loudness, much more "noise," because we are much better trained to listen for the *reason in it* than our ancestors were. In fact, all of our senses have become somewhat dulled precisely because they immediately inquire for the reason, that is, for what "it means," and no longer for what "it is": such dulling betrays itself, for example, in the absolute dominance of tonal tempering; for ears that still make the finer distinctions, between C sharp and D flat for example, are now among the exceptions. In this regard our ear has become coarser. Then, too, the ugly side of the world, originally inimical to the senses, has been conquered for music; its sphere of power, especially to express the sublime, fearful, and mysterious, has grown astonishingly wide; our music now brings into speech things that earlier had no tongue. In a similar way, some painters have made the eye more intellectual and have gone far beyond what was formerly called pleasure in colors and forms. Here, too, the side of the world that was originally considered ugly has been conquered by the aesthetic understanding. — What is the consequence of all this? The more capable of thoughts the eye and ear become, the closer they come to the limits where they become unsensuous: pleasure is displaced into the brain, the sensory organs themselves become dull and weak, the symbolic more and more takes the place of what exists — and so we arrive at barbarism as surely by this path as by any other. Meanwhile it is still said: the world is uglier than ever, but it *signifies* a more beautiful world than there has ever been. But the more the ambergris odor of meaning is diffused and dispersed, the rarer are those who still perceive it: and the others finally remain fixed beside what is ugly and try to enjoy it directly, at which attempt, however, they will inevitably fail. So there is in Germany a double stream of musical development: here a crowd of ten thousand with ever higher, more refined demands, ever more attentive to what "it means," and there the enormous majority who every year become more incapable of understanding what is meaningful, even in the form of sensory ugliness, and therefore learn to grab with ever more satisfaction for what is intrinsically ugly and disgusting in music, that is, for what has a vulgar sensuousness.

218

Stone is more stony than before. — In general, we no longer understand architecture, at least not nearly as well as we understand music. We have outgrown the symbolism of lines and figures, just as we have lost the habit of recognizing the effects of rhetorical tone and no longer suck this sort of cultural mother's milk from the first moment of our lives. Everything in a Greek or Christian building originally signified something, and indeed, did so by reference to a higher order of things: this atmosphere of inexhaustible significance lay upon the building like a magical veil. Beauty came only incidentally into the system, without essentially affecting the fundamental sensation of the uncanny sublime, of things consecrated by proximity to the gods and to magic; at most, beauty *mitigated* the *dread*—but this dread was everywhere the presupposition.—What is the beauty of a building to us now? The same thing as the beautiful face of a woman without spirit: something masklike.

219

Religious origin of modern music.—Music of the soul arises in the restored Catholicism after the Council of Trent thanks to Palestrina, who assisted the newly awakened, deeply moved inner spirit to expression; later, with Bach, in Protestantism as well, insofar as it was made more profound by the Pietists and released from its original, fundamentally dogmatic character. The presupposition and necessary preliminary step for both developments is the preoccupation with music that characterized the period of the Renaissance and pre-Renaissance, especially that learned involvement with music, that basically scientific pleasure in artistic feats of harmonics and counterpoint. On the other hand, opera also had to precede this: in which the laity made known its protest against an excessively learned, cold music and wished to grant a soul to Polyhymnia once more.—Without that deeply religious change in mood, without that ringing out of the most inwardly aroused disposition, music would have remained learned or operatic; the spirit of the Counter-Reformation is the spirit of modern music (for the Pietism in Bach's music is also a sort of Counter-Reformation). So deeply are we indebted to the religious life.—Music was the *Counter-Renaissance* in the field of art, to which the later painting of Murillo belongs, and perhaps the Baroque style as well: more so, in any case, than the architecture of the Renaissance or of antiquity. And yet we might now ask: if our modern music could move stones, would it assemble them into an architecture like antiquity's? I very much doubt it. For what reigns in this music—affect, pleasure in elevated, all-encompassing moods, the desire for liveliness at any price, the rapid change of sensations, strong effects of relief in light and shadow, the juxtaposition of ecstasy and naiveté—all that reigned once already in the plastic arts and created new laws of style:—but it was neither in antiquity nor in the time of the Renaissance.

220

The idea of the beyond in art.—Not without deep pain do we admit to ourselves that the artists of all ages have in their highest flights carried to heavenly transfiguration precisely those conceptions that we now recognize as false: they are the glorifiers of the religious and philosophical errors of humanity, and they could not have done this without their belief in the absolute truth of these errors. Now if the belief in such truth generally diminishes, if the rainbow colors at the outermost ends of human knowing and imagining fade: then the species of art that, like the *Divina commedia*, Raphael's pictures, Michelangelo's frescoes, the Gothic cathedrals, presupposes not only a cosmic, but also a metaphysical significance for art objects can never blossom again. A touching tale will come of this, that there once was such an art, such belief by artists.

221

The revolution in poetry.—The strict constraint that the French dramatists imposed upon themselves in regard to unity of action, of place, and of time, as in style, verse- and sentence-structure, selection of words and thoughts, was as important a schooling as that of counterpoint and fugue in the development of modern music or that of Gorgian tropes in Greek rhetoric. To bind oneself in such a way can seem absurd; nevertheless, there is no other means for getting past naturalizing impulses than first to limit oneself in the most severe (perhaps most arbitrary) way. Thus we gradually learn how to step gracefully even upon narrow footbridges spanning dizzying chasms and we bring home the highest suppleness in movement as our profit: as the history of music demonstrates to the eyes of everyone now living. Here we see how step by step the fetters become looser until they can finally seem to have been wholly thrown off: this *appearance* is the highest result of a necessary development in art. In modern poetry, no such fortunate, gradual extrication from self-imposed fetters took place. Lessing made the French form, that is, the only modern art form, an object of mockery in Germany and made Shakespeare his point of reference, and thus we lost the steadying continuity of that unfettering and made a leap into naturalism — that is, back into the beginnings of art. Goethe attempted to save himself from this by always knowing how to bind himself in ever new and varied ways; but even the most gifted get only as far as continual experimentation once the thread of development has been torn. Schiller owes the relative sureness of his form to having involuntarily respected, if also repudiated, French tragedy as a model and to having kept himself fairly independent from Lessing (whose dramatic experiments he rejected, as is well known). After Voltaire, the French themselves suddenly lacked the great talents who would have led the way in developing tragedy from constraint into the appearance of freedom; following the German model, they, too, later made the leap into a sort of Rousseauean state of nature in art and began experimenting. Simply read Voltaire's *Mahomet* from time to time in order to perceive clearly what was lost once and for all to European culture by that break from tradition. Voltaire was the last of the great dramatists who used Greek moderation to restrain a polymorphic soul that could encompass the greatest tragic thunderstorms — he was able to do what no German was yet capable of doing because the French are by nature much more closely related to the Greeks than are the

Germans—just as he was the last great writer who had a Greek ear, a Greek aesthetic conscientiousness, a Greek simplicity and charm in his handling of prose discourse; just as he was one of the last of those people who could combine in themselves the highest freedom of the spirit and an absolutely unrevolutionary disposition without being inconsistent and cowardly. Since then, the modern spirit, with its restlessness, its hatred of moderation and restraint, has come to dominate in every area, first unleashed by the fever of revolution, and then reining itself in again when seized by fear and dread of itself—but with the reins of logic, no longer with those of aesthetic moderation. To be sure, when thus unfettered we can enjoy for a while the poetries of all peoples, everything that has grown up in hidden places, primeval growth, wildly blossoming, wonderfully beautiful and gigantically irregular, from folk songs up through the "great barbarian" Shakespeare; we taste the joys of local color and period costume, which have until now been alien to all artistic peoples; we make ample use of the "barbaric advantages" of our time that Goethe asserted against Schiller in order to set the formlessness of his Faust in the most favorable light. But for how much longer? The encroaching flood of poetries of all styles and all peoples *must* gradually wash away the soil in which a quiet, concealed growth might still have been possible; all poets *must* become experimenting imitators, reckless copiers, however great their strength at the start; the public, finally, which has forgotten how to see a genuinely aesthetic act in the restraining of the power of representation, in the organizing mastery of every aesthetic technique, *must* more and more value force for the sake of force, color for the sake of color, thought for the sake of thought, even inspiration for the sake of inspiration; accordingly, this public cannot enjoy the elements and conditions of the work of art at all except *in isolation*, and finally it makes the natural demand that the artist *must* also present them to it in isolation. To be sure, we threw off the "unreasonable" fetters of Franco-Greek art, but imperceptibly accustomed ourselves to finding all fetters, all limitation unreasonable;—and so art moves toward its dissolution and thereby touches—admittedly in a very instructive way—upon every phase of its beginnings, its childhood, its incompletion, its one-time gambles and extravagancies: it interprets, as it descends toward destruction, its emergence, its becoming. One of the great ones, upon whose instinct we can surely rely and whose theory lacked nothing except thirty *more* years of practice—Lord Byron once said: "With regard to poetry in general I am convinced the more I think of it that we are all on the wrong path, one as much as another. We are all upon an inwardly wrong revolutionary system—our generation or the next will finally be of this opinion." This is the same Byron who says: "I look upon Shakespeare as the worst model, though as the most extraordinary of writers." And basically, doesn't Goethe's mature aesthetic insight from the second half of his life say exactly the same thing?—that insight, with which he made such a leap across a series of generations that one can on the whole maintain that Goethe has not yet had his effect and that his time is still to come? Precisely because his nature held him for a long time firmly within the path of the poetic revolution, precisely because he savored most deeply all the discoveries, prospects, and resources that were indirectly uncovered by that break from tradition and had been unearthed, as it were, from beneath the ruins of art, therefore his later transformation and conversion carries so much weight: it means that he felt the deepest desire to regain the artistic tradition and to ascribe, at least with the eye of imagination, the ancient perfection and wholeness to the still standing ruins and colonnades of the temple, even if the strength of his arms should prove itself far too weak to build anything where such tremendous forces had been necessary for destruction. Thus he lived in art as though in recollection of true art: his writing became a means of recollecting, of understanding ancient, long-departed artistic eras. To be sure, his demands were unfulfillable, considering the strength of the new age; the pain of this was, however, amply compensated by his joy in the fact that they once *had been* fulfilled, and that we, too, can still participate in this fulfillment. Not individuals, but more or less ideal masks; no reality, but an allegorical generality; historical types, local color attenuated almost to invisibility and made mythic; contemporary sensibility and the problems of contemporary society compressed to the simplest forms, stripped of their stimulating, absorbing, pathological characteristics, made *ineffectual* in any sense other than an artistic one; no new materials and characters, but the ancient, long-familiar ones in everlasting reanimation and transformation: that is art as Goethe later *understood* it, as the Greeks and the French, too, *practiced* it.

222

What remains of art. — It is true that art has much greater value under certain metaphysical presuppositions; for example, if one holds the belief that character is unchangeable and that the essence of the world continually expresses itself in all characters and actions: then the artist's work becomes an image of something *everlasting*, whereas in our conception, the artist can give his image validity only for a certain time, because humanity as a whole has come to be and is changeable, and even the individual human being is neither fixed nor enduring. — The same holds true under another metaphysical presupposition: granting that our visible world is only appearance, as the metaphysicians presume, art would then come fairly close to the real world: for there would then be all too much similarity between the world of appearance and the artist's world of dream images; and the remaining difference would put the significance of art even higher than the significance of nature because art would represent the uniformity of nature, its types and exemplars. — Those presuppositions, however, are false: what place still remains for art after coming to know this? Above all, it has taught us over thousands of years to look upon life in all its forms with interest and pleasure and to bring our sensibility sufficiently far that we can finally cry: "life, however it may be, is good." This teaching of art — to take pleasure in existence and, without too fervent an engagement with it, to view human life as a piece of nature, as an object whose development is governed by laws—this teaching has grown up within us, and now it comes to light again as an omnipotent need to know. We could give up art, but would not thereby forfeit the capacity we have learned from it: just as we have given up religion, but not the heightening of sensibility and the exaltation acquired from it. Just as the plastic arts and music are the measure of the wealth of feeling really acquired and obtained from religion, so would the intense and manifold delight in life that has been implanted by art still demand satisfaction after its disappearance. The scientific human being is a further development of the artistic one.

223

Twilight of art.—As in old age we recall our youth and celebrate festivals of remembrance, so humanity will soon stand in relation to art, seeing it as a touching recollection of the joys of youth. Perhaps never before has art been so profoundly and tenderly grasped as now, when the magic of death seems playfully to surround it. Think of that Greek city in southern Italy, which on a single day of the year still celebrated its Greek festivals amid sorrow and tears that foreign barbarism was triumphing more and more over the customs brought along from Greece; never did anyone so savor the Hellenic, nowhere did anyone quaff this golden nectar with such intense pleasure, as among these declining Hellenes. We will soon view the artist as a magnificent relic and show him the honor that we would not readily grant to anyone of our own kind, as if honoring a wonderful stranger upon whose strength and beauty the happiness of earlier times depended. What is best in us has perhaps been inherited from the sensations of earlier times, which we can scarcely approach in an immediate way any more; the sun has already gone down, but the heaven of our life still glows and shines from its presence, even though we no longer see it.

Chapter 5

Signs of Higher and Lower Culture

224

Refinement through degeneration. — History teaches that *the* most self-sustaining branch of a people will be the one where most individuals have a sense of community as a result of the similarity in their habitual and indiscussible principles, that is, as a result of their common beliefs. Here good, sound customs are strengthened, here the subordination of the individual is learned and character is already given steadiness as a gift at birth and has it afterward reinforced by upbringing. The danger for these strong communities based upon individuals who all share a similar character is a gradual increase in inherited stupidity, which trails all stability like its shadow. It is the more unconstrained, the much more uncertain and morally weaker individuals upon whom *spiritual progress* depends in such communities: these are the people who attempt new things and, in general, many different things. Because of their weakness, countless individuals of this kind perish without much visible effect; but in general, especially when they have descendants, they loosen things up and inflict from time to time a wound upon the stable element of a community. Precisely in this wounded and weakened spot, the collective being is *inoculated*, as it were, with something new; but its strength as a whole must be great enough to absorb this new thing into its blood and to assimilate it. Degenerate natures are of the highest significance wherever progress is to ensue. A partial weakening has to precede every large-scale advance. The strongest natures *maintain* the type; the weaker ones help to *develop* it *further*. — Something similar occurs in the individual human being; seldom is any degeneration, any mutilation, even a vice or any physical or moral damage whatsoever without an advantage in some other respect. For instance, a more sickly individual who lives among a warlike and restless tribe will perhaps have more occasion to be by himself and thereby become calmer and wiser; someone with one eye will have *one* stronger eye; a blind person will see more deeply within and will in any case have sharper hearing. To that extent, the renowned struggle for existence does not seem to me to be the only point of view from which the progress or strengthening of an individual or a race can be explained. Instead, two things must come together: first, an increase in the stabilizing force brought about by uniting minds in belief and in communal feeling; and second, the possibility of attaining higher goals as degenerate natures turn up and, in consequence, partial weakenings and woundings of the stabilizing force occur; it is precisely the weaker nature, as the more delicate and free, that makes any progress possible at all. A people that has begun to crumble and weaken somewhere, but is on the whole still strong and healthy, can absorb the infection of what is new and incorporate it advantageously. For the individual human being, the task of education involves this: putting him so firmly and securely on track that he can as a whole no longer be diverted from his path. Then, however, the educator has to inflict wounds upon him or to use the wounds that fate inflicts, and when pain and need have resulted from this, something new and refined can be inoculated into the wounded places. His whole nature will take it in and later, in its fruits, make the traces of its refinement visible. — As for what concerns the state, Machiavelli says that "the form of government has very little significance, although half-educated people think otherwise. The great goal of the art of politics should be *durability*, which outweighs everything else, since it is much more valuable than freedom." Only when the maximum durability has been securely grounded and guaranteed is steady development and refining inoculation possible at all. Admittedly, the dangerous associate of all durability, authority, will generally resist that.

225

Free spirit a relative concept. — We call someone a free spirit who thinks differently from what we expect of him on the basis of his origin, environment, his social rank and position, or on the basis of the prevailing views of the time. He is the exception, the constrained spirits are the rule; they reproach him by saying that his free principles either have their origin in the desire to attract attention or logically lead to free actions, that is, to ones that are irreconcilable with any secure morality. Occasionally someone also says that these or those free principles derive from perverseness and intellectual exaggeration; yet only a maliciousness that does not itself believe what it says, but simply wants to cause some harm, speaks thus: for proof of the greater excellence and keenness of his intellect is usually written so legibly upon the free spirit's face that the constrained spirits understand it well enough. But both of the other derivations of free-spiritedness are sincerely meant; and in fact, many free spirits do originate in one of these ways. Yet the principles that they reach upon those paths might therefore be truer and more reliable than those of the constrained spirits. With knowledge of the truth, what matters is whether one *has* it, not what induced one to seek it or the way in which one found it. If the free spirits are right, then the constrained spirits are wrong, regardless of whether the former came to the truth via immorality and whether the others have up until then held fast to untruth out of morality. — Moreover, what is essential in the free spirit is not that his views be more correct, but instead, that he has freed himself from tradition, whether the outcome has been a success or a failure. Generally, though, he will in fact have truth, or at least the spirit of truthful inquiry, on his side: he demands reasons, the others, faith.

226

Origin of faith. — The constrained spirit adopts his position not due to reasons, but out of habit; he is a Christian, for example, not because he has had any insight into the various religions or any choice among them; he is an Englishman not because he decided for England, but instead because he found Christianity and Englishness at hand and adopted them without any reasons, as someone born in a country producing wine becomes a drinker of wine. Later, when he was a Christian and an Englishman, he may have also discovered a few reasons favorable to his habits; we may overturn these reasons, but do not thereby overturn his entire position. Compel a constrained spirit to produce his reasons against bigamy, for example, and then you will find out whether his holy zeal for monogamy rests upon reasons or upon habit. Habituation to spiritual principles without reasons is what we call faith.

227

Reasoning backward from consequences to the reason, or the lack of one. — All states and social orders: social ranks, marriage, education, law, all these get their strength and durability solely from the faith that the constrained spirits have in them — hence from the absence of reasons, or at least from fending off the inquiry for reasons. The constrained spirits will not readily concede this, doubtless feeling that it is a *pudendum*. Christianity, which was very innocent in its intellectual notions, perceived nothing of this *pudendum*, demanding faith and nothing but faith and passionately turning aside the demand for reasons; it pointed to the success of faith: you shall soon perceive the advantage of faith, it suggested, you shall be made blessed by it. Actually, the state behaves just the same, and every father raises his son in the same way: just take this as true, he says, and you will soon perceive how much good it does. But this means that the *truth* of an opinion is supposed to be proved by the personal *benefit* that it yields, that the advantageousness of a doctrine is supposed to stand surety for its intellectual certainty and solidity. This is as if a defendant were to say in court: my counsel is speaking the whole truth, for just look at what follows from his speech: I will be acquitted. — Because the constrained spirits adopt their principles on account of their utility, they presume that the free spirit likewise seeks his own advantage with his views and takes to be true only whatever directly benefits him. Since, however, what seems to benefit him is the opposite of what benefits his countrymen or others of the same social rank, these people assume that his principles are dangerous for them; they say or feel: he must not be right, for he is harmful to us.

228

The strong, good character. — A narrowness of views that has, out of habit, become instinctive leads to what we call strength of character. When someone acts on the basis of just a few motives, but always the same ones, his actions attain great energy; if these actions are in harmony with the principles of the constrained spirits, they are honored and engender moreover in the one who performs them the sensation of a good conscience. Few motives, energetic action, and a good conscience make up what we call strength of character. Someone with strength of character lacks any knowledge of the many possibilities for action and the many directions it can take; his intellect is unfree, constrained, because in any given case it indicates perhaps only two possibilities to him; he must by necessity choose between them in a way that conforms to his whole nature, and he does this easily and quickly because he does not have to choose among fifty possibilities. The environment in which they are raised tries to make every human being unfree by always keeping the smallest number of possibilities in front of them. The individual is treated by those who raise him as if he were admittedly something new, but ought to become a *repetition*. If every human being initially appears as something unfamiliar, never before existing, still he ought to be made into something familiar, already existing. We describe a child as having a good character when its narrow adherence to what already exists becomes visible; by putting itself on the side of the constrained spirits, the child testifies to its awakening sense of community; on the basis of this sense of community, it will later become useful to its state or its class.

229

The measure of things among constrained spirits.—There are four classes of things that the constrained spirits say are justified. First: all things that have lasted over time are justified; second: all things that are not inconvenient for us are justified; third: all things that bring us advantage are justified; fourth: all things for which we have made sacrifices are justified. The last one explains, for example, why a war that was begun against the will of the people is pursued with enthusiasm as soon as the first sacrifices have been made.—The free spirits who plead their cause in the forum of the constrained spirits have to prove that there have always been free spirits, thus, that free-spiritedness has lasted over time, and then, that they do not want to cause inconvenience, and finally, that on the whole, they provide advantages to the constrained spirits; but because they cannot convince the constrained spirits of this last thing, it is of no use to them to have proven the first and second points.

230

Esprit fort.—Compared with someone who has tradition on his side and needs no reasons for his actions, the free spirit is always weak, especially in action; for he is acquainted with too many motives and points of view and therefore has an uncertain, inexperienced hand. What means exist, then, to make him *relatively strong* despite this, so that he can at least assert himself and not perish without effect? How does the strong spirit (*esprit fort*) come to be? This is in an individual case the question of how to beget genius. Where do the energy, the unbending strength, the persistence come from, with which the individual, in opposition to tradition, strives to acquire a wholly individual knowledge of the world?

231

The origin of genius.—The ingenuity with which a prisoner searches for the means of deliverance, the most cold-blooded and tedious effort to use every tiny advantage, can teach us what maneuvers nature employs in order to bring genius—a word that I ask you to understand without any mythological or religious flavor—into being: nature traps the genius in a prison and stimulates to the utmost his desire to free himself.—Or with a different image: someone who has completely lost his way in a forest, but struggles with uncommon energy to find any direction at all leading to open air, sometimes discovers a new path that nobody knows: thus arise those geniuses who are afterward praised for originality.—I have already mentioned that a mutilation, crippling, a significant defect in some organ often causes another organ to develop unusually well because it has to perform its own function and another one besides. Here we can guess at the origin of many splendid talents.—Apply, then, these general indications about the emergence of genius to the special case, the emergence of the perfect free spirit.

232

Conjecture about the origin of free-spiritedness.—Just as glaciers increase in size when in the equatorial regions the sun burns down upon the seas with greater heat than before, so, too, a very strong and expansive free-spiritedness may well be evidence that the heat of sensibility has somewhere grown exceptionally strong.

233

The voice of history.—In general, history *seems* to provide the following instruction about engendering genius: mistreat and torture people—thus it calls out to the passions of envy, hatred, and rivalry—drive them to extremes, one against the other, one people against another, and do it for centuries; then perhaps, from a spark of the terrible energy that has thus been ignited, as it flies off to the side, the light of genius will suddenly flare up; the will, driven wild like a horse under the rider's spur, will then break out and spring over to a different area. — Anyone who became aware of how genius has been engendered and also wanted to put into practice nature's usual procedure would have to be exactly as malicious and ruthless as nature. — But perhaps we have misunderstood.

234

Value of the middle of the path. — Perhaps the engendering of the genius is reserved for only a limited period of human history. For we cannot expect the future of humanity to produce all at once everything that only very particular conditions were able to bring about in any past period; not, for example, the astonishing effects of religious feeling. This has had its time, and many fine things can never grow again because they were able to grow only from it. Thus, there will never again be a religiously circumscribed horizon of life and of culture. Perhaps even the saint's type is only possible given a certain constraint of the intellect that is apparently over and done with forever. Thus, too, the high point of intelligence has perhaps been reserved for one particular age of humanity: it came forth — and comes forth, for we still live in this age — when an extraordinary, long-gathered energy of will extended itself by inheritance to *spiritual* goals in a way that was exceptional. That high point will be over and done with when this wildness and energy are no longer widely cultivated. Humanity will perhaps come closer to its real goals in the middle of its path, in the middle period of its existence, than at the end. Forces upon which art, for example, depends could actually die out; the pleasure in lies, in imprecision, in the symbolic, in intoxication, in ecstasy, could come to be disdained. Indeed, if life were ever arranged within the perfect state, no themes for poetry could be drawn from the present any more, and only backward people would desire poetic unreality. These people, in any case, would then look back with longing to the times of the imperfect state, of the half-barbaric society, to *our* times.

235

Genius and the ideal state in contradiction.—The socialists crave to produce a good life for as many people as possible. If the lasting site of this good life, the perfect state, really were attained, that good life would ruin the soil from which great intellect and any powerful individual grow: by which I mean great energy. If this state ever were attained, humanity would have become too feeble to be able to engender genius. Don't we then have to wish that life should maintain its violent character and that savage powers and energies be called forth again and again? Now the warm, sympathetic heart longs for the *elimination* of precisely that violent and savage character, and the warmest heart that we can imagine would desire it the most passionately: even though it is precisely this passion that has taken its fire, its heat, its very existence from the savage and violent character of life; the warmest heart thus wants to eliminate its own foundation, to destroy itself, which is to say: it wants something illogical, it is not intelligent. The highest intelligence and the warmest heart cannot coexist in any single person, and the sage who pronounces judgment on life also sets himself above goodness and regards it as only one thing to be appraised in taking account of life as a whole. The sage must resist those excessive desires for unintelligent goodness because he is concerned with the survival of his type and with the eventual emergence of the highest intellect; at least he will not promote the founding of the "perfect state," insofar as only enfeebled individuals have a place in it. By contrast, Christ, whom we like to think of as having the warmest of hearts, promoted human stupidity, put himself on the side of the poor in spirit, and delayed the engendering of the greatest intellect: and was consistent in doing so. His reverse image, the perfect sage—we may indeed predict this—will just as necessarily obstruct the engendering of a Christ.—The state is a clever arrangement for the protection of individuals from one another: but if we push its refinement too far, we will finally weaken the individual, even dissolve him—and thus the original purpose of the state will be most thoroughly thwarted.

236

The zones of culture.—Metaphorically speaking, we can say that the ages of culture correspond to the various climatic belts, except that they lie one after the other and not, like the geographic zones, beside one another. In comparison with the temperate zone of culture into which it is our task to cross, the zone of the past gives on the whole the impression of a *tropical* climate. Violent contrasts, abrupt changes between day and night, heat and splendid colors, the reverence for everything sudden, mysterious, terrible, the speed with which storms break out, everywhere the lavish overflow of nature's cornucopias: and by contrast in our culture, a bright, yet not luminous sky, clear, generally unvarying air, sharpness, even occasionally coldness: thus the two zones contrast with each other. If in the former we see how the most raging passions are overpowered and shattered by the uncanny force of metaphysical conceptions, we feel as if savage tropical tigers were being crushed before our eyes in the coils of colossal serpents; our spiritual climate has no such occurrences, our imagination has been tempered, even in dreams we scarcely come close to what earlier peoples beheld while awake. But shouldn't we be happy about this change, even conceding that artists have been significantly impaired by the vanishing of tropical culture and find us nonartists to be a little too sober? To that extent, artists no doubt have the right to deny "progress," for in fact: whether the last three millennia exhibit a progressive advance in the arts seems at least doubtful; just as a metaphysical philosopher such as Schopenhauer would have no cause to perceive any progress if he surveyed the last four millennia with regard to metaphysical philosophy and religion.—For us, however, the very *existence* of the temperate zone of culture counts as progress.

237

Renaissance and Reformation.—The Italian Renaissance contained within itself all the positive forces to which we owe modern culture: that is, liberation of thought, disdain for authorities, the triumph of cultivation over the arrogance of lineage, an enthusiasm for science and the scientific past of humanity, an unfettering of the individual, an ardor for veracity and an aversion against appearance and mere effect (an ardor that blazed forth in a whole array of artistic characters who, with the highest moral purity, demanded from themselves perfection and nothing but perfection in their works); indeed, the Renaissance had positive forces that, *up until now*, have never since become as powerful in our modern culture. It was the golden age of this millennium, despite all its flaws and vices. In contrast, the German Reformation distinguishes itself as an energetic protest of the spiritually backward, who were by no means sated with the medieval worldview and sensed the signs of its dissolution, the exceptional flattening and superficializing of religious life, with profound displeasure rather than with the rejoicing that would have been appropriate. With their northern strength and stubbornness they threw humanity backward, compelled the Counter-Reformation to take place, that is, compelled Catholic Christianity to adopt a defensive position against the violence besieging it, and thus delayed for two or three centuries the complete awakening and supremacy of the sciences, just as they have perhaps made any growing together of the ancient and the modern spirit forever impossible. The great task of the Renaissance could not be brought to completion, the protest of a German nature that had meanwhile remained backward (whereas in the Middle Ages it had had sense enough to seek salvation by climbing over the Alps again and again) hindered this. It was the accidental result of an exceptional constellation of political events that Luther was preserved at that time and that the protest gained strength: for the emperor protected him in order to use his innovation as an instrument for pressuring the pope, and likewise the pope favored him in secret in order to use the Protestant imperial princes as a counterweight against the emperor. Without this singular interplay of intentions, Luther would have been burned like Huss—and the Enlightenment would perhaps have dawned somewhat earlier and with a more beautiful luster than we can now conceive.

238

Justice for the god who is becoming.—If the whole history of culture opens itself to our gaze as a tangle of evil and noble, true and false conceptions, and if the sight of these breaking waves makes us feel almost seasick, then we grasp how much comfort lies in the conception of a *god who is becoming*: he discloses himself more and more in the transformations and destinies of humanity, everything is not just blindly mechanical, a senseless and purposeless interplay of forces. The deification of becoming is a metaphysical outlook—from a lighthouse down at the sea of history, as it were—in which a generation of scholars all too prone to historicizing took comfort; we should not be angry at this, however erroneous that conception may be. Only someone who, like Schopenhauer, denies development will also feel nothing of the misery of these breaking historical waves and may therefore, because he knows nothing and feels nothing of that god who becomes and of the need to assume his existence, be justified in giving vent to his mockery.

239

Fruits after their season.—Every better future that we wish upon humanity is also in many respects necessarily a worse future: for it is pure fantasy to believe that a new, higher stage of humanity will unite in itself all the merits of earlier stages and, for example, that it must also engender the highest form of art. Instead, every season has its own merits and charms and excludes those of other seasons. What grew out of religion and in proximity to it cannot grow again if religion has been destroyed; at most, stray, late-sprouting shoots can mislead and deceive us, as can the temporary outbreak of recollections of the old art: a condition that doubtless betrays the feeling of loss and deprivation, but is no evidence for the strength from which a new art could be born.

240

Increasing severity of the world. — The higher a person's culture ascends, the more areas are removed from mirth and mockery. Voltaire thanked Heaven from his heart for the invention of marriage and the church: for thus taking such good care for our amusement. But he and his time, and before him the sixteenth century, mocked these themes into the ground; every joke that anyone makes in this area now is passé, and above all, far too cheap to be able to attract the customers' interest. Today we inquire about causes; it is the age of seriousness. Who cares anymore about seeing the differences between reality and pretentious appearance, between what a person is and what he wants to imagine, in a ludicrous light; the feeling for these contrasts works quite differently as soon as we seek for reasons. The more thoroughly someone understands life, the less he will mock, except that eventually he may still mock the "thoroughness of his understanding."

241

The genius of culture. — If someone wanted to imagine a genius of culture, how would such a being be constituted? He manipulates lies, force, the most ruthless self-interest as his tools with such assurance that he could only be called an evil, demonic being; but his goals, shining through here and there, are great and good. He is a centaur, half beast, half human, and has angelic wings on his head besides.

242

Miraculous education. — The interest in education will reach great intensity only from the moment when one gives up the belief in a God and in his solicitude: just as the art of medicine could flourish only when the belief in miraculous cures ceased. But up to the present, the whole world still believes in a miraculous education: for we *saw* the most fertile and powerful human beings grow out of the greatest disorder, confusion of aims, unfavorable circumstances: how could this happen normally? — Now in these cases as well, we will soon look more closely, examine more carefully: we will never discover miracles there. Given the same circumstances, countless human beings continually perish; the single individual who has been saved has usually become stronger as a result because he endured these terrible circumstances by virtue of an indestructible innate strength that he exercised and increased: thus is the miracle to be explained. An education that no longer believes in miracles will have to attend to three things: first, how much energy has been inherited? second, how can more new energy be ignited? third, how can the individual accommodate himself to those extremely diverse claims of culture without their unsettling him and splintering his uniqueness — in short, how can the individual be integrated into the counterpoint of private and public culture, how can he play the melody and accompany the melody at the same time?

243

The future of the physician. — There is at present no profession that could be so greatly enhanced as that of the physician; especially since the spiritual physicians, those described as ministering to the soul, no longer have public approval to engage in their conjurer's arts and cultivated people avoid them. The highest spiritual training of a physician has not yet been reached when he knows and has practical experience in the best and newest methods and understands how to make those rapid deductions from effects to causes for which diagnosticians are famed: he must in addition possess an eloquence that adapts itself to every individual and addresses itself to the heart, a manliness the mere sight of which chases away despondency (the worm that gnaws at all sick people), a diplomat's smoothness in mediating between those who require joy for their recovery and those who for reasons of health must (and can) create joy for others, the subtlety of a police agent and lawyer in understanding the secrets of a soul without betraying them—in short, a good physician now requires the tricks and artistic license of every other professional class: thus equipped, he is then in a position to become a benefactor to all of society by increasing good works, spiritual joy, and fruitfulness, by preventing evil thoughts, designs, knaveries (whose disgusting source is so frequently the lower body), by establishing a spiritual-bodily aristocracy (as maker and obstructer of marriages), by benevolently amputating all so-called tortures of the soul and remorse: thus for the first time he turns from being a "medicine man" into a savior and yet does not need to do any miracles, nor to let himself be crucified.

244

In proximity to madness.—The sum of sensations, knowledge, experiences, that is, the whole burden of culture, has become so great that an overstimulation of the nervous and intellectual powers is a universal danger; indeed, the cultivated classes in European countries are thoroughly neurotic and almost all of their great families have come close to insanity in one of their branches. Now admittedly we try today to maintain health in every possible way; but what remains essential is diminishing the tension of feeling, the crushing cultural burden that, even if it were to be purchased with heavy losses, nonetheless gives us room for great hopes of a *new Renaissance*. We have Christianity, the philosophers, poets, and musicians to thank for an overabundance of deeply moving sensations: but to keep them from overgrowing us, we have to conjure up the spirit of science, which makes us on the whole somewhat colder and more skeptical, and in particular, cools down the scorching stream of a faith in final, definitive truths that has become so fierce, principally due to Christianity.

245

Bell-casting of culture.—Culture has come into being like a bell, within a sheath of coarser, commoner material: untruth, violence, the unlimited dilation of every individual ego, of every individual people, were what made up this sheath. Has the time now come to remove it? Has the molten matter solidified, have the good, useful drives, the habits of the nobler disposition become so secure and general that no reliance on metaphysics and the errors of religion is necessary any longer, none of the harshness and violence that were the means for binding one person or one people most powerfully to another?—There is no divine sign to assist us any more in answering this question: our own insight must decide. Humanity must itself take in hand the earthly governance of all humanity, its "omniscience" must watch over the further destiny of culture with a sharp eye.

246

The cyclopses of culture.—Anyone who sees those furrowed hollows where glaciers have lain finds it scarcely possible that a time will come when a valley of meadows, forests, and streams will occupy that same place. So it is in the history of humanity as well; the fiercest forces break the way, destructively at first, but nevertheless their activity was necessary so that a milder cultural dispensation could later establish itself here. The fearsome energies—what we term evil—are the cyclopean architects and road builders of humanity.

247

Orbit of humanity.—The whole of humanity is perhaps only a developmental phase of a certain animal species of limited duration: so that human beings came from apes and will again become apes, while there is nobody who takes any interest whatsoever in this wonderful comic ending. Just as with the decline of Roman culture and its most important cause, the spread of Christianity, a general tendency toward human repulsiveness gained the upper hand within the Roman Empire, so, too, the decline of universal world culture might some day lead to a even more heightened repulsiveness and eventual bestialization of humanity to the point of apishness. — Precisely because we can envision this perspective, we are perhaps in a position to prevent the future from reaching such an end.

248

Comforting words for those despairing of progress. — Our age gives the impression of an interim state; the old worldviews, the old cultures, still exist in part, the new ones are not yet secure and habitual and hence lack decisiveness and consistency. It appears as if everything were becoming chaotic, the old being lost, the new worth nothing and becoming ever feebler. But so it is for the soldier who is learning to march; for a time he is more uncertain and awkward than ever because the muscles are being moved now according to the old system, now according to the new one, and neither has yet decisively claimed victory. We stagger, but it is necessary not to let this frighten us and possibly make us surrender what we have newly achieved. Besides, we *cannot* go back to the old, we *have* burned our boats; all that remains is to be bold, regardless of what may result. — Let us simply *step forward*, let us simply move on! Perhaps our behavior will at least look like *progress*; but if not, Frederick the Great's phrase might also be said to us by way of comfort: *Ah, mon cher Sulzer, vous ne connaissez pas assez cette race maudite, à laquelle nous appartenons.*

249

Suffering from the cultural past. — Anyone who has made the problem of culture clear to himself suffers from a feeling similar to that of someone who has inherited a fortune acquired by unlawful means, or of the prince who reigns as a result of the violent deeds of his ancestors. He thinks of his origin with sorrow and is often ashamed, often irritable. The whole sum of strength, will for living, and joy that he devotes to his possessions is often balanced by a profound weariness: he cannot forget his origin. He regards the future with sadness; his descendants, he knows in advance, will suffer from the past as he does.

250

Manners.—Good manners disappear to the extent that the influence of the court and of a closed aristocracy grows weaker: we can clearly observe this decrease from decade to decade if we keep an eye upon public actions: these are visibly becoming more and more plebeian. No one understands any more how to pay homage and to flatter in a spirited way; this results in the ludicrous fact that in cases nowadays where someone *has to* pay homage (for example, to a great statesman or artist), he borrows the language of deepest feeling, of candid and respectful honesty—out of embarrassment and a lack of wit and grace. Thus, the public, ceremonial encounters among people seem ever more awkward, yet also more deeply felt and sincere, without this being the case.—But do manners have to go downhill forever? It seems to me instead that manners follow a steep curve and that we are approaching their lowest point. If society ever does become more certain of its purposes and principles so that these work in a formative way (whereas now the acquired manners of earlier formative states are passed on and acquired ever more feebly), there will be manners for the interactions, gestures, and expressions of social intercourse that will seem as necessary and straightforward as those purposes and principles will be. An improved distribution of time and work, gymnastic exercise transformed to accompany every lovely leisure hour, an increased and more rigorous reflectiveness that confers shrewdness and suppleness even upon the body, will bring all this about.—Now we might admittedly pause here, somewhat derisively, to think of our scholars and whether they, who want to be the precursors of that new culture, do in fact distinguish themselves by their better manners. This is certainly not the case, though their spirit may be willing enough: for their flesh is weak. The past is still too powerful in their muscles: they are still standing in a constrained position and are half worldly priests, half the dependent educators of aristocratic people and classes, and furthermore are crippled and deadened by the pedantry of science and by outdated, uninspired methods. They are therefore, at least in regard to their bodies and often in regard to three-quarters of their spirit as well, still the courtiers of an aged, indeed senile culture, and as such senile themselves; meanwhile, the new spirit that occasionally rumbles inside these ancient receptacles serves only to make them more uncertain and fearful. The ghosts of the past walk within them as well as the ghosts of the future: is it any wonder, given this, if they do not make the best appearance or have the most pleasing demeanor?

251

Future of science.—Science gives great satisfaction to the one who does work and research in it, but very little to the one who *learns* its results. But since all the important truths of science must gradually become everyday, ordinary things, even this slight satisfaction comes to an end: just as we have long since ceased to take any pleasure in learning the quite remarkable multiplication tables. Now if science gives us less and less pleasure in doing it and takes more and more pleasure away by casting suspicion on the comfort provided by metaphysics, religion, and art: then the greatest source of pleasure, the one to which humanity owes almost all it means to be human, will be impoverished. A higher culture must therefore give people a dual brain, two compartments of the brain, as it were, the one to experience science, the other to experience nonscience: lying next to each other, without confusion, separable, each able to be closed off from the other; this is a requirement for health. In the one region lies the power source, in the other the regulator: illusions, one-sidedness, and passions must be used to create heat, while the pernicious and dangerous consequences of overheating must be averted with the aid of scientific knowledge. — If this requirement of higher culture is not satisfied, the future course of human development can be predicted with near-certainty: the interest in what is true will cease to the extent that it provides less pleasure; illusion, error, and fantasy will reconquer step by step the terrain they once controlled, because they are associated with pleasure: the ruination of the sciences and a sinking back into barbarism will result next; humanity will have to begin weaving its tapestry all over again after having, like Penelope, destroyed it by night. But who can guarantee us that it will always find the strength for this once again?

252

The pleasure in knowing. — Why is knowing, the element of the researcher and the philosopher, connected with pleasure? First and above all, because we thereby become conscious of our strength, hence for the same reason that gymnastic exercises are pleasurable even without spectators. Second, because in the process of acquiring knowledge we get beyond older conceptions and their advocates, become victors, or at least believe that we are. Third, because we feel ourselves to be raised above *everyone else* by even the tiniest new piece of knowledge and feel that we are the only one who knows what is correct in this matter. These three reasons for pleasure are the most important ones, yet there are many other secondary reasons, according to the nature of the knower. — A not inconsiderable list of such reasons is given in a place where one would not look for it, in my paraenetic essay on Schopenhauer: an inventory that can satisfy every experienced servant of knowledge, although he may wish that the ironic tinge that seems to lie upon those pages were not there. For if it is true that "a host of very human drives and petty passions must have been mixed together" for a scholar to emerge, that the scholar is admittedly a very fine, but hardly a pure metal and "consists of a confused tangle of very different impulses and stimuli": yet the same holds true likewise for the emergence and nature of the artist, the philosopher, the moral genius—however the great names glorified in that essay are called. *Everything* human deserves to be viewed ironically in regard to its *origin*: that is why there is such an *excess* of irony in the world.

253

Loyalty as proof of validity. — It is the consummate sign of the excellence of a theory if its originator has no misgivings about it for *forty* years; but I maintain that there has not yet been any philosopher who has not eventually looked down upon the philosophy he invented in his youth with disdain—or at least with suspicion.—But he may not have spoken publicly about this change of mind, out of ambition or—as is more probable for noble natures—out of tender consideration for his adherents.

254

Increase in what is interesting. — In the course of becoming more highly cultivated, a person comes to see everything as interesting; he knows how to find the instructive side of something quickly and how to specify the point where this can fill a gap in his thinking or confirm one of his thoughts. Thus, boredom disappears more and more, as does the excessive excitability of his disposition. Eventually he goes around among human beings as a naturalist does among plants and perceives even himself as a phenomenon that strongly stimulates only his drive for knowledge.

255

Superstition about simultaneity. — We tend to suppose that whatever happens simultaneously is connected. A relative dies somewhere far away and at the same time we dream of him— and so! But countless relatives die without our dreaming of them. It is the same as with people who make vows in a shipwreck: we do not afterward have in the temple the votive tablets of those who perished. — A person dies, an owl screeches, a clock stands still, all in a single hour of the night: shouldn't there be a connection there? Such intimacy with nature as is assumed by this surmise flatters human beings. — This class of superstition can also be found in a refined form among historians and those who portray culture, who tend to have a sort of hydrophobia about all the meaningless juxtapositions with which, however, the life of individuals and peoples is so rich.

256

The capacity to do, not to know, is what science trains. — The value of having for some time rigorously pursued a *rigorous science* does not rest directly upon the results of this pursuit: for they will be a tiny, vanishing drop in relation to the sea of what is worth knowing. But there does result an increase in energy, in deductive capacity, in tenacity of perseverance; one has learned how to attain a *purpose purposefully*. To that extent it is very valuable, in regard to everything that one later does, to have been a scientist at one time.

257

Youthful charm of science. — The search for truth still has the charm of contrasting strongly everywhere against gray and tedious error; this charm is vanishing more and more; to be sure, we still live at present in the youthful age of science and tend to pursue truth like a beautiful girl; but what if she one day changes into a glowering old woman? In almost every science the fundamental insight has either been discovered at a very early point or continues still to be sought; how differently this stirs us than when everything essential has been discovered and only a meager autumnal gleaning remains for the researcher (a sensation with which we can acquaint ourselves in certain historical disciplines).

258

The statue of humanity.—The genius of culture behaves like Cellini when he cast his statue of Perseus: the fluid mass threatened not to suffice, but it *had* to: so he tossed in bowls and plates and whatever else came to hand. In just the same way, the genius tosses in errors, vices, hopes, hallucinations, and other things made of baser or finer metal, for the statue of humanity must come out of this and be finished; what does it matter if here and there some inferior material was used?

259

A culture of men.—Greek culture of the classical period is a culture of men. As far as women are concerned, Pericles says it all with the words of his funeral oration: they are at their best when men speak of them as little as possible.—The erotic relation of the men to the youths was, to a degree inaccessible to our comprehension, the sole necessary prerequisite of all male education (somewhat in the way that for a long time all higher education for women was brought about by love affairs or marriage); all the idealism in the strength of the Greek nature threw itself into that relationship, and young people have probably never since been treated so attentively, so affectionately, so completely with regard to what might be best for them (*virtus*) as in the sixth and fifth centuries—that is, in accordance with the beautiful phrase of Hölderlin's, "for in loving the mortal gives of his best." The more important this relationship was taken to be, the lower sank the importance of social intercourse with women: the aspect of procreation and sexual pleasure—nothing further was considered; there was no spiritual intercourse, not even genuine affairs of love. If one further considers that women themselves were excluded from contests and spectacles of every kind, only the religious cults remain as the sole higher entertainment for women.—Of course, when Electra and Antigone were represented in tragedy, they *put up with* this in art, although they did not care for it in life: just as now we cannot endure any pathos in *life*, but like to see it in art. — Women had no further duties than producing beautiful, powerful bodies in which the character of the father could live on in as unbroken a way as possible, and thereby to counteract the overexcitation of nerves increasingly prevalent in such a highly developed culture. This kept Greek culture young for such a relatively long time; for in the Greek mothers, the Greek genius returned again and again to nature.

260

The prejudice in favor of what is large. — People clearly overestimate everything that is large and conspicuous. This results from the conscious or unconscious insight that they find it very useful if any one person throws all his strength into a single area and makes himself as it were into a single monstrous organ. For the individual person, a *balanced* development of his powers is certainly more useful and fortunate; for every talent is a vampire that sucks blood and strength from the other powers, and its excessive production can bring the most gifted person almost to madness. In the arts, too, the extreme natures attract far too much attention; but we must be at a much lower level of culture to let ourselves be fascinated by them. People subject themselves out of habit to anything that wants power.

261

The tyrants of the spirit. — Only where the ray of myth falls does the life of the Greeks light up; elsewhere it is gloomy. Now the Greek philosophers rob themselves of precisely this myth: isn't it as if they wanted to remove themselves from the sunshine and go into the shadows, into the gloom? But no plant avoids the light; basically, those philosophers were only seeking a *brighter* sun, the myth was not clear and luminous enough for them. They found this light in their knowledge, in what every one of them called his "truth." At that time, however, knowledge still had a greater luster; it was still young and still knew little of all the difficulties and dangers of its paths; at that time it could still hope to reach the center of all being with a single leap and from there to solve the riddle of the world. These philosophers had a robust faith in themselves and in their "truth," which they used to overthrow all their contemporaries and predecessors; each of them was a contentious, violent *tyrant*. Never, perhaps, was there greater happiness in this world from believing oneself in possession of the truth, but never were the harshness, the arrogance, the tyrannical and evil results of such a belief greater either. They were tyrants, hence what every Greek wanted to be and what everyone was whenever he *could* be. Perhaps only Solon was an exception; in his poems he tells how he scorned personal tyranny. But he did it out of love for his work, for his setting down of laws; and to be a lawgiver is a more sublimated form of tyranny. Parmenides, too, set down laws, as Pythagoras and Empedocles probably did as well; Anaximander founded a city. Plato was the incarnate desire to become the supreme philosophical giver of laws and founder of states; he seems to have suffered terribly from the nonfulfillment of his nature, and toward the end his soul was filled with the blackest bile. The more power Greek philosophy lost, the more it suffered inwardly from this biliousness and slanderous rage; when for the first time the various sects fought for their truths in the streets, the souls of all these free men of truth were completely choked with jealousy and venom, the tyrannical element raged as poison in their bodies. These numerous petty tyrants would have liked to eat one another raw; not a single spark of love and all too little pleasure in their own knowledge remained inside them. — In general, the principle that tyrants are usually murdered and that their posterity has a short life also holds true for tyrants of the spirit. Their history is short, violent, their influence abruptly broken off. We can say of almost all the great Hellenes that they seem to have come too late, the same for Aeschylus as for Pindar, for Demosthenes, for Thucydides; one generation after them — and then it is all over. That is what makes Greek history turbulent and uncanny. Nowadays, to be sure, we admire the gospel of the tortoise. To think historically now means nothing more than thinking that history has always been made according to the principle: "as little as possible in the longest possible amount of time!" Alas, Greek history races so fast! No one since has ever lived so profligately, so immoderately. I cannot convince myself that the history of the Greeks took that *natural* course for which it has been so much praised. They were far too manifoldly endowed to be *gradual* in the step-by-step fashion of the tortoise in its race with Achilles: and that is what we call natural development. With the Greeks, things went forward quickly, but just as quickly downward; the movement of the whole machine is so accelerated that a single stone thrown into its gears makes it fly to pieces. Socrates, for instance, was such a stone; in one night, the development of the philosophical science, up until then so amazingly regular, though admittedly all too rapid, was destroyed. It is no idle question whether Plato, had he remained free of the Socratic enchantment, might not have discovered a still higher type of philosophic being, one that we have lost forever. We can see such types in the ages preceding him, as if in a sculptor's studio. Yet the sixth and fifth centuries seem to promise still more and higher things than they themselves brought forth; but they got no further than promising and announcing them. And yet there is scarcely any loss more severe than the loss of a type, of a new, heretofore undiscovered, supreme *possibility of the philosophical life*. Even of the older types, most have been imperfectly transmitted to us; all the philosophers from Thales to Democritus seem to me extraordinarily hard to perceive, but whoever succeeds in recreating these figures will wander among images of the most powerful and purest type. This capacity, admittedly, is rare; even the later Greeks who were concerned with the lore of the older philosophy lacked it; Aristotle in particular seems not to have any eyes in his head when he stands before depictions of them. And so it seems as if these splendid philosophers lived in vain or as if they are simply supposed to have prepared the way for the contentious and loquacious hordes of the Socratic schools. As I have said, there is a gap, a break in development here; some tremendous calamity must have occurred and the only statue from which we would have been able to recognize the sense and purpose of that great exercise of creative powers broke apart or miscarried: what really happened has forever remained a secret of the workshop.—What took place among the Greeks—that every great thinker, believing himself to be the possessor of absolute truth, became a tyrant, so that among the Greeks the history of the spirit also acquired the violent, precipitate, and dangerous character that their political history displays—this kind of event was not thereby exhausted: many similar things occurred, on into the most recent times, although gradually less frequently and now hardly able any more to maintain the clear, naive conscience of the Greek philosophers. For on the whole, contending dogmas and skepticism now speak too powerfully, too loudly. The period of the tyrants of the spirit is over. In the spheres of higher culture, admittedly, there must always be some form of mastery, but this mastery lies henceforth in the hands of the *oligarchs of the spirit*. Despite all spatial and political divisions, they form a cohesive society, whose members *recognize* and *acknowledge* one another, whatever favorable or unfavorable evaluations of them may be circulated by public opinion and the judgments of those who write for mass-circulation newspapers and magazines. The spiritual superiority that previously produced division and enmity now tends to *unite*: how could individuals assert themselves and swim on their own course through life, against the tide, if they did not here and there see others like them, living under the same conditions, and did not take their hands in a struggle that is as much against the ochlocratic character of the half-spirited and the half-cultivated as against the occasional attempts to establish a tyranny by manipulating the masses? The oligarchs need one another, they have their greatest joy in one another, they understand their insignia—but nevertheless, each of them is free; he struggles and triumphs in *his own* place and would rather perish than submit.

262

Homer. — The greatest fact in the cultivation of the Greeks is still that Homer became pan-Hellenic at such an early point. All the spiritual and human freedom that the Greeks attained can be traced back to this fact. But at the same time, this was actually the fatal destiny of Greek cultivation, for Homer made Greek culture more shallow by centralizing it and dissolved the more serious instincts of independence. From time to time, opposition to Homer rose up from the deepest foundation of Hellenism; but he always remained victorious. All great spiritual powers exert a repressive as well as a liberating influence; but admittedly it makes a difference whether Homer or the Bible or science tyrannizes human beings.

263

Talent. — In a humanity as highly developed as the present one, everyone acquires by nature access to many talents. Everyone has *innate talent*, but only a few are born with and trained to a sufficient degree of tenacity, persistence, and energy that any one of them really becomes a talent, that is, *becomes* what he *is*, which is to say: discharges it in works and actions.

264

Cleverness of spirit either overestimated or underestimated. — Unscientific but talented people esteem every indication of spirit, whether it follows a true or a false trail; above all, they want the person with whom they associate to use his cleverness to entertain them well, to spur them on, inflame them, carry them away in seriousness and jest, and in any case to be the strongest amulet preserving them from boredom. Scientific natures, by contrast, know that the talent for having all sorts of ideas occur to them must be strictly curbed by the spirit of science; it is not the fruit that gleams, shines, and stimulates, but instead the often plain, unpretentious truth that he wants to shake from the tree of knowledge. Like Aristotle, he should make no distinction between what is "boring" and what is "clever"; his daimon leads him through the desert as well as through tropical vegetation, so that he will everywhere take pleasure only in what is real, valid, genuine. — In insignificant scholars, this results in a disdain for and suspicion of clever people in general, and clever people in turn often have an aversion for science: as, for example, almost all artists do.

265

Reason in school.—Schooling has no task more important than teaching rigorous thinking, careful judging, and logical reasoning: therefore it must disregard everything that is not useful for these operations, such as religion. It can count upon human obscurity, habit, and need to later relax the bow of thought stretched all too tautly. But as far as its influence reaches, it should forcefully promote what is essential and distinctive in human beings: "reason and science, the *supreme* powers of man"—as Goethe, at least, judges.—The great naturalist von Baer finds the superiority of all Europeans in comparison to Asians in the capacity that the former develop in school to be able to provide reasons for what they believe, something that the latter are wholly incapable of doing. Europe has been schooled in logical and critical thinking; Asia still does not know how to distinguish between truth and fiction and is not aware whether its convictions stem from personal observation and rule-governed thinking or from fantasies.— Reason in the schools has made Europe into Europe: in the Middle Ages, it was on the way to becoming once again a part and an appendage of Asia—hence to forfeiting the scientific sense that it owed to the Greeks.

266

Underestimated effect of Gymnasium instruction.—We rarely look for the value of the *Gymnasium* in the things that really are learned there and indelibly instilled by it, but instead in the things that are taught but that the student assimilates only reluctantly and shakes off as quickly as he can. Reading the classics—every educated person concedes this—is a monstrous procedure everywhere that it is carried on: with young people who are in no respect mature enough for it, by teachers whose every word and often whose mere appearance casts a blight upon a good author. But therein lies the value that is usually misconstrued—that these teachers speak the *abstract language of higher culture*, unwieldy and difficult to understand though it is, but a higher gymnastics for the head; that there occur in their speech concepts, technical terms, methods, and allusions that the young people almost never hear in the conversation of their families or in the street. If the students only *listen*, their intellects will involuntarily be preformed along the lines of a scientific way of seeing things. It is not possible to emerge from this training wholly untouched by abstraction, as a pure child of nature.

267

Learning many languages.—Learning many languages fills the memory with words instead of with facts and ideas, while memory is a receptacle that in each person can absorb only a certain, limited amount of content. Then, too, learning many languages does harm insofar as it awakens the belief that we possess certain accomplishments and really does lend someone a certain seductive appearance in social intercourse; and it does harm indirectly by working against the acquisition of a thorough grounding for our knowledge and the intention of earning the respect of others in an honest way. Finally, it strikes like an ax at the root of any more subtle linguistic feeling for our mother tongue: this feeling is thereby irreparably damaged and destroyed. The two peoples that produced the greatest stylists, the Greeks and the French, did not learn any foreign languages.—But because human intercourse is inevitably becoming ever more cosmopolitan, and a good tradesman in London, for example, now has to make himself understood in writing and in speech in eight languages, the learning of many languages is admittedly a necessary *evil*: but one that will eventually reach an extreme and force humanity to find a cure for it: and in some far-off future there will be a new language for everyone, at first as a commercial language, then as the language of spiritual commerce generally, just as certainly as there will some day be air travel. For what other purpose has the science of languages studied the laws of language for a century and appraised what is necessary, valuable, and successful in every individual language!

268

On the military history of the individual. — We find concentrated within an individual human life that passes through several cultures the struggle that is otherwise played out between two generations, between father and son: the closeness of the relationship *intensifies* this struggle, because each party pitilessly draws into it the inner traits of the other party that it knows so well; and so this struggle will be the most bitter within a single individual; here, every new phase strides on past earlier ones, cruelly unjust in misunderstanding their means and goals.

269

A quarter hour earlier. — We occasionally find someone who stands ahead of his own time in his views, and yet only so far ahead that he anticipates the vulgar views of the next decade. He adheres to public opinion before it is public, that is to say: he has fallen into the arms of a view that deserves to become trivial a quarter hour sooner than other people. His reputation, however, tends to be noised about much more than the reputation of those who really are great and superior.

270

The art of reading. — Every strong orientation is one-sided: it approximates the orientation of a straight line and is like it exclusive, that is, it does not touch many other orientations, as do weak parties and natures in their wavering to and fro: we must therefore also excuse philologists for being one-sided. The production of texts and their preservation from corruption, along with their exegesis, carried on in a guild for centuries, has finally allowed us to discover the right methods; the whole of the Middle Ages was profoundly incapable of a rigorously philological exegesis, that is, of the simple desire to understand what an author is saying—it really was something to discover these methods, let us not underestimate it! All of science attained continuity and steadiness only when the art of reading correctly, that is, philology, had reached its peak.

271

The art of drawing conclusions.—The greatest advance that human beings have made lies in having learned to draw conclusions correctly. That is by no means something as natural as Schopenhauer assumes when he says: "everyone is capable of drawing conclusions, only a few of making judgments," but is instead acquired late and even now has not yet attained predominance. Drawing conclusions that are false is the rule in more ancient times: and the mythologies of all peoples, their magic and their superstition, their religious cults, their law, are the inexhaustible sites for evidence of this principle.

272

Growth rings of individual culture.—The strength and weakness of spiritual productivity is connected far less to inherited talent than to the degree of *vigor* that goes along with it. Most educated young people of thirty go backward at this early solstice in their lives and are averse to changing spiritual direction from then on. Therefore a new generation is immediately essential for the welfare of a steadily thriving culture, which likewise, however, does not advance things very far: for in order to *draw even with* his father's culture, the son has to use up almost the same amount of inherited energy that the father himself possessed at the stage of life when he engendered his son; with the small surplus, he gets farther (since things go forward a bit more quickly because the path here is being traveled for the second time; in order to learn what the father knew, the son does not expend quite as much energy). Extremely vigorous men, such as Goethe for example, traverse as much distance as four successive generations can scarcely manage; but they therefore get so far ahead that other people catch up to them only in the next century, even then perhaps not fully, because frequent interruptions weaken the continuity of a culture, the logical coherence of its development.—People recapitulate ever more quickly the usual phases of the spiritual culture that has been attained in the course of history. At present, they begin by entering culture as children who are moved by religion, with these sensations reaching perhaps their greatest liveliness at the age of ten; they then pass over into attenuated forms (pantheism) while they are approaching science, get completely beyond God, immortality, and the like, but lapse into the enchantment of a metaphysical philosophy. This, too, eventually loses credibility for them; art, by contrast, seems to impart more and more, so that for a time metaphysics does just barely persist and survive, transformed into art or into an aesthetically transfiguring disposition. But the scientific sense becomes ever more imperious and leads the man away toward natural science and history and especially toward the most rigorous methods of knowledge, whereas an ever milder and more unpretentious significance devolves upon art. All of this now tends to occur within the first thirty years of a man's life. It is the recapitulation of a lesson at which humanity has toiled for perhaps thirty thousand years.

273

Gone backward, not left behind.—Anyone who presently commences his development from religious sensations and perhaps for a long time afterward lives in metaphysics and art has gone a good way backward and begins his race against other modern people under unfavorable provisions: he seemingly loses both space and time. But by pausing in those regions where ardor and energy are unfettered and where power continuously flows forth like a volcanic stream from inexhaustible sources, he moves forward much more quickly as soon as he has dissociated himself at the proper time from those regions; his feet have wings, his breast has learned to breathe more serenely, deeply, and with better endurance. — He has pulled back only in order to have sufficient space for his leap: hence, there may even be something dreadful and threatening in this movement backward.

274

A slice of our self as artistic object. — It is a sign of superior culture to consciously hold on to certain phases of development that lesser people live through almost thoughtlessly and then erase from the tablet of their soul, sketching for ourselves a faithful image of them: for this is the higher genre of painterly art, which only a few understand. To do this, it is necessary to isolate those phases artificially. Historical studies cultivate the capacity for this sort of painting, for they constantly challenge us, when prompted by a piece of history or by the life of a people or of an individual, to imagine a very specific horizon of thoughts, a specific intensity of sensations, the predominance of this and the insignificance of that. The sense for history consists of being able to quickly reconstruct such systems of thought and feeling on a given occasion, as if we were reconstructing the total impression of a temple from a few columns and ruined walls that have remained standing by chance. The most immediate result of this is that we understand our fellow human beings as very specific systems of this kind and as representatives of different cultures, that is to say, as necessary, but as changeable. And conversely, that we can separate out pieces of our own development and represent them independently.

275

Cynic and Epicurean. — The Cynic perceives the connection between the multiplied and magnified pains of more highly cultivated people and the abundance of their needs; he therefore conceives that the host of opinions about what is beautiful, proper, seemly, delightful must give rise to copious sources not only of enjoyment, but also of displeasure. In accordance with this insight, he moves backward in his development by relinquishing many of these opinions and withdrawing from certain demands made by culture; he thereby obtains a feeling of freedom and empowerment; and gradually, once habit has made his way of life tolerable for him, he will in fact have fewer and weaker sensations of displeasure than cultivated people and will become very much like a domestic animal; in addition, everything that he does feel has the charm of contrast and — he can also curse to his heart's content, so that he thereby gets well beyond the animal's world of sensations. — The Epicurean adopts the same point of view as the Cynic; generally, only a difference of temperament sets them apart. And so the Epicurean uses his higher culture to make himself independent of prevailing opinions; he raises himself above them, whereas the Cynic merely continues to negate them. It is as if the former were strolling along in windless, well-protected, twilight avenues, while above him the treetops were being tossed in the wind and betrayed to him how violently the world outside was moving. The Cynic, on the other hand, acts as if he were going naked outside into the blowing wind and hardens himself to the point of insensibility.

276

Microcosm and macrocosm of culture. — Human beings make the best discoveries about culture within themselves when they find two heterogeneous powers ruling there. Given someone who is as much in love with the plastic arts or music as he is enraptured by the spirit of science and who sees it as impossible to suspend this contradiction by annulling the one and completely liberating the other: the only possibility remaining for him is to shape himself into a cultural edifice big enough for both those powers to inhabit, albeit at opposite ends, while between them there reside mediating powers with sufficient strength to smooth over, if necessary, any strife that might break out. Any such cultural edifice in a single individual, though, will have the greatest resemblance to the cultural structure of an entire era and will by analogy furnish continuous instruction about it. For wherever the great architecture of culture has been developed, its task has been to compel mutually contentious powers into harmony by assembling an overwhelming array of other, less incompatible powers, yet without repressing them or putting them in chains.

277

Happiness and culture.—Seeing the surroundings of our childhood leaves us deeply moved: the garden house, the church with its graves, the pond and the woods—we always suffer in seeing these things again. Pity for ourselves grips us, for how much we have suffered through since then! And here everything still stands so quietly, so eternally: only we have become so different, so agitated; we even find once again a few people upon whom time has no *more* whetted its tooth than upon an oak tree: farmers, fishermen, forest people—they are the same.—Being moved and feeling self-pity at the sight of lower culture is the sign of higher culture; from which it follows that higher culture does not in any event increase happiness. Whoever wants to harvest happiness and contentment from life need only keep away from higher culture.

278

Metaphor of the dance.—It should now be considered the decisive sign of great culture when someone possesses enough strength and flexibility to be just as clear and rigorous in acquiring knowledge as he is capable at other moments of letting poetry, religion, and metaphysics get a hundred feet ahead of him, as it were, and still appreciating their power and beauty. This sort of position between two such different claims is very difficult to maintain, for science presses for the absolute predominance of its methods, and if one does not give in to this pressure, the different danger arises of feebly wavering back and forth between different impulses. Nonetheless: in order to offer a glimpse of the solution for this difficulty, at least with a metaphor—remember that *dancing* is not the same thing as staggering weakly back and forth between different impulses. High culture will look like an audacious dance: which is why, as noted, much strength and flexibility are necessary.

279

On making life easier.—One principal means of making life easier is idealizing all of its events: but we make it quite clear to ourselves by looking at painting what idealizing means. The painter demands that the viewer not look too carefully, too sharply; he forces him back a certain distance, so that he observes from there; he is required to presume a very specific distance of the observer from the picture; indeed, he must even assume an equally specific degree of sharpness in his viewer's vision; in such things he must absolutely not dare to waver. Everyone who wants to idealize his life must therefore not wish to look at it too carefully and must always banish his gaze back a certain distance. Goethe, for instance, understood this trick.

280

Making things harder as making them easier, and the reverse.—Many things that make human life harder at certain stages serve to make it easier at a higher stage because such people have come to know even harder things in life. The reverse occurs as well: thus, religion, for example, has a double face according to whether someone looks up at it in order to have his burden and distress removed or looks down at it as at a chain placed upon him so that he may not ascend too high into the air.

281

Higher culture is necessarily misunderstood.—Whoever has strung his instrument with only two strings, such as scholars, who besides their *drive for knowledge* have only an acquired *religious* one, does not understand those people who can play upon more strings. It lies in the nature of the higher, *many-stringed* culture that it is falsely interpreted by lower cultures; as occurs, for example, if art is valued only as a disguised form of religiosity. Indeed, people who are only religious understand even science as a search for religious feeling, just as deaf-mutes do not know what music is if not visible movement.

282

Song of lament.—It is perhaps the advantages of our times that bring with them a diminishing and an occasional underestimating of the *vita contemplativa*. But we must concede that our time is poor in great moralists, that Pascal, Epictetus, Seneca, Plutarch are little read any more, that work and diligence—once in the retinue of the great goddess health—sometimes seem to rage like a disease. Because time for thinking and tranquility while thinking are lacking, we no longer ponder divergent views: we content ourselves with hating them. With the tremendous acceleration of life, the spirit and the eye have grown accustomed to seeing and judging partially or falsely, and everyone resembles the traveler who gets to know a land and its people from the train. We deprecate an independent and careful attitude toward knowledge almost as a form of madness; the free spirit has been discredited, especially by scholars, who miss in the art with which he observes things their thoroughness and antlike diligence and would happily banish him to a solitary corner of science: whereas he has the quite different and higher task of commanding from an isolated site all the scientists and scholars who have been called to arms and of showing them the paths and goals of culture.—A lament such as the one that has just been sung will probably have its time and eventually go silent by itself when the genius of meditation makes a forceful return.

283

Primary deficiency of active people. — Active people generally lack the higher mode of activity: I mean individual activity. They are active as officials, businesspeople, scholars, that is to say, as species beings, but not as fully distinctive individual and unique human beings; in this respect they are lazy. — It is the misfortune of active people that their activity is almost always a little unreasonable. We dare not ask the banker who is busy accumulating money, for example, about the purpose of his restless activity: it is unreasonable. Active people roll along as a stone rolls along, according to the stupidity of the laws of mechanics. — As at all times, all human beings now fall into the categories of the enslaved and the free; for whoever does not have two-thirds of his day for himself is a slave, whatever else he may be: statesman, businessman, official, scholar.

284

In favor of the idle. — As a sign that esteem for the meditative life has decreased, scholars now compete with active people in a sort of hurried pleasure, so that they appear to esteem this sort of pleasure more highly than the kind that really is their due and that is in fact much more pleasurable. Scholars are ashamed of *otium*. Yet there is something noble about leisure and idleness. — If idleness really is the *beginning* of all vices, at least it therefore finds itself in the closest proximity to all virtues; the idle person is always a better person than the active one. — But you surely do not think that in speaking of leisure and idleness I am referring to you, you sloths? —

285

Modern restlessness. — The agitation of modern life becomes ever greater as we go westward, so that on the whole, the inhabitants of Europe present themselves to Americans as tranquil and pleasure-loving, even though they flit about like bees and wasps. This agitation has become so great that higher culture can no longer let its fruits ripen; it is as if the seasons followed one another too swiftly. Due to its lack of tranquility, our civilization is heading toward a new barbarism. At no time have active people, that is to say, restless people, counted for more. Among the necessary corrections in the character of humanity that we must therefore undertake is a considerable strengthening of its contemplative element. Every individual who is tranquil and steady in heart and head has the right to believe that he possesses not only a good temperament, but a generally useful virtue as well, and that he even fulfills a higher duty by preserving this virtue.

286

To what extent the active person is lazy. — I believe that everyone must have his own opinion about everything on which opinions are possible, because he is himself an individual, unique thing that adopts a new, unprecedented position toward every other thing. But the laziness that lies at the bottom of an active person's soul prevents him from drawing water from his own well. — It is the same with the freedom of opinions as with health: both are individual; no generally valid conception of either one can be established. What one individual needs for his health serves to make someone else sick, and many ways and means leading to freedom of the spirit may count as ways and means to unfreedom for more highly developed natures.

287

Censor vitae. — The fluctuation between love and hate describes for a long time the inner state of someone who wants to be free in his judgment of life; he does not forget and keeps track of everything, good and evil alike. When in the end the entire tablet of his soul has been written full of experiences, he will not despise and hate existence, but he will not love it, either, and will instead pore over it, now with a joyful eye, now with a sorrowful eye and, like nature, be now in a summer, now in an autumn mood.

288

Ancillary success.—Whoever seriously wants to become free, will in the process lose any propensity for faults and vices without having been compelled to do so; annoyance and irritation will assail him less frequently as well. His will wants nothing more earnestly than knowledge and the means to obtain it, that is to say: the lasting state in which he is most fit for gaining knowledge.

289

The value of illness.—The person who lies sick in bed sometimes discovers that it is his official position, his occupation, or his society that makes him sick and that they have made him lose his presence of mind: he gains this wisdom from the leisure that his illness forced upon him.

290

Sensibility in the countryside.—If someone does not have firm, restful lines on the horizon of his life, the sort of lines marked by mountains and forests, his innermost will itself becomes restless, distracted, and covetous, much like the nature of someone living in the city: he has no happiness and gives none to others.

291

Cautiousness of free spirits.—Free-minded people who live only for knowledge will quickly find they have reached their external goal in life, their final position in relation to society and the state, and will, for example, be content with a small official position or with only as much property as barely suffices for living; for they will arrange their lives in such a way that neither a great transformation in economic circumstances nor even the overthrow of the political order will overturn their life along with it. They expend as little energy as possible on all these things so that they can dive with all their collected forces and with a deep breath, as it were, into the element of knowledge. Thus, they can hope to dive deeply and even to see to the very bottom. — Such a spirit prefers to take in only the fringes of an event; he does not love things in all the breadth and vastness of their folds: for he does not want to entangle himself in them. — He, too, knows the weekdays of unfreedom, of dependence, of servitude. But from time to time a Sunday of freedom must come to him, or else he will not be able to endure life. — It is likely that even his love for humanity will be cautious and somewhat shortwinded, for he wants to have only as much to do with the world of inclinations and blindness as is necessary for the purpose of knowledge. He must trust that the guiding spirit of justice will say something on behalf of its adherent and protégé if accusing voices describe him as poor in love. — There is in his way of living life and of thinking a *refined heroism* that disdains offering itself to the reverence of the masses, as his coarser brothers do, and that tends to pass quietly through and out of the world. Through whatever labyrinths he may wander, through whatever rocks his stream may make its torturous way — when he reaches the light, he goes his way clearly, lightly, and almost soundlessly and lets the sunlight play down into his depths.

292

Forward. — And with that, forward on the track of wisdom with a firm step and a steady confidence! Whatever you are, serve as your own source of experience! Throw off the dissatisfaction with your nature, pardon yourself for your own self, for in every case you have in yourself a ladder with a hundred rungs on which you can climb to knowledge. The age into which you mournfully feel you have been thrown considers you blessed for this good fortune; it calls to you that you are even now taking part in experiences that people of a later age will perhaps have to do without. Do not disdain it for still being religious; explore fully the extent to which you still have genuine access to art. Can't you, with the help of precisely these experiences, retrace tremendous stretches of the human past with greater understanding? Haven't many of the most splendid fruits of more ancient cultures grown from precisely *this* soil that sometimes displeases you so much, from the soil of unclear thinking? We have to have loved religion and art like a mother and a nurse—otherwise we cannot become wise. But we must be able to look outward beyond them and be able to outgrow them; if we remain under their spell, we do not understand them. You must likewise be familiar with history and with the cautious balancing of these scales: "on the one hand—on the other." Turn back, treading in the footsteps where humanity made its great, sorrowful way through the desert of the past: thus you are instructed with the greatest certainty as to where all later humanity neither can nor dare go again. And because you want with all your might to peer ahead and to see how the knot of the future will be tied, your own life acquires the value of a tool for and a means to knowledge. You have it in your own hands to succeed in dissolving everything you live through—the experiments, wrong turns, errors, delusions, passions, your love and your hope—into your goal without any remainder. This goal is that you yourself become a necessary chain of the rings of culture and from this necessity draw conclusions about the necessity in the course of culture in general. When your gaze has become strong enough to see to the bottom of the dark well of your being and of your knowledge, then perhaps the distant constellations of future cultures will also be visible for you in that mirror. Do you believe that such a life with such a goal is too strenuous, too lacking in all amenities? Then you have not yet learned that no honey is sweeter than that of knowledge and that the clouds of affliction hanging over you must serve as the udder from which you will squeeze the milk for your own refreshment. When old age comes, you will really notice for the first time how you have given ear to the voice of nature, the nature that rules the whole world through pleasure: the same life that has its apex in old age also has its apex in wisdom, in the gentle sunshine of a continuous spiritual joyfulness; you encounter both old age and wisdom on the same crest of life, as nature wished it to be. Then it is time for the mist of death to approach, nor is there any cause for anger. Toward the light—your final movement; an exulting shout of knowledge—your final sound.

Chapter 6

In Relations with Others

293

Benevolent dissimulation. — In our relations with other people, a benevolent dissimulation is frequently required, as if we did not see through the motives for their actions.

294

Copies. — Not infrequently, we encounter copies of important people; and as with paintings, here too, most people are better pleased with the copies than with the originals.

295

The speaker. — We can speak very much to the point and yet in such a way that everyone in the world shouts the opposite: when, that is, we are not speaking to everyone in the world.

296

Lack of intimacy. — A lack of intimacy among friends is a mistake that cannot be censured without becoming irreparable.

297

On the art of giving. — Having to refuse a gift simply because it was not offered in the right way embitters us against the giver.

298

The most dangerous party member. — In every party there is someone whose far too credulous expression of the party's principles provokes the others to defect.

299

Adviser to the sick. — Whoever gives advice to someone who is sick acquires for himself a feeling of superiority over that person, whether the advice is taken or rejected. Hence, sick people who are sensitive and proud hate those who give advice even more than their sickness.

300

Two sorts of equality. — The passion for equality can express itself by someone either wanting to pull everyone else down to his level (by disparaging them, keeping secrets from them, or tripping them up) or wanting to pull himself up along with everyone else (by giving them recognition, helping them, taking pleasure in their success).

301

Against embarrassment. — The best means of coming to the assistance of people who are extremely embarrassed and of reassuring them consists in praising them with conviction.

302

Preference for particular virtues. — We do not put any special value upon possessing a virtue until we perceive its complete absence in our opponent.

303

Why we contradict. — We often contradict an opinion even though it is really only the tone in which it was expressed that we find disagreeable.

304

Trust and intimacy. — Whoever zealously seeks to force another person to be intimate with him is generally not certain whether he possesses that person's trust. Whoever is certain that he is trusted puts little value upon intimacy.

305

Equilibrium of friendship. — In our relationship with another person, we sometimes recover the appropriate equilibrium of friendship if we place a few grains of fault on our own side of the scale.

306

The most dangerous physicians. — The most dangerous physicians are those who, as born actors, have perfected the art of deception by which they imitate the born physician.

307

When paradoxes are in order. — To gain the assent of clever people to some proposition, we sometimes need only to present it in form of a tremendous paradox.

308

How courageous people are won over. — We persuade courageous people to undertake some action by representing it as more dangerous than it is.

309

Courtesies. — We count the courtesies shown to us by people whom we do not like as offenses.

310

Making people wait. — A sure way to provoke people and to put malicious thoughts in their heads is to make them wait for a long time. This makes people immoral.

311

Against trusting people.—People who grant us their complete trust believe that they thereby gain a right to ours. This is a false conclusion; we acquire no rights by making gifts.

312

Means of compensation.—Giving to someone whom we have injured the opportunity for a witticism at our expense is often enough to provide satisfaction for him personally, or even to make him well-disposed toward us.

313

Vanity of the tongue.—Whether someone conceals his bad qualities and vices or admits them openly, what his vanity desires in both cases is to gain an advantage thereby: just observe how acutely he distinguishes between those from whom he conceals these qualities and those toward whom he is honest and sincere.

314

Considerate.—Wanting to offend nobody, to cause nobody harm, can as easily be the mark of a just disposition as of a fearful one.

315

Requisite for disputing.—Anyone who does not know how to put his thoughts on ice should not head into the heat of battle.

316

Association and arrogance.—We forget arrogance when we know that we are always among deserving people; being alone breeds presumption. Young people are arrogant because they associate with others like themselves, all of whom are nothing, but would like to be something important.

317

Motive of attack. — We often attack not only in order to do someone harm, to overcome him, but perhaps only in order to become conscious of our strength.

318

Flattery. — People who wish to use flattery to deaden our caution in dealing with them are employing a dangerous means, a sleeping potion, as it were, which if it does not put us to sleep, only keeps us all the more awake.

319

Good letter writers. — Someone who does not write any books, thinks a lot, and has insufficient society about him will generally be a good letter writer.

320

What is ugliest. — It is doubtful whether a much-traveled person will have found any parts of the world uglier than those in the human face.

321

Sympathetic people. — Natures that are sympathetic and always helpful in misfortune are rarely as likely to share in joy: when others are fortunate, they have nothing to do, are superfluous, feel as if they no longer possess their superior position, and hence easily manifest discontent.

322

Relatives of a suicide. — The relatives of a suicide hold it against him that he did not remain alive out of concern for their reputations.

323

Foreseeing ingratitude.—Someone who gives a large gift does not get any gratitude; for the recipient has already been burdened too much by accepting it.

324

In dull society.—Nobody thanks a clever person for his politeness in putting himself on their level in a social circle where it is not polite to show one's cleverness.

325

Presence of witnesses.—We leap all the more readily after someone who has fallen into the water if people are present who do not dare to do so.

326

Keeping silence.—For both parties involved, the most unpleasant way to respond to a polemic is to get annoyed and keep silent: for the attacker generally interprets silence as a sign of contempt.

327

The secret of a friend.—There are few people who, when they are at a loss for subject matter in conversation, will not reveal the secret affairs of their friends.

328

Humanity.—The humanity of famous people consists in graciously putting themselves in the wrong when they are among people who are not well known.

329

The self-conscious person.—People who do not feel sure of themselves in society use every opportunity for publicly displaying their superiority to anyone near at hand who is inferior to them, through teasing, for example.

330

Thanks. — A refined soul is oppressed by knowing anyone is under obligation to it; a coarse soul, by knowing itself under obligation to anyone.

331

Mark of alienation. — The strongest sign of alienation in the views that two people hold is when both speak ironically to the other, but neither senses the irony therein.

332

Arrogance of the meritorious. — Arrogance in those with merit gives even more offense than arrogance in those without merit: for the merit already gives offense by itself.

333

Danger in the voice. — Sometimes in conversation the sound of our own voice disconcerts us and misleads us into making assertions that do not correspond at all to our opinion.

334

In conversation. — In conversation, whether we tend to agree or disagree with the other person is completely a question of habit: the one makes as much sense as the other.

335

Fear of our neighbor. — We fear the hostile disposition of our neighbor because we are afraid that this disposition will enable him to penetrate our secrets.

336

To distinguish by reproving.—Highly respected people confer even their reproofs as if they wished to distinguish us in this way. These are supposed to make us aware of how earnestly they concern themselves with us. We misunderstand them completely if we take their reproofs objectively and defend ourselves against them; we annoy them by behaving in this way and alienate them from us.

337

Vexation at the goodwill of others.—We are mistaken about the degree to which we believe ourselves to be hated or feared: because we are ourselves quite cognizant of the degree to which we diverge from a person, position, or party, but those other people only know us very superficially and therefore also only hate us superficially. We often encounter goodwill that is inexplicable to us; if we do understand it, however, it offends us because it shows that someone does not take us seriously enough or as having much importance.

338

Clashing vanities.—Two people who meet will, if their vanity is equally great, afterward retain a negative impression of each other because each was so preoccupied with the impression that he wanted to produce in the other person that the other person made no impression upon him; both eventually notice that their effort has been in vain and each places the blame on the other.

339

Bad manners as a good sign.—The superior spirit takes pleasure in the tactlessness, arrogance, even hostility toward him of ambitious youths; these are the bad manners of fiery steeds that have not yet carried any rider and that will nonetheless soon be proud to carry one.

340

When it is advisable to be in the wrong.—We do well to accept without refutation even those accusations that do us wrong in any case where the accuser would see a still greater wrong on our part if we were to contradict him, much less to refute him. In this way, admittedly, someone can always be in the wrong and still maintain that he is right and finally with the best conscience in the world become the most unbearable tyrant and nuisance; and what holds true for the individual can also occur in whole classes of society.

341

Too little respected.—Extremely conceited people to whom we have shown signs of a slighter regard than they expected to receive attempt for a long time to mislead themselves and others about this and become cunning psychologists in order to make it seem as if other people really did show them sufficient respect: if they do not attain their goal, if the veil of deception is torn, they give themselves over to an even greater rage.

342

Primal circumstances still echoing in speech.—In the way that men put forth their assertions in today's society, we can often perceive an echo of the times when they were more expert with weapons than with anything else: they handle their assertions sometimes as if they were marksmen aiming their weapons; at other times, we can practically hear the whistling and clashing of swords; and some men send an assertion crashing down like a heavy club.—Women, on the other hand, speak like creatures who have for millennia sat at the loom, or guided a needle, or been childish with children.

343

The narrator.—Anyone who narrates something makes it readily discernible whether he narrates the events because they interest him or because he wants his narration to attract the interest of others. In the latter case, he will exaggerate, use superlatives, and do other similar things. He generally narrates worse in this case because he is thinking not so much of the subject matter as of himself.

344

Reading aloud.—Anyone who reads dramatic texts aloud makes discoveries about his own character: he finds his voice more natural for certain moods and scenes than for others, for everything pathetic, or for the farcical, for instance, whereas in ordinary life he has perhaps simply not had the opportunity to display pathos or buffoonery.

345

A scene from comedy that occurs in life.—Someone thinks up a clever opinion on some topic in order to deliver it in some social setting. Now in a comedy, we would listen and observe how he tries to set full sail for a certain point and to steer the conversation toward a place where he can make his remark: how he continually pushes the conversation toward a single destination, occasionally losing his direction, then regaining it, finally reaching the right moment: his breath almost fails him —and then someone else in the group takes the remark right out of his mouth. What will he do? Oppose his own opinion?

346

Unintentionally impolite.—When someone unintentionally treats another person impolitely, not greeting him, for instance, because he does not recognize him, this rankles inside him even though he cannot reproach himself for his own intentions; the bad opinion that he has engendered in the other person vexes him, or he fears the consequences of ill feeling, or it causes him pain to have injured the other person—hence vanity, fear, or pity can be stirred, perhaps all of them together.

347

Betrayer's masterpiece. — To express to a fellow conspirator the insulting suspicion that one might be betrayed by him and to do this at the exact moment when one is oneself engaged in betrayal is a masterpiece of malice because it keeps the other person occupied with himself and forces him to behave for a time quite unsuspiciously and openly, so that the real betrayer has given himself a free hand.

348

Giving offense and being offended. — It is much more pleasant to give offense and later to ask for forgiveness than to be offended and to grant forgiveness. The one who does the former gives a sign of power and afterward a sign of his goodness of character. The other person, if he does not want to be considered inhuman, *must* forgive; because of this compulsion, there is only a slight pleasure in someone else's humiliation.

349

In a dispute. — If we simultaneously contradict an opinion and lay out our own, our continual consideration of that other opinion generally disturbs the natural delivery of our own: it appears more purposeful, more severe, perhaps somewhat exaggerated.

350

A trick. — Anyone who wants to obtain something difficult from someone else must not grasp the matter as a problem, but simply lay out his plan as if it were the only possibility; if he sees any objection or contradiction dawning in his opponent's eye, he must know how to break off quickly and how not to allow him any time for reflection.

351

Pangs of conscience after social gatherings.—Why do we have pangs of conscience after ordinary social gatherings? Because we have taken important things lightly, because in speaking of other people we have not spoken with complete truthfulness, or because we have kept silent where we ought to have said something, because we did not take an occasion to spring to our feet and run away, in short, because we have behaved in society as if we belonged to it.

352

We are misjudged.—Anyone who continually listens to hear how he is being judged will continually be annoyed. For we are misjudged even by those who are nearest to us (who "know us best"). Even good friends sometimes give vent to their ill humor in an envious word; and would they be our friends if they knew us exactly as we are?—The judgments of indifferent people hurt a great deal because they sound so unconstrained, almost objective. But if we notice that someone who is hostile to us knows a concealed point about us as well as we know it ourselves, then how great is our dismay!

353

Tyranny of the portrait.—Artists and diplomats who can quickly construct a complete picture of a person or of an event by combining a few individual traits are the most unfair of all in afterward demanding that the event or the person really must be the way that they painted them; they actually demand that someone be as gifted, as cunning, as unjust as he is in their representation of him.

354

The relative as the best friend.—The Greeks, who knew so well what a friend is—they alone of all peoples have had a deep, many-sided philosophical discussion of friendship; so that they were the first and up until now the last people to whom the friend appeared as a problem worth resolving—these same Greeks designated *relatives* by an expression that is the superlative of the word "friend." This remains inexplicable to me.

355

Misunderstood honesty.—When someone cites himself in conversation ("as I said," "as I tend to say") this gives an impression of arrogance, whereas it more frequently proceeds from the opposite source, or at least from an honesty that does not want to embellish and adorn this moment with ideas that belong to an earlier moment.

356

The parasite.—It indicates a complete lack of refined sensibility when someone prefers to live in dependency and at the expense of others simply in order not to have to work, and generally with a concealed animosity against those upon whom he depends.—Such a disposition is much more frequent among women than among men and also much more excusable (for historical reasons).

357

On the altar of reconciliation.—There are circumstances in which we can obtain something from someone only by offending him and making an enemy of him: this feeling of having an enemy torments him so much that he readily utilizes the first sign of a softened mood to propose a reconciliation and sacrifices upon the altar of this reconciliation the thing that previously meant so much to him that he did not want to give it up at any price.

358

Demanding pity as a sign of arrogance.—There are people who, when they become irate and offend other people, demand first, that we not hold this against them, and second, that we pity

359

Bait.—"Every person has his price"—that is not true. But it is possible to find for everyone some sort of bait that he cannot help but take. Thus, we can win many people's support for something simply by giving it a sheen of philanthropy, nobility, benevolence, self-sacrifice—and is there anything to which we could not give this sheen?—These are what *their* souls find sweet and delectable; others have different tastes.

360

Demeanor when praised.—When good friends praise someone with a talented nature, he will often act as if he were pleased out of politeness and goodwill, while in truth being indifferent to it. His real nature is quite lethargic toward this, so it cannot move him a single step away from the sun or the shade in which he lies; but people want to cause pleasure with their praise, and we would distress them if we did not take joy in their praise.

361

Socrates' experience.—If someone has mastered any one thing, he has for that very reason generally remained completely inept at most other things; but he believes exactly the opposite, as Socrates already found out. This is the drawback that makes associating with masters unpleasant.

362

Means of brutalization.—In struggling against stupidity, the most reasonable and gentle people eventually become brutal. They have perhaps thus found the right line of defense, for by rights, the appropriate argument against a stupid brow is a clenched fist. But because, as noted, their character is gentle and reasonable, they cause themselves more suffering by this means of self-defense than they inflict upon others.

363

Curiosity. — If curiosity did not exist, little would be done for the welfare of our neighbors. But curiosity sneaks into the house of the unfortunate and needy under the name of duty or pity. — Perhaps there is a good bit of curiosity even in the maternal love that is so highly praised.

364

Miscalculation in society. — This person wishes to be considered interesting on account of his judgments, that person on account of his inclinations and aversions, a third on account of his acquaintances, a fourth on account of his isolation — and they all miscalculate. For the one before whom this spectacle is being performed believes that he is himself the only spectacle to be considered here.

365

Duel. — In favor of all affairs of honor and duels, we can say that if someone has such sensitive feelings that he does not want to live when some person or other says or thinks this or that about him, then he has a right to make the matter depend upon the death of one or the other of them. We cannot remonstrate against his being so sensitive, for in this regard we are the heirs of the past, of its greatness, as well as its excesses, without which no greatness ever existed. Now if there is a code of honor that allows blood to count in place of death, so that the spirit is relieved after fighting a duel according to the rules, this is a great benefit, because otherwise many human lives would be in danger. — Moreover, such an institution educates people to be careful in their expressions and makes it possible to associate with them.

366

Refinement and gratitude. — A refined soul will gladly feel itself obliged to be grateful and not anxiously avoid occasions in which it incurs obligations; it will likewise be composed in its subsequent expressions of gratitude; whereas commoner souls resist becoming obligated in any way or are afterward excessive and all too assiduous in their expressions of gratitude. This latter also occurs, moreover, among people of common origins or in depressed circumstances: doing *them* a favor seems to them like a miracle of grace.

367

The hours of eloquence.—In order to speak well, one person may need someone who is recognized as decidedly superior to him, while someone else can find complete liberty of speech and well-chosen, eloquent turns of phrase only in the presence of someone whom he surpasses: the reason is in both cases the same; each of them speaks well only when he speaks *sans gêne*, the one because he does not feel any competitive drive or rivalry in the presence of his superiors, the other similarly in regard to his inferiors.—Now there is a completely different species of people who speak well only when they speak competitively, with the aim of gaining a victory. Which of the two species is the more ambitious: the one that speaks well from aroused ambition, or the one that speaks badly or not at all from exactly the same motive?

368

The talent for friendship.—Among people who have a special gift for friendship, two types stand out. The one is continually ascending and finds a friend who is precisely appropriate for each phase of his development. The series of friends that he acquires in this way is seldom coherent with itself, sometimes discordant and contradictory: completely in accordance with the fact that later phases of his development suspend or go against the earlier phases. Such a person might in jest be called a *ladder*. The other type is represented by someone who exerts a force of attraction upon quite various characters and talents, so that he gains a whole circle of friends; because of him, however, they do come into friendly contact with one another despite all their differences. We might call such a person a *circle*: for in him that congruity between such various dispositions and natures must somehow be prefigured. — One might add that the gift for having good friends is in many people much greater than the gift for being a good friend.

369

Tactics in conversation. — After a conversation with someone, we are best disposed toward our interlocutor if we have had the opportunity to display before him our wit and charm in all their splendor. Clever people who want to gain someone's favor make use of this during the conversation by passing along to him the best opportunities for a good witticism and the like. One can imagine an amusing conversation between two extremely clever people, both of whom want to gain the other person's favor, both therefore tossing the fine opportunities in the conversation back and forth with neither person taking them up: so that the conversation as a whole proceeds without any wit or charm because each concedes to the other the opportunity for wit and charm.

370

Discharging ill humor. — Any person who fails at something prefers to attribute this failure to the ill will of someone else, rather than to chance. His stimulated sensibility is relieved by thinking of a person and not of a thing as the reason for his failure; for we can revenge ourselves on people, but we have to choke down the injuries of chance. Therefore, when a prince has failed at something, his circle tends to designate some individual as the ostensible cause and to sacrifice that person in the interest of all the courtiers; for otherwise, the ill humor of the prince would be vented on all of them, since he cannot take any revenge on the goddess of fate herself.

371

Taking on the color of our surroundings. — Why are inclination and aversion so infectious that we can hardly live in proximity to a person of strong feelings without being filled like a cask with his pros and cons? First, completely refraining from judgment is very difficult, sometimes outright unbearable for our vanity; it appears in the same light as a poverty of thought and feeling or as timidity and effeminacy: and so we are at least moved to take sides, perhaps against the prevailing orientation, if this position provides more satisfaction for our pride. Ordinarily, though — this is the second possibility — we are not even consciously aware of the transition from indifference to inclination or aversion, but instead gradually habituate ourselves to feeling the same way as those around us, and because sympathetic agreement and mutual understanding are so pleasant, we soon bear all the signs and partisan colors of our surroundings.

372

Irony. — Irony has its place only as a pedagogical technique to be used by a teacher when interacting with any sort of pupil: its aim is to arouse humiliation and shame, but only of the salutary sort that awakens good intentions and enjoins us to offer respect and gratitude to the person who treated us in this way, as we would to a physician. The ironist presents himself as ignorant so effectively, in fact, that the pupils who converse with him are deceived, become audacious in their confident belief that they know better, and expose themselves in all sorts of ways; they abandon their cautiousness and show themselves as they are — until the moment when the rays of the lamp that they have held in their teacher's face fall back upon them in a very humiliating way. — Wherever a relationship like that between teacher and students does not exist, irony shows bad manners and is a vulgar sort of affectation. All ironic writers count upon the foolish species of people who like to feel as if they share with the author a superiority to everyone else, regarding him as the mouthpiece of their arrogance. — Moreover, habituation to irony, just like habituation to sarcasm, corrupts one's character, gradually lending it the quality of a malicious superiority: one finally resembles a snappish dog that has learned how to laugh as well as how to bite.

373

Arrogance. — There is nothing against which we should guard more carefully than against the growth of the weed that is called arrogance and that spoils all we reap; for there is an arrogance in affection, in signs of respect, in benevolent familiarity, in caresses, in friendly advice, in admission of errors, in pity for others, and all these beautiful things arouse repugnance if that weed sprouts among them. An arrogant person, that is, anyone who wants to seem more important than he is *or is considered to be*, always miscalculates. To be sure, he has a momentary success in his favor, insofar as those people in whose presence he behaves arrogantly generally pay him the degree of honor that he demands, whether out of fear or indolence; but they take a terrible revenge for this by subtracting exactly as much from the value that they previously ascribed to him as there is excess in the amount that he has demanded. There is nothing for which people make us pay more dearly than humiliating them. An arrogant person can make his genuinely great merit so suspect and so small in the eyes of others that they trample it into the dust. — Even a proud demeanor is something that we should allow ourselves only where we can be quite certain not to be misunderstood or to be considered arrogant, in front of friends or wives, for example. For there is no greater folly in our relations with other people than acquiring a reputation for being arrogant; it is even worse than not having learned how to tell lies politely.

374

Dialogue. — The dialogue is the perfect conversation because everything that the one person says obtains its specific color, its tone, its accompanying gesture *from a strict regard for the other person* with whom he is speaking and is therefore much like what occurs in correspondence, where one and the same person manifests ten ways of expressing his soul according to whether he is writing to this or to that person. There is in a dialogue only a single refraction of any thought: this is produced by the interlocutor, who serves as the mirror in which we wish to see our thoughts reflected back to us as beautifully as possible. But what is it like with two, three, or more interlocutors? There, the conversation loses its individualizing subtlety, the various motives work at cross purposes and annul one another; the turn of phrase that pleases one person does not suit the disposition of someone else. Hence, any person interacting with several others is forced to withdraw into himself, to set out the facts as they are, but to remove from topics the playful, ethereal air of humanity that makes a conversation into one of the most pleasant things in the world. Simply listen to the tone in which men tend to speak when conversing with a whole group of men; it is as if the refrain of everything said were: "this is what *I* am, this is what *I* say, now make of it whatever you please!" This is the reason why clever women generally leave an alienating, painful, forbidding impression upon anyone whom they have met in society: it is having to speak to many people and in front of many people that robs these women of all spiritual charm and exhibits in a glaring light their conscious reliance upon themselves, their tactics, and their design for public victory: whereas in a dialogue, the same women become feminine once again and recover their spiritual charm.

375

Posthumous fame.—Hoping for recognition from a distant future makes sense only if we assume that humanity will remain essentially unchanged and that everything great must be felt to be great not for one age, but for all ages. But this is an error; in all of its feeling and judging about what is beautiful and good, humanity changes quite drastically; it is mere fancy to believe that we are a mile farther along the way and that all humanity is taking *our* road. Besides: a scholar who goes unrecognized can definitely count upon his discovery also being made by others, so that at the very best, some later historian will acknowledge that he knew this thing or that before its general acceptance, but was not in a position to gain credence for his thesis. Not having been recognized is always interpreted by posterity as a lack of strength. — In short, we should not speak so readily in favor of an arrogant isolation. There are exceptions, of course; but usually it is our failures, weaknesses, and follies that keep people from recognizing our great qualities.

376

Of friends. — Just reflect for yourself sometime how various are the sensations and how divided the opinions even among the closest acquaintances; how even the same opinions have a wholly different place or intensity in the heads of your friends than in your own; how hundredfold occasions arise for misunderstanding or for hostile evasion of one another. After all this you will say to yourself: how uncertain is the ground upon which all our affiliations and friendships rest, how near are cold downpours or foul weather, how isolated is every human being! If someone perceives this and realizes in addition that all the opinions held by his fellow human beings as well as their type and their intensity are just as necessary and irresponsible as their actions are, if he acquires an eye for how this inner necessity of opinions arises from the indissoluble interweaving of character, occupation, talent, environment — he will perhaps get rid of the bitterness and severity of feeling with which that sage cried out: "Friends, there are no friends!" He will instead admit to himself: yes, there are friends, but their errors and delusions about you are what led them to you and they must have learned to keep silent in order to remain your friend; for such human relationships almost always depend upon a few things never being said, indeed, upon their never being touched upon; but if these pebbles do begin to roll, the friendship follows along behind them and shatters. Are there people who would not be mortally wounded if they were to find out what their most intimate friends actually know about them?— By getting to know ourselves and seeing our own nature as a changing sphere of opinions and moods and thus learning a little self-deprecation, we bring ourselves once again into equilibrium with other people. It is true that we have good reasons to pay very little respect to each of our acquaintances, even the greatest among them, but we have equally good reasons to turn this feeling against ourselves.—And so let us put up with one another since we put up with ourselves; and perhaps everyone will sometime arrive at the more joyous hour when he will say:

> "Friends, there are no friends!" thus cried the dying sage;
> "Foes, there is no foe!"—I cry, the living fool.

Chapter 7

Woman and Child

377

The perfect woman. — The perfect woman is a higher type of human being than the perfect man: also something much rarer. — The natural science of animals offers a means to establish the probable truth of this proposition.

378

Friendship and marriage. — The best friend will probably obtain the best wife, because a good marriage rests upon the talent for friendship.

379

Perpetuation of the parents. — The unresolved dissonances of character and disposition in the parents' relationship resonate in their child's nature and constitute the history of his inner sufferings.

380

From the mother. — Everyone carries inside himself an image of woman drawn from his mother: this determines whether he will revere women or despise them or generally be indifferent to them.

381

Correcting nature. — If someone does not have a good father, he should provide himself with one.

382

Fathers and sons. — Fathers have a great deal to do in order to make up for having had sons.

383

Error of refined women. — Refined women think that something simply does not exist if it is not possible to speak of it in society.

384

A male sickness. — What is most certain to counteract the male sickness of self-contempt is for the man to be loved by a clever woman.

385

One kind of jealousy. — Mothers easily become jealous of their sons' friends when these friends are particularly successful. A mother generally loves *herself* in her son more than she does the son himself.

386

Reasonable unreason. — In the maturity of their life and of their understanding, the feeling comes over everyone that their father was wrong to have engendered them.

387

Maternal goodness. — Some mothers need happy, respected children, some need unhappy ones: otherwise they cannot manifest their goodness as mothers.

388

Different sighs. — Some men have sighed over the abduction of their wives, most men, however, because nobody wanted to abduct them.

389

Match of love. — Marriages made for love (the so-called love-matches) have error as a father and penury (need) as a mother.

390

Women's friendship. — Women can be quite good at entering into friendship with a man; but in order to maintain it — for this, some assistance from a slight physical antipathy is required.

391

Boredom. — Many people, especially women, do not feel any boredom because they have never really learned how to work.

392

An element of love. — In every type of female love some trace of maternal love also appears.

393

The unity of place and drama. — If spouses did not live together, good marriages would be more frequent.

394

The usual consequences of marriage. — Every association that does not raise us up pulls us downward, and vice versa; therefore men usually sink a little when they take wives, whereas women are slightly elevated. Men who are too spiritual in nature require marriage just as much as they resist it like an unpleasant medicine.

395

Teaching to command. — Children from modest families must be educated in how to command, just as other children must be educated in how to obey.

396

Wanting to fall in love. — People who have become engaged as a matter of convenience often work hard at *falling* in love in order to avoid being reproached for cold, calculating utility. Likewise, those people who have turned to Christianity for their own advantage work hard at really becoming pious; for this makes the religious pantomime easier for them.

397

No standstill in love. — A musician who *loves* a slow tempo will take the same pieces of music more and more slowly. There is no point where any love stands completely still.

398

Modesty. — In general, the modesty of women increases along with their beauty.

399

A lasting marriage. — A marriage in which each person wants to attain an individual goal through the other person will last; for example, if the wife wants to become famous through her husband and the husband wants to become popular through his wife.

400

Protean nature. — Out of love, women become exactly what the men who love them imagine them to be.

401

Loving and possessing. — Women most often love an important man in such a way that they want to have him for themselves alone. They would gladly put him under lock and key if their vanity did not advise against it: this vanity wants his importance to be evident to other people as well.

402

Test of a good marriage. — A marriage proves its excellence by being able to put up with an occasional "exception."

403

A means for getting anyone to do anything. — We can make anyone so fatigued and weakened from commotion, anxieties, and an overload of work and thinking that he no longer resists something that seems to be complicated, but gives in to it — this is known both to diplomats and to women.

404

Respectability and honesty. — Those girls who want to rely solely upon their youthful charms to maintain them for their entire lives and whose cunning is further prompted by their mothers' shrewdness want exactly the same thing as courtesans, the only difference being that the former are more clever and more dishonest than the latter.

405

Masks. — There are women who, wherever we may search, have nothing inside, but are instead wholly masks. A man who gets involved with these almost spectral, necessarily unsatisfying beings is to be pitied, but it is precisely these women who are able to arouse the man's desire most strongly: he searches for her soul — and goes on searching forever.

406

Marriage as a long conversation. — In entering into a marriage we should put the question to ourselves: do you believe that you will enjoy conversing with this woman all the way into old age? Everything else in marriage is transitory, but most of the time together is spent in conversation.

407

Girls' dreams. — Inexperienced girls flatter themselves by imagining that it lies in their power to make a man happy; later they learn that assuming a man requires only a girl to make him happy really means thinking very little of him. — The vanity of women demands that a man be more than a happy spouse.

408

The dying out of Faust and Gretchen. — As a scholar has very astutely remarked, the cultivated men of contemporary Germany resemble a mixture of Mephistopheles and Wagner, but certainly not Faust, whom their grandfathers (in their youth at least) felt rumbling within them. There are therefore — to continue that proposition — two reasons why *Gretchens* do not suit them. And because they are no longer desired, it seems that they are dying out.

409

Girls in the Gymnasium. — Above all else, do not extend our *Gymnasium* education to girls! An education that often turns clever, inquisitive, fiery youths into — copies of their teachers!

410

Without rivals. — Women easily perceive whether a man's soul has already been possessed by something else; they want to be loved without rivals and reproach him for the goals of his ambition, for his political duties, for his sciences and arts if he has a passion for such things. Unless, of course, he shines because of these things — then they hope that a liaison with him would make *them*, too, shine more brightly; if that is the case, they encourage their lover.

411

The female intellect. — The intellect of women manifests itself as perfect self-control, presence of mind, and utilization of every advantage. This is the primary trait that they pass along to their children, to which the father adds the darker background of the will. His influence determines the rhythm and harmony, as it were, with which the new life will be played out; but its melody stems from the woman. — Or rephrased for those who know how to construe such things: women have intelligence, men have spirit and passion. This is not contradicted by the fact that men actually get so much further with their intelligence: they have the deeper, stronger drives, which carry their intelligence a very long way, even though it is in itself something passive. Women are often secretly amazed at the great respect that men pay to their spirit. If in their choice of spouse men are above all searching for someone who has great depth and spirit, but women are searching for someone who has cleverness, presence of mind, and brilliance, we can clearly see how a man is basically searching for an idealized man and a woman for an idealized woman, hence not for a complement to themselves, but instead for the perfection of their own virtues.

412

A judgment of Hesiod's confirmed. — A sign of women's cleverness is that they have almost everywhere understood how to have themselves supported like drones in a beehive. Yet consider what that originally means and why men do not let themselves be supported by women. This is surely because male vanity and ambition are greater than female cleverness; for women have understood how to secure a preponderant advantage, even mastery for themselves, through their subordination. Even caring for children could originally have been used by women's cleverness as a pretext for avoiding as much work as possible. Even at present, when they really are busy, for example as housekeepers, they understand how to make a bewildering fuss about it: so that men tend to overestimate the worth of their activity tenfold.

413

Near-sighted people are smitten. — Sometimes simply having stronger eyeglasses suffices to cure someone smitten with love; and anyone who had the imaginative power to represent a face or a figure twenty years older than it is would perhaps go through life quite undisturbed.

414

Women in hatred. — In a state of hatred, women are more dangerous than men; in the first place because they are not constrained by any considerations of fairness once their feeling of hostility has been aroused, but instead allow their hatred to swell without interruption to its final consequences, and second because they are practiced in finding sore spots (which every human being and every party has) and stabbing there: for which purpose their dagger-sharp intelligence does splendid service (whereas men hold back at the sight of wounds and are often disposed to be magnanimous and conciliatory).

415

Love. — The idolatrous attitude toward love that women promote is basically and originally an invention of their cleverness, insofar as all those idealizations of love enhance their power and let them present themselves as more and more desirable in men's eyes. But the habituation over centuries to this exaggerated estimation of love has led them to fall into their own net and to forget its origin. They themselves are now the ones who are deceived more than men are, and they therefore suffer more from the disillusionment that will almost inevitably enter into the life of every woman — insofar as she has enough imagination and intelligence for her to be able to be deceived and disillusioned.

416

On the emancipation of women. — Can women be at all just when they are so accustomed to loving and to immediately feeling for or against everything? Hence, they take an interest in causes more seldom than in people: but once they are for some cause they immediately become its partisans and thereby spoil its pure, innocent influence. Thus, there arises a not inconsiderable danger if politics and particular branches of science are entrusted to them (history, for example). For what would be rarer than a woman who really knew what science is? The best of them even nourish a secret disdain for it in their bosoms, as if they were somehow superior to it. Perhaps all this may change, but for now this is how it is.

417

Inspiration in women's judgments. — Those sudden decisions for or against something that women tend to make, the lightning-quick illumination of personal relations as their inclinations and aversions break forth, in short, the proofs of feminine injustice, have been suffused with a glow by amorous men, as if all women were inspired with wisdom even without the Delphic cauldron and the laurel wreath: and their utterances are interpreted and construed for a long time afterward, like Sibylline oracles. Yet if we consider that something can be said in favor of any person or thing, but that something can just as readily be said against them, and that everything has not just two sides, but three or four, then it is practically impossible for these sorts of sudden decisions to be completely mistaken; indeed, we could say: the nature of things is arranged in such a way that women are always in the right.

418

Letting ourselves be loved. — Because it is usually one of the two people in a loving pair who is the lover, the other the beloved, the belief has arisen that there is a constant amount of love in every love affair: the more the one grabs for himself, the less remains for the other. Exceptions do occur where vanity convinces each of the two persons that he or she must be the one who is loved, so that both want to let themselves be loved: which results in many scenes that are half amusing and half absurd, especially in marriage.

419

Contradictions in female heads.—Because women are so much more personal than objective, they can tolerate positions in their circle of ideas that are logically in contradiction with one another: they tend to become enthused for the representatives of these positions one after another and to accept their systems wholesale; yet in such a way that a dead spot is produced where a new personality can later obtain predominance. It may happen that all the philosophy in the head of an old woman consists of nothing but this sort of dead spot.

420

Who suffers more?—After any personal discord and quarrel between a woman and a man, one of them will suffer most at the thought of having caused the other pain; whereas the other will suffer most at the thought of not having caused the first person pain enough, so that the latter tries to use tears, sobs, and an air of consternation to keep the other person downhearted even after the quarrel.

421

Occasion for female magnanimity.—If we could ever get ourselves to think beyond the claims of custom, we might well consider whether nature and reason do not direct a man toward multiple marriages in succession, perhaps taking the form of an initial marriage at the age of twenty-two years to a girl somewhat older than him, one who is spiritually and morally superior to him and who can be his guide through the dangers of his twenties (ambition, hatred, self-contempt, passions of all kinds). Her love would later become wholly maternal and she would not only tolerate it, but would promote it in the most salutary way if in his thirties the man were to form a relationship with a very young girl whose education he would himself take in hand. — Marriage is an institution that is essential for those in their twenties, useful but not essential for those in their thirties: for later life, it is often harmful and promotes regression in a man's spiritual cultivation.

422

Tragedy of childhood. — Not infrequently, it may happen that noble-minded and ambitious people have to undergo their hardest struggle during childhood: perhaps by having to maintain their convictions against a low-minded father given over to pretense and deceit or, like Lord Byron, by living in a continual struggle with a childish and wrathful mother. Anyone who has experienced something like this will never in his life get over knowing who has really been his greatest, most dangerous enemy.

423

Parental folly. — The grossest errors in judging a person are made by his parents: this is a fact, but how can we explain it? Do the parents have too much experience of their child and can they no longer bring it together in any coherent way? It has been observed that those traveling among foreign peoples manage to grasp the general, distinctive features of a people only during the initial period of their residence; the more they come to know that people, the less skilled they become at seeing what is typical and distinctive about them. As soon as they become nearsighted, their eyes cease to be farsighted. Might the parents therefore misjudge their child because they have never stood far enough away from him? — Or we might explain this completely differently in the following way: people tend not to reflect upon what lies nearest at hand, what surrounds them, but simply to accept it. Perhaps the habitual thoughtlessness of parents is the reason why, if they are ever forced to make a judgment about their child, that judgment is so skewed.

424

From the future of marriage.—Those noble, free-minded women who take as their task the education and elevation of the female sex should not overlook one consideration: marriage conceived in its higher form, as a friendship of the soul between two human beings of different sex, that is, as we can hope it will be in the future, entered into for the purpose of engendering and educating a new generation—such a marriage, using sensuality as if it were only a rare, occasional means toward a greater end, will probably require us to provide some natural assistance from *concubinage*; for if, for reasons of the man's health, the wife is also supposed to serve as the sole source of satisfaction for his sexual needs, then an erroneous consideration, opposed to the aims just indicated, will already be determinative in selecting a wife: the producing of offspring will be a matter of chance and their successful education highly improbable. A good wife, who ought to be friend, helpmate, bearer of children, mother, household head, and manager, who perhaps even has to oversee her own business and official duties separately from her husband, cannot at the same time be a concubine: this would in general mean asking too much of her. Consequently there might occur in the future the reverse of what happened in Pericles' Athens: men who at that time had little more than concubines in their wives turned to the Aspasias on the side because they desired the charms of a sociability that liberated head and heart, a sociability that only the charm and spiritual resilience of women can create. All human institutions such as marriage allow only a moderate degree of practical idealization, failing which, crude remedies immediately become necessary.

425

Storm and stress period of women.—In the three or four civilized countries of Europe, a few centuries of education would suffice to make women into anything we want, even into men—

not in the sexual sense, admittedly, but at least in every other sense. Acted upon in this way, they will at some point have assumed all the male virtues and strengths, at the same time, of course, having to assume their weaknesses and vices as part of the bargain: this much, as noted, we can accomplish by force. But how will we endure the intermediate state that this will bring about and that might itself last for a few centuries, during which female follies and injustices, their age-old birthrights, will still assert their supremacy over all that has been newly won and acquired? This will be the time when anger will comprise the essential male affect, anger at the fact that all the arts and sciences have been inundated and clogged with an unprecedented dilettantism, that philosophy has been talked to death by bewildering chatter, that politics have become more fantastic and partisan than ever, that society is completely dissolving because the keepers of the old morality have become ridiculous to themselves and are striving to stand outside of morality in every possible way. For if women had their greatest power *in* morality, what would they have to grasp in order to regain a comparable amplitude of power after having given up morality?

426

The free spirit and marriage. — Will free spirits live with women? In general, I believe that they, like the prophetic birds of antiquity, as the true-thinking and truth-speaking men of the present, must prefer *to fly alone*.

427

Happiness in marriage. — Everything habitual pulls an ever tighter net of spider webs around us; and soon we notice that the threads have become ropes and that we ourselves are sitting in the middle as the spider that has caught itself and must feed on its own blood. That is why the free spirit hates all habits and rules, everything lasting and definitive, that is why he painfully rips apart the net around him again and again: although he will as a consequence suffer numerous small and large wounds—for he must tear those threads *away from himself*, away from his body and his soul. He must learn to love where he previously hated, and vice versa. Indeed, nothing should be impossible for him, not even sowing dragon's teeth in the same field where he previously let the cornucopias of his kindness flow forth.—From this we can determine whether he is made for the happiness of marriage.

428

Too near.—If we live too closely together with another person, it is as if we were to repeatedly handle a good engraving with our bare hands: one day we have a miserable, dirty piece of paper in our hands and nothing more. So, too, the soul of a human being is eventually worn out by constant handling; at least it eventually *seems* that way to us—we never see its original design and beauty again.—We always lose something by associating all too intimately with women and friends; and sometimes we lose the pearl of our life.

429

The golden cradle.—The free spirit will always breathe more freely once he has finally decided to shake off the maternal care and vigilance through which the women around him hold sway. For what harm is there to him in the cold draft of air from which they so anxiously preserve him, what significance is there in having one real disadvantage, loss, accident, illness, error, or infatuation more or less in his life, compared with the unfreedom of the golden cradle, the peacock-tail fan, and the oppressive sensation of having to be grateful besides because he is waited on and spoiled like an infant? That is why the milk given to him by the maternal disposition of the women around him can so easily turn to gall.

430

Willing animal sacrifice.—Nothing that women of significance do for their husbands, if they are men of renown and greatness, does more to make their lives easier than becoming the receptacle, as it were, for the general disfavor and occasional ill humor of other people. Contemporaries tend to overlook many mistakes and follies and even actions of gross injustice in their great men if they can just find someone whom they can mistreat and slaughter as a true sacrificial animal in order to relieve their own feelings. Not infrequently, a woman finds within herself the ambition to offer herself for this sacrifice, and then the man can of course be quite content—provided that he is enough of an egoist to put up with having this sort of willing conducting rod for lightning, storms, and rain near him.

431

Pleasant adversaries.—The natural inclination of women toward a peaceful, regular, happily harmonious existence and society, their accomplishment in spreading a soothing sheen upon the sea of life, unintentionally works contrary to the heroic inner impulse of the free spirit. Without noticing it, women act like someone removing stones from the path of a wandering mineralogist so that his foot does not stumble upon them—whereas he has set out precisely *in order to* stumble upon them.

432

Dissonance of two accords.—Women want to serve and find their happiness in doing so: and the free spirit does not want to be served and finds his happiness in this.

433

Xanthippe.—Socrates found the sort of wife that he needed—but even he would not have sought her had he known her well enough: the heroism of even this free spirit would not have gone that far. Xanthippe actually drove him more and more into his characteristic profession by making his house and home inhospitable and unhomely for him: she taught him to live in the streets and everywhere that one could chat and be idle and thus shaped him into the greatest Athenian street dialectician: who finally had to compare himself to an obtrusive gadfly that some god had placed upon the neck of that beautiful horse, Athens, in order to keep it from finding any peace.

434

Blind to what is far off. — Just as mothers can really sense and see only the visible and palpable pains of their children, so the wives of ambitious men cannot bring themselves to see their spouses suffering, starving, or even disregarded — whereas all this may not only be a sign that these men have chosen their way of life correctly, but even the guarantee that their great goals *must* someday be attained. Women are always secretly intriguing against the higher souls of their husbands; they want to cheat them of their future for the sake of a painless, comfortable present.

435

Power and freedom. — However highly women revere their husbands, they still revere the powers and ideas recognized by society even more: for millennia, they have been accustomed to going around bowed down before every ruler, with their hands folded upon their breasts, and they disapprove of every rebellion against public authority. That is why, without even intending to do so, but instead out of instinct, they fasten themselves like brakes onto the wheels of any free-spirited, independent striving and in certain circumstances render their husbands highly impatient, especially if the latter talk themselves into believing that it is basically love that drives the women to do this. Disapproving of the methods that women use while magnanimously honoring the motives behind these methods — that is a man's way, and often enough a man's despair.

436

Ceterum censeo. — It is ridiculous when a society of people who have nothing decrees the abolition of the right of inheritance, and it is no less ridiculous when people without children engage in the practical work of making laws for a country — they do not in fact have enough ballast in their ship to be able to sail safely into the ocean of the future. But it seems just as nonsensical if someone who has chosen as his task the acquisition of the most universal knowledge and the appraisal of existence as a whole burdens himself with the personal considerations of family, sustenance, safety, or maintaining the respect of his wife and child and thus spreads before his telescope a gloomy veil that hardly any rays of distant galaxies are able to penetrate. So I, too, arrive at the proposition that in matters of the highest philosophical kind, anyone who is married is suspect.

437

Finally. — There are many sorts of hemlock and fate usually finds an occasion for placing a cup of this poisonous drink to the lips of a free spirit — in order to "punish" him, as the whole world then says. What do the women around him do then? They will scream and lament and perhaps disturb the thinker's sunset calm: as they did in the prison of Athens. "O Crito, tell someone to take these women away!" Socrates finally said.

Chapter 8

A Glance at the State

438

Requesting the floor. — A demagogic character and an intention of influencing the masses is common to all political parties today: because of that intention, all of them are compelled to transmute their principles into great frescoes of stupidity and to paint them thus upon the wall. None of this can be changed any more, indeed, it is superfluous to raise even a single finger against it; for what Voltaire said holds true in this domain: *quand la populace se mêle de raisonner, tout est perdu.* Since this has already occurred, we must adapt ourselves to the new conditions, as we adapt when an earthquake has displaced the old boundaries and contours of the land and changed the value of our property. Moreover: if all politics is now a question of making life tolerable for the greatest number, then this greatest number might also be allowed to determine what they understand a tolerable life to be; if they believe that the intellect is capable of discovering the appropriate means for attaining this goal, what good would it do to doubt it? They now *want* for once to forge their happiness and unhappiness themselves; and if this feeling of self-determination, this pride in the five or six ideas that their heads contain and bring to light, does in fact make their lives so pleasant for them that they will gladly endure the fatal consequences of their narrow-mindedness: there is little to object to here, provided their narrow-mindedness does not go so far as to demand that *everything* should become politics in this sense, or that *everyone* should live and work according to this standard. For above all, now more than ever, some people must be allowed to refrain from politics and to step a bit out of the way: they, too, are impelled by the pleasure of self-determination in doing this, and there may also be a bit of pride connected to remaining silent when too many people, or simply many people, are speaking. And then we must excuse these few if they do not take the happiness of the many all that seriously, whether we take this to mean many peoples or many social classes, and if they are guilty now and then of adopting an ironic air; for their seriousness lies elsewhere, their idea of happiness is quite different, their goal cannot be encompassed by every clumsy hand that happens to have five fingers. There finally arrives—this will be the hardest to allow to them, but also must be allowed to them—an occasional moment when they emerge from their silent isolation and try out once again the power of their lungs: then they call to one another like people lost in a forest in order to make their presence known and to encourage one another; in the course of which, admittedly, many things become audible that sound bad to those ears for which they are not intended.—Soon afterward, it is silent once again in the forest, so silent that we can once again clearly perceive the buzzing, humming, and fluttering of the countless insects that live in and above and beneath it.

439

Culture and caste.—A higher culture can arise only where there are two different castes in society: that of the workers and that of the idlers, those who are capable of true leisure; or more strongly expressed: the caste of those who are forced to work and the caste of those who are free to work. How happiness gets divided is not an essential consideration when it is a matter of engendering a higher culture; but in any case, the caste of idlers is the one that is more capable of suffering and does suffer more, its pleasure in existence is less, its task greater. Now if it is even possible for some movement between the two castes to take place, so that the duller, less intelligent families and individuals from the upper caste can be demoted to the lower one and the freer people from the lower caste can in turn gain admission to the higher one: then a state has been reached beyond which only an open sea of indefinite wishes can be seen. — Thus the fading voice of days gone by speaks to us; but where are there still ears to hear it?

440

Of blood lineage. — What provides men and women of noble blood with an advantage over others and gives them an unquestionable right to be esteemed more highly are two arts that are augmented more and more by hereditary transmission: the art of being able to command and the art of proud obedience. — Now wherever commanding is part of daily affairs (as in the world of business and industry), there arises something similar to those "noble bloodlines," but they lack the aristocratic bearing in obedience that those people inherited from feudal conditions and that will no longer grow in our cultural climate.

441

Subordination. — Subordination, which is so highly esteemed in the military and bureaucratic state, will soon seem as unbelievable to us as the resolute tactics of the Jesuits already seem; and when this subordination is no longer possible, there will no longer be any way to attain a whole host of the most amazing effects, and the world will be a poorer place. It must vanish because its foundation is vanishing: the belief in absolute authority, in definitive truth; even in military states physical compulsion does not suffice to produce it, for it derives instead from an inherited adoration of princely qualities as if they were something superhuman. — In *freer* circumstances, people subordinate themselves only under certain conditions, as a result of a mutual contract, hence, with every possible reservation made for their self-interest.

442

Conscript armies. — The greatest disadvantage of the conscript armies that are so highly extolled today consists in the fact that they squander some of the most highly civilized individuals; only when every circumstance is favorable do they exist at all — how frugally and anxiously we should deal with them, since it requires great stretches of time to create the conditions that might chance to produce such delicately organized brains! But just as the Greeks wallowed in Greek blood, so do the Europeans today in European blood: and indeed, it is always relatively more of the most highly cultivated individuals who will be sacrificed, the very ones who would guarantee an extensive and excellent posterity; such people stand in the front lines of battle as the commanders and moreover expose themselves most to danger because of their greater ambition. — The crude patriotism of the Romans is today, when quite different and higher tasks than *patria* and *honor* stand before us, either something dishonest or a sign of backwardness.

443

Hope as a presumption. — Our social order will slowly melt away, just as all earlier orders have done, as soon as the suns of new opinions shine with a new heat over humanity. We can *wish for* this melting away only if we have hope: and we may reasonably be hopeful only if we give to ourselves and to others like us credit for more strength in our hearts and heads than we do to the representatives of what presently exists. This hope will therefore usually be a *presumption*, an *overestimation*.

444

War. — Against war it can be said: it makes the victor stupid and the vanquished malicious. In favor of war: both of these effects make people more barbaric and thus more natural; war is a time of sleep or of winter for culture, from which humanity emerges with more strength for good and for evil.

445

In the prince's service. — In order to act with complete ruthlessness, a statesman might best perform his work not for himself, but for a prince. The eye of any observer will be blinded by the radiance of this general disinterestedness, so that he does not see the malice and harshness that accompany the work of the statesman.

446

A question of power, not of justice. — For people who see everything in terms of its higher utility, socialism, provided it *really* is a rebellion against the oppressors of those who have been oppressed and held down for millennia, does not involve a problem of *justice* (with its ridiculous, feeble question: "how far *should* we give in to its demands?"), but only a problem of *power* ("how far *can* we make use of its demands?"); it is therefore the same as a force of nature, as steam, for example, which people can either force to serve them as a machine god or else, should the machine fail, that is, should human calculation err in constructing it, can blow the machine to pieces and the people along with it. To resolve that question of power, we must know how strong socialism is and in what modified form it can still be used as a powerful lever within the present play of political forces; under certain circumstances, we must ourselves do everything we can to strengthen it. For with every great force — even the most dangerous ones — humanity must reflect upon how to make it into an instrument of human intentions. — Socialism gains certain rights only if it seems that war is about to break out between the two powers that represent the old and the new, but a prudent calculation of how to maximize self-preservation and advantage by both parties then gives rise to the desire for a settlement. Without a contract, no rights. Up until now, however, there has been neither war nor contract in the designated territory, therefore no rights either, no "ought."

447

Making use of the slightest dishonesty. — The power of the press consists in the fact that every individual who serves it feels only a very slight sense of responsibility and obligation. He generally does express *his* opinion, but on occasion does *not* express it, in order to benefit his party or the political aims of his country or even himself. These slight lapses into dishonesty or perhaps only into dishonest reticence are not hard to put up with as individual behavior, yet their consequences are extraordinary because these slight lapses are committed by many people at the same time. Each of them says to himself: "By doing some very slight services, I can improve my life and make a living: by failing to give due regard to these minor considerations, I make my life impossible." Because it seems almost indifferent in moral terms whether one does or does not write one additional line, which may in any case not even have one's signature, someone who has money and influence can make the public share any opinion. Anyone who knows that most people are weak in small matters and who wants to attain his own goals through them is always a dangerous person.

448

Complaining too loudly. — Representing a crisis in a strongly exaggerated way (for example, the defects of an administration, corruption and arbitrary favoritism in political or scholarly organizations) admittedly diminishes its effect upon those who know something about the situation, but creates an even greater effect among those who do not know anything about it (and who would have remained indifferent to a cautious, moderate exposition). But since the latter make up a significant majority and harbor within themselves greater strength of will and a more vehement passion for action, that exaggeration will give rise to investigations, punishments, promises, reorganizations. — To that extent, it is useful to represent crises in an exaggerated way.

449

The apparent weathermakers of politics.—Just as the common people privately assume that someone who knows about the weather and can predict it a day in advance actually makes the weather, so do even cultivated and educated people display their superstitious faith by attributing to great statesmen the personal responsibility for all the important changes and fluctuations that occur while they are in power, when it is quite clear that those statesmen simply knew something about them a bit earlier than others did and made their calculations accordingly: hence, they, too, are taken as weathermakers—and this belief is not the least significant instrument of their power.

450

New and old conception of government.—To differentiate between the government and the people as if two separate spheres of power, one stronger and higher, the other weaker and lower, were negotiating and reaching agreement is a piece of inherited political sensibility that even today corresponds exactly to the historical arrangement of power relations in *most* states. When Bismarck, for example, describes the constitutional form as a compromise between government and people, he speaks in accordance with a principle that has its reason in history (and for the very same reason, admittedly, an admixture of unreason as well, without which nothing human can exist). On the other hand, we are now supposed to learn—in accordance with a principle that has sprung purely from the *head* and is now supposed to *make* history—that the government is nothing but an organ of the people, not a provident, venerable "above" in relation to a habitually diffident "below." Before we accept this hitherto unhistorical and arbitrary, if also more logical formulation of the concept of government, we really ought to consider the consequences: for the relationship between people and government is the strongest model for other relationships, the pattern from which interactions between teacher and pupil, head of household and servants, father and family, commander and soldier, master and apprentice have instinctively taken their shape. All these relationships are now being slightly reformulated under the influence of the prevailing constitutional form of government: they are *becoming* compromises. But how greatly they will have to be transformed and displaced, changed in both name and essence, once that newest concept of all has everywhere made itself master of people's minds! — which may, however, still require another century. During this process, nothing is *more* desirable than caution and slow development.

451

Justice as a party lure. — Noble (if not particularly discerning) representatives of the ruling class may well vow: "we want to treat people as equals and to grant them equal rights"; to that extent, a socialist way of thinking based upon *justice* is possible, but as noted, only within the ruling class, which in this case *practices* justice with its sacrifices and renunciations. By contrast, the *demand* for equality of rights made by socialists of the subjected caste never flows from a sense of justice, but instead from greed. — If someone holds bloody chunks of meat near an animal and then yanks them away until finally it roars: do you think that this roaring signifies justice?

452

Possession and justice. — When the socialists demonstrate that the division of property among present-day humanity is the consequence of countless acts of injustice and violence and *in summa* deny any obligation toward something so unjustly grounded, they are seeing only one isolated thing. The entire past of the old culture was built upon force, slavery, deceit, error; but we, as the heirs of all these circumstances, indeed as concrescences of that entire past, cannot erase ourselves by decree and should not wish to remove any one part of it. Unjust sentiments are also fixed in the souls of those without property; they are no better than the proprietors and have no moral prerogative, for at some point their ancestors were also proprietors. What is necessary is not the forcible redistribution of property, but instead the gradual transformation of sensibility; the sense of justice must become greater in everyone, the instinct for violence weaker.

453

The helmsman of the passions.—The statesman generates public passions in order to profit from the counterpassions that are thereby awakened. To take an example: a German statesman knows perfectly well that the Catholic Church will never have the same designs as Russia and that it would in fact much rather be allied with the Turks than with Russia; he likewise knows that Germany would be greatly endangered by an alliance between France and Russia. Now, if he manages to make France the hearth and home of the Catholic Church, he will have eliminated this danger for a long time to come. Consequently, he has an interest in displaying hatred toward Catholics and using every sort of animosity to transform those who acknowledge the pope's authority into an impassioned political power, one that is hostile to German policies and must naturally merge with France, the adversary of Germany: he aims just as necessarily at Catholicizing France as Mirabeau saw the salvation of his fatherland in its de-Catholicizing.—One state therefore wants millions of minds in another state to be shrouded in darkness in order to gain an advantage from this darkness. It is the same attitude that supports the republican form of government in a neighboring state—*le désordre organisé*, as Mérimée said—solely because it assumes that this government will make the people weaker, more disunited, and less capable of war.

454

The dangerous ones among revolutionary spirits.—We can divide those who intend the overthrow of society into those who want to attain something for themselves and those who want to attain something for their children and grandchildren. The latter are the more dangerous, for they have the faith and the good conscience of disinterestedness. The others can be bought off: the ruling elements of society are still rich and clever enough for that. The danger begins as soon as the goals become impersonal; those who are revolutionaries from impersonal interests can regard all defenders of the status quo as personally interested and can therefore feel superior to them.

455

Political value of fatherhood.—If a man has no sons, he does not have the full right to participate in discussions about what any affair of state requires. We must ourselves, along with other people, have risked what is dearest to us; only this binds us firmly to the state; we must have the happiness of our posterity in view, hence, first and foremost have posterity, in order to take the proper, natural interest in institutions and in their alteration. The development of a higher morality in someone depends upon his having sons; this makes him unegoistically disposed, or more accurately: it spreads out his egoism over time and allows him seriously to pursue goals beyond his individual lifetime.

456

Pride in ancestry.—We may justly take pride in having an unbroken line of *good ancestors* down through our fathers—but not in the line itself, for everyone has this. Descent from good ancestors constitutes genuine nobility of birth; a single break in that chain, a single evil ancestor, therefore cancels nobility of birth. We should ask everyone who speaks of his nobility: do you have no violent, avaricious, licentious, malicious, cruel people among your forebears? If he can in certainty and good conscience respond with a No, we should seek out his friendship.

457

Slaves and workers. — That we set more value upon satisfying vanity than upon all other sorts of well-being (security, shelter, pleasures of every kind) is evident to a ridiculous degree in the way that (quite apart from political reasons) everyone desires the abolition of slavery and absolutely detests reducing people to this condition: whereas everyone must concede that slaves live more securely and happily in every respect than the modern worker and that the work of slaves involves very little work compared with that of the "worker." We protest in the name of "human dignity": but this, expressed more plainly, is that cherished vanity, which feels that the hardest fate is not to be treated as an equal or to have less public esteem than someone else. — The Cynic thinks differently about this because he disdains honor: — and so Diogenes was for a time a slave and a tutor.

458

Leading spirits and their instruments. — We see great statesmen, and in general all those who must make use of many people to carry out their plans, proceed sometimes in one way, sometimes in another: either they very subtly and carefully select people who are suitable for their plans and then allow them a relatively great degree of freedom because they know that the nature of those they have selected will move them in the direction that they themselves want them to take; or else they choose badly, taking whatever comes to hand, but then forming this clay into something that suits their purposes. The latter sort of person is more forceful and also desires more submissive instruments; he generally has much less knowledge of people and much greater contempt for them than the first-mentioned spirits, but the machine that he constructs usually works better than the machine from the former's workshop.

459

Arbitrary law necessary.—Jurists disagree as to whether the legal code that has been most completely thought through or the legal code that is easiest to understand prevails. The first sort, whose highest model is the Roman law, appears to the lay person as incomprehensible and therefore not as an expression of his sense of justice. Popular codes of law, such as the Germanic, were crude, superstitious, illogical, in part foolish, but they did correspond to quite specific, inherited, indigenous customs and feelings.—But wherever the law is no longer a tradition, as it no longer is for us, it can function only by *command* or compulsion; none of us has a traditional feeling for the law any more, so we must therefore be content with *arbitrary laws* that are the expression of the necessity that there *must be* some law. In this case, then, whatever is the most logical is the most acceptable because it is the *most impartial*: even conceding that in every case the smallest unit of measure in the relationship between transgression and punishment is arbitrarily established.

460

The great man of the masses.—The recipe for what the masses call a great man can easily be given. One should in any case provide them with something they find quite agreeable or first put it in their heads that this or that thing would be quite agreeable and then give it to them. But not immediately, not at any price whatsoever: one should instead gain it by great exertion, or seem to gain it thus. The masses must have the impression that a powerful, indeed invincible force of will is present; at least it must seem to be present. Everyone admires strength of will because nobody has it, and everyone tells himself that if he did have it, there would no longer be any limits for him and for his egoism. Now if it appears that a strong will of this kind does accomplish something that the masses find agreeable instead of attending to the wishes of its own desire, we are even more amazed and congratulate ourselves. In other respects, the great man should have all the traits of the masses: the less ashamed they are before him, the more popular he is. Therefore: let him be violent, envious, exploitative, designing, flattering, fawning, arrogant, whatever the circumstances demand.

461

Prince and god.—People often deal with their princes much in the same way they do with their god, and indeed, the prince was often the representative of the god, or at least his high priest. This almost uncanny mood of reverence and fear and shame has already become and is becoming much weaker, but it sometimes flares up and attaches itself to powerful people in general. The cult of genius is an echo of this reverence for gods and princes. Wherever one strives to raise individual human beings into something superhuman, there will also be a tendency to conceive of entire classes of the people as coarser and lower than they really are.

462

My utopia.—In a better-ordered society, the hard labor and exigencies of life would be assigned to the one who suffers least from them, that is, to those who are most insensible, and thus step-by-step upward to the one who is most sensitive to the highest, most sublimated species of suffering and who therefore still suffers even when his life has been made as easy as possible.

463

A delusion in the doctrine of revolution.—There are political and social visionaries who ardently and eloquently demand the overthrow of all social order in the belief that the most splendid temple of a beautified humanity would immediately be raised, as if by itself. In these dangerous dreams, we can still hear an echo of Rousseau's superstition, which believes in the marvelous, primordial, but as it were *stifled* goodness of human nature, and which ascribes all the blame for this stifling to the institutions of culture embodied in society, state, and education. Unfortunately, we know from historical experience that every such revolution brings with it a new resurrection of the most savage energies in the form of the long-buried horrors and excesses of the most distant ages: that a revolution can therefore certainly be a source of energy when humanity has grown feeble, but never an organizer, architect, artist, perfecter of human nature.—It is not *Voltaire's* moderate nature, inclined to organizing, purifying, and reconstructing, but instead *Rousseau's* passionate follies and half-lies that have roused the optimistic spirit of revolution, and against which I cry: "*Ecrasez l'infâme!*" This spirit has for a long time frightened off the *spirit of enlightenment and of progressive development*: let us look to see—everyone within himself—whether it is possible to call it back again!

464

Moderation.—Complete decisiveness in thought and inquiry, that is, free-spiritedness that has become an attribute of character, makes us moderate in our actions: for it weakens the faculty of desire, draws a great deal of the available energy to itself in order to further spiritual purposes, and demonstrates the partial utility or the uselessness and danger of all sudden changes.

465

Resurrection of the spirit.—When lying upon the political sickbed, a people generally rejuvenates itself and rediscovers the spirit that it gradually lost in the pursuit and assertion of power. Culture owes its highest achievements to times of political weakness.

466

New opinions in an old house.—The overthrow of institutions does not follow immediately upon the overthrow of opinions; instead, the new opinions live for a long time in the desolate and strangely unfamiliar house of their predecessors and even preserve it themselves, since they need some sort of shelter.

467

Schooling. — Schooling will always be mediocre at best in large states for the same reason that the cooking in large kitchens is mediocre at best.

468

Innocent corruption. — In all institutions where the sharp wind of public criticism does not blow, an innocent corruption grows up like a fungus (thus, for example, in scholarly bodies and senates).

469

Scholars as politicians. — Scholars who become politicians are generally assigned the comic role of having to be the good conscience of a political policy.

470

The wolf hidden behind the sheep. — Almost every politician will in certain circumstances need an honest man so badly that, like a ravenous wolf, he breaks into a sheepfold: not, however, in order to eat the stolen ram, but in order to hide himself behind its woolly back.

471

Times of happiness. — An age of happiness is simply not possible because people want only to wish for it, but not to have it, and every individual learns during his good days to actually pray for disquiet and misery. The destiny of human beings is adapted to *happy moments* — every life has such moments — but not to happy ages. These will nevertheless continue to persist in the human imagination as "what lies beyond the mountains," as a legacy from our forefathers; for since time primordial the concept of an age of happiness has doubtless been taken from that state in which someone who has greatly exerted himself in hunting and in war gives himself over to rest, stretches out his limbs, and hears the wings of sleep rustle around him. It is a false conclusion if, in accord with that ancient habit but *after long stretches of time* filled with misery and distress, someone imagines that he could now participate in that state of happiness, *correspondingly intensified and prolonged*.

472

Religion and government. — As long as the state, or more clearly, the government, knows itself to be constituted as guardian on behalf of a multitude still short of maturity and considers for their sake the question of whether religion ought to be maintained or abolished, it will quite probably always decide in favor of maintaining religion. For religion satisfies the individual spirit in times of loss, deprivation, fear, or mistrust, that is, precisely when the government feels itself incapable of doing anything to directly soothe the spiritual suffering of the private man: indeed, even amid universal, unavoidable, and for the present inevitable evils (famines, economic crises, wars) religion imparts a calming, patient, trusting attitude to the multitude. Wherever the inevitable or accidental deficiencies of the state government or the dangerous consequences of dynastic interests become noticeable for an attentive observer and make him more inclined to recalcitrance, less insightful people will think that they see the hand of God and submit patiently to arrangements from *above* (a concept in which divine and human modes of government are usually fused): thus, internal civil peace and the continuity of development are preserved. The power that lies in the unity of popular sentiment, in everyone having the same opinions and goals, is protected and sealed by religion, except for those rare cases where a priesthood cannot reach agreement with the governmental power on the price of its adherence and enters into conflict with it. Ordinarily, the state knows how to win over the priests because it needs their deeply private and concealed education of souls and it knows how to value servants who seem outwardly to represent a completely different interest. Without the assistance of the priests, no power can become "legitimate" even today: as Napoleon understood.—Hence, absolute tutelary government and the careful maintenance of religion necessarily go together. This presupposes that the ruling people and classes are enlightened about the advantages that religion provides for them and consequently feel to a certain degree superior to it, insofar as they are using it as a means: which is why free-spiritedness has its origin here. But what if that completely different conception of government, as it is taught in *democratic* states, begins to prevail? If people see in it nothing but the instrument of the popular will, not as an Above in comparison with a Below, but simply as a function of the sole sovereign, the people? In this case, the government can only take the same position toward religion as that taken by the people; every diffusion of enlightenment will have to be echoed in its representatives, any utilization and exploitation of the religious drives and consolations for governmental purposes will not be quite as easy (unless powerful party leaders temporarily exert an influence similar to that of enlightened despotism). But if the state can no longer derive any advantage from religion itself, or if the people think in far too varied ways about religious things to permit the government to adopt any uniform, unified plan with regard to religious measures—then the necessary expedient will be to treat religion as a private matter and to turn it over to the conscience and practice of every individual. The very first consequence of this is that the religious sensibility seems to grow stronger, insofar as certain concealed and suppressed impulses associated with it, to which the state had unintentionally or deliberately granted no room to breathe, now burst forth in extreme and excessive ways; it later turns out that religion has become overrun with sects and that an abundance of dragon's teeth were sown in the moment when religion was made a private matter. The sight of conflict, the hostile exposure of all the weaknesses of religious creeds, finally allows no other expedient than for every better and more gifted person to make irreligion his private affair: a disposition that even now is gaining the upper hand in the spirit of those who rule and, almost against their will, is giving their measures a character hostile to religion. As soon as this occurs, the attitude of those people who are still moved by religion and who previously adored the state as something partly or wholly sacred changes into something decidedly *hostile to the state*; they lie ready to ambush governmental measures, attempt to obstruct or to thwart or to disrupt them as much as they can and by the ardor of their opposition drive the other, irreligious party into an almost fanatical enthusiasm *for* the state; this process is secretly abetted by the fact that those who belong to their circles sense an emptiness since their separation from religion and seek to create a temporary substitute for that, a sort of completion, in their devotion to the state. After these transitional struggles, which may last a long time, it will finally be decided whether the religious parties are still strong enough to restore the old state of affairs and to turn back the wheel: in which case the state will inevitably fall into the hands of an enlightened despotism (perhaps less enlightened and more fearful than before)—or whether the nonreligious parties will prevail and restrict the propagation of their opponents for several generations, perhaps through schools and education, finally making it impossible. But then their enthusiasm for the state will also diminish: it will become ever clearer that, along with the religious adoration that sees the state as a mystery, an entity endowed with otherworldly force, the reverential and pious relationship with it has also been deeply shaken. Henceforth, individuals will see only the side of it that can be useful or harmful to them and will push themselves forward, using every possible means to obtain influence over it. But this competition will soon become too great, people and parties will change too quickly and savagely throw one another from the summit after having scarcely reached the top. No government will be able to guarantee the duration of any of the measures that it puts into place; people will shy away from undertakings that would require quiet growth over decades or centuries in order to bring their fruit to maturity. Nobody will feel any further obligation toward a law than that of bowing momentarily to the power that introduced the law: they will immediately proceed to undermine it by means of a new force, the formation of a new majority. Finally—we can say this with certainty—the distrust of all ruling powers, the insight into the futile and destructive nature of these short-winded struggles, will impel people to a completely new decision: to do away with the concept of the state, to abolish the opposition between "private and public." Step by step, private companies will absorb the functions of the state: even the most tenacious remnants of the old work of governing (the activity, for example, that is supposed to protect private persons against one another) will finally be taken care of by private entrepreneurs. The disregard for, decline, and *death of the state*, the liberation of the private person (I take care not to say: of the individual) is the consequence of the democratic concept of the state; herein lies its mission. Once it has fulfilled its task—which like everything human bears much reason and unreason in its womb—once all relapses into the old sickness have been overcome, a new page will be opened in the storybook of humanity, where we will read all sorts of strange tales, some of them perhaps good ones.—To briefly repeat what I have said: the interests of tutelary government and the interests of religion go hand in hand with each other, so that if the latter begins to die out, the foundation of the state will also be deeply shaken. The belief in a divine order of political things, in a mystery concerning the existence of the state, is of religious origin: if religion vanishes, the state will inevitably lose its ancient Isis veil and no longer arouse reverence. Seen from nearby, the sovereignty of the people also serves to scare away the last traces of magic and superstition from this realm of feelings; modern democracy is the historical form of the *decline of the state*.—The prospect that results from this assured decline is, however, not in every respect an unhappy one: the cleverness and self-interest of human beings are the best developed of all their characteristics; if the state no longer corresponds to the demands of these forces, chaos is the least likely thing to emerge; instead, an invention even more to the purpose than was the state will triumph over the state. How many organizing forces has humanity already seen die out—for example, hereditary clans, which for millennia were much more powerful than the family, and indeed ruled and organized society long before the latter appeared. We ourselves are seeing the idea that attributes significant legal and political power to the family, which once held sway as far as the Roman way of life reached, becoming ever fainter and feebler. Thus, a later generation will likewise see the state become insignificant in certain areas of the world—an idea that many people today can scarcely conceive without fear and abhorrence. To *work* toward the diffusion and realization of this idea is admittedly something else: we would have to be quite arrogant about our rational capacity and hardly understand history halfway to put our hand to the plow right away—at a point when nobody can yet exhibit the seeds that later are to be strewn upon the rended earth. Let us therefore trust to "the cleverness and self-interest of human beings" that the state will *still* persist for a good while yet and that the destructive experiments of overzealous and premature half-knowers will be repelled!

473

Socialism in regard to its means.—Socialism is the visionary younger brother of an almost decrepit despotism whose heir it wants to be; its aspirations are therefore in the deepest sense reactionary. For it desires an abundance of governmental power such as only despotism has ever had and indeed outdoes the entire past by striving for the outright annihilation of the individual: this it perceives as an unjustified luxury of nature that it ought to improve into a purposeful *organ of the community*. Being related to every excessive manifestation of power, it always appears in proximity to them, just as the typical old socialist Plato did at the court of the Sicilian tyrants; it longs for (and under certain circumstances promotes) the powerful Caesarean state of this century because it would like to be its heir, as I have said. But even this inheritance would not suffice for its purposes; it requires the most total subjection and suppression of all citizens by the absolute state, the like of which has never before existed; and since it can no longer count upon the old religious piety for the state and must instead involuntarily, yet continuously, work to abolish that piety—because, of course, it is working for the abolition of all existing *states*—it can only hope to exist here and there for short periods of time by utilizing the most extreme terrorism. Therefore, it prepares itself in secret for a rule of terror and pounds the word "justice" like a nail into the heads of the half-educated masses in order to rob them completely of their understanding (after this understanding has already suffered a great deal from their partial education) and to create in them a good conscience for the evil game that they are to play.—Socialism can serve to instruct us quite brutally and forcefully about the danger of all accumulations of governmental power and to that extent to instill in us a distrust of the state itself. When its harsh voice joins in the battle cry "*as much government as possible*," this becomes at first louder than ever: but soon the opposing cry presses forward with an even greater force: "*as little government as possible*."

474

The development of the spirit, feared by the state.—Like every organizing political power, the Greek polis resisted and mistrusted the growth of culture; its powerful basic impulse manifested itself almost exclusively in efforts to cripple and obstruct it. It did not want to allow any space in culture for history or becoming; the education prescribed by state law should be seen as a duty by every generation and should keep them all at the same stage of development. Nor did Plato want things to be any different for his ideal state. Culture therefore developed *despite* the polis: of course the polis did assist it indirectly and against its will because the ambition of the individual was so highly stimulated in the polis that, once entered upon the path of spiritual cultivation, he continued along it to its furthest extremes. We should not appeal to Pericles' panegyric as evidence to the contrary: for that is nothing more than a grandly optimistic, deceptive image of the supposedly necessary connection between the polis and Athenian culture; Thucydides allows it to shine forth one more time, like a transfiguring sunset just before night falls upon Athens (the plague and the breakdown of tradition), whose light is supposed to make us forget the horrible day that preceded it.

475

The European and the destruction of nations. — Commerce and industry, the circulation of books and letters, the commonality of all higher culture, rapid changes of place and of scenery, the present nomadic existence of all those who do not own land — these conditions are inevitably bringing along with them a weakening and finally a destruction of nations, at least of the European ones: so that as a consequence of these changes and the continual crossbreeding they occasion, a mixed race, the European, must come into being. The isolation of nations works consciously or unconsciously against this goal by engendering *national* animosities, yet the process of mixing goes forward slowly nonetheless, despite those occasional countercurrents: this artificial nationalism is moreover as dangerous as artificial Catholicism once was, for it is in essence a state of distress and beleaguerment forcibly inflicted by the few upon the many, requiring artifice, deceit, and force to maintain its authority. It is not the interests of the many (of the various peoples), as some might claim, but above all the interests of certain princely dynasties and of certain commercial and social classes that push us toward this nationalism; once we have recognized this, we should simply present ourselves fearlessly as *good Europeans* and in our actions work for the melting together of nations: a process that the Germans' ancient, proven trait of being the *interpreters and intermediaries between peoples* makes them able to assist. — Incidentally: the whole problem of the *Jews* exists only within national states, since it is here that their energy and higher intelligence, the accumulated capital of spirit and will that they have built up from generation to generation in a long school of suffering, must reach a degree of preponderance where it awakens envy and hatred, so that in almost every existing nation — and more and more as these nations come to behave nationalistically once again — the literary incivility of leading the Jews to the slaughterhouse as scapegoats for every possible public and personal misfortune gains the upper hand. As soon as it is no longer a matter of conserving nations, but instead of engendering the strongest possible European racial mixture, the Jew is just as usable and desirable an ingredient as the remains of any other nation. Every nation, every person has unpleasant, even dangerous qualities; it is cruel to demand that the Jew should be an exception. Those qualities may even be especially dangerous and forbidding in him; and the youthful stock-exchange Jew is perhaps the most repulsive invention of the whole human species. Nevertheless, I would like to know how much we have to overlook in any final reckoning for a people whose history has entailed more suffering than any other, for which all of us share the guilt, and to whom we owe the noblest human being (Christ), the purest sage (Spinoza), the mightiest book, and the most effective moral code in the world. Moreover: in the darkest periods of the Middle Ages, when a band of Asiatic clouds hung heavily over Europe, it was the Jewish freethinkers, scholars, and physicians who held fast to the banner of enlightenment and of spiritual independence while under the harshest personal pressure and defended Europe against Asia; it is not least thanks to their efforts that a more natural, rational, and in any case unmythical explanation of the world could once again emerge triumphant and that the ring of culture that now unites us with the enlightenment of Greek and Roman antiquity remained unbroken. If Christianity has done everything to orientalize the Occident, then Judaism has helped in an essential way to occidentalize it once again: which in a certain sense means making Europe's mission and history into a *continuation of the Greeks'*.

476

Seeming superiority of the Middle Ages. — The Middle Ages display in the church an institution with a completely universal goal encompassing all of humanity, moreover, one that was concerned — ostensibly — with their highest interests: by contrast, the goals of states and nations displayed by modern history make a discouraging impression; they seem petty, mean, materialistic, and limited in extent. But this differing impression upon our imagination should not determine our judgment; for that universal institution conformed to artificial needs resting upon fictions, ones that, where they did not previously exist, first had to be engendered (the need for salvation); modern institutions remedy real states of distress, and the time is coming when institutions will arise to serve the shared, true needs of all human beings and to put that imaginary archetype, the Catholic Church, into shadow and oblivion.

477

War indispensable. — It is vain dreaming and mystical fancy to expect much more (or even: to expect much at all) from humanity once it has forgotten how to wage war. At present, we know no other means by which that raw energy of encampments, that deep, impersonal hatred, that murderer's coldbloodedness accompanied by a good conscience, that shared, organizing ardor in the destruction of the enemy, that proud indifference toward great losses, toward our own existence and that of our friends, that muffled, earthquakelike shuddering of the soul, could be imparted as strongly and securely to exhausted peoples as they are by every great war: the brooks and streams that burst forth here, though they carry all sorts of stones and rubbish along with them and destroy the fields of delicate cultures, will afterward under favorable circumstances turn the wheels in the workshops of the spirit with new energy.

Culture simply cannot do without passions, vices, and acts of malice. — When the imperialized Romans became rather tired of war, they tried to obtain new energy from animal baiting, gladiatorial contests, and the persecution of Christians. Present-day Englishmen, who seem on the whole also to have renounced war, adopt a different means to engender anew their fading energies; those dangerous voyages of discovery, circumnavigations, ascents of mountains, are undertaken for scientific purposes, they claim, but really in order to bring back home the surplus energy from all these sorts of adventures and dangers. People will discover many more such surrogates for war, but perhaps more and more perceive from them that a humanity as highly cultivated and therefore as inevitably exhausted as is the present European one requires not only wars, but the greatest and most terrible wars — and thus, temporary relapses into barbarism — if the means of culture are not to cost them their culture and their very existence.

478

Industriousness in south and north. — Industriousness arises in two quite different ways. Workers in the south become industrious not from any acquisitive impulse, but as a result of the constant neediness of others. The blacksmith is industrious because someone is always coming along who wants to have a horse shod or a wagon repaired. If nobody were to come, he would lounge around in the marketplace. Obtaining his subsistence is not very difficult in a fertile land, requiring only a very slight amount of work from him, in any case no industriousness; in the end, he would go begging and be content. — The industriousness of English workers, by contrast, has behind it the sense for acquisition: it is conscious of itself and of its goals and wants power along with property, and along with power the greatest possible freedom and individual distinction.

479

Wealth as the origin of a nobility of blood. — Wealth necessarily engenders an aristocracy of race, for it allows one to select the most beautiful women, to pay the best teachers, and it permits a person to have cleanliness, time for physical exercise, and above all, to avoid deadening physical labor. To that extent, it creates all the conditions for producing within a few generations people whose movements and even actions are noble and beautiful: the greater freedom of temperament, the absence of anything pitiful or petty, of any abasement before employers, of any penny-pinching mentality. — Precisely these negative qualities are the richest gift that fortune can give to a young person; anyone who is really poor will generally be destroyed by nobility of disposition; he does not gain advancement and acquires nothing; his race is incapable of life. — But we should reflect that wealth has almost the same effects whether someone is able to spend three hundred or thirty thousand talers a year: there is no further essential progression of the favorable circumstances. But to have less, to beg and demean oneself as a boy, is terrible: although for those who seek their happiness in the glitter of a court, in subordination to powerful and influential people, or who want to become leading figures in the church, it may be the right starting point. (— It teaches one how to bow down in order to creep into the hollowed corridors of favor.)

480

Envy and indolence in different directions. — Both of the opposing parties, the socialist and the national ones — or whatever their names may be in the different countries of Europe — are worthy of each other: envy and laziness are the motive forces in both of them. In the former camp, people want to work as little as possible with their hands, in the latter one, as little as possible with their heads; in the latter, they hate and envy the prominent, self-made individuals who are not willing to let themselves be lined up in the ranks of those pursuing some mass action; in the former, they hate and envy the better, outwardly more favorably placed caste of society whose real task, the production of the highest cultural goods, makes their inner lives so much harder and more painful. To be sure, if one did succeed in making that spirit of mass action into the spirit of the higher classes of society, then the socialist multitudes would be quite right to also seek to level the outward differences between themselves and the others, since they would already be inwardly level with one another in head and heart.—Live as higher human beings and always do the deeds of higher culture—then everything that lives will acknowledge your rights and the social order, whose summit you represent, will be proof against every evil eye and hand.

481

Great politics and its costs.—Just as the greatest costs that a people sustain from war and from maintaining a state of readiness for war lie not in the expenses of war, nor in the obstructions in trade and commerce, nor even in maintaining a standing army—however great these costs may be at present when eight European states spend the sum of two to three billions upon them annually—but from the fact that year after year an exceptional number of the most capable, most energetic, most industrious men are taken away from their real occupations and professions in order to be soldiers: so, too, a people that prepares to engage in great politics and to secure for itself a decisive voice among the most powerful states does not sustain its greatest costs where we usually locate them. It is true that from this point on, a host of the most eminent talents will continually be sacrificed on the "altar of the fatherland" or of national ambition, whereas other spheres of action previously stood open to the talents that are now devoured by politics. But off to the side of these public hecatombs and fundamentally much more horrible than them, a drama is going on that plays itself out continuously in a hundred thousand acts at once:

every capable, industrious, spirited, ambitious person who is part of a people coveting political laurels is mastered by this covetousness and no longer belongs wholly to his own affairs, as he did before: every day, new questions and concerns about the public welfare devour a daily tribute from the mental and emotional capital of every citizen: the sum of all these sacrifices and costs in individual energy and labor is so tremendous that the political blossoming of a people almost inevitably brings with it a spiritual impoverishment and exhaustion, a lessened capacity for undertaking works that require great concentration and single-mindedness. In the end, we might ask: are all these blooms and this splendor of the whole (which really show up only in the fear of other states for the new colossus and in the more favorable conditions for national commerce and trade that have been wrested from foreign countries) *worth* it, if all of the more noble, more delicate, more spiritual plants and growths in which this nation's soil had previously been so rich must be sacrificed to this coarse and gaudy flower of the nation?

482

To say it once again. — Public opinions — private laziness.

Chapter 9

By Oneself Alone

483

Enemies of truth. — Convictions are more dangerous enemies of truth than are lies.

484

Upside down world. — We criticize a thinker more sharply when he presents us with a displeasing proposition; and yet it would be more reasonable to do this when his proposition pleases us.

485

Strong in character. — It is much more often the case that a person appears to have strength of character because he continually follows his temperament than because he continually follows his principles.

486

The one thing that is necessary. — A person must have one of these two things: either a naturally light-hearted disposition or a disposition lightened by art and knowledge.

487

The passion for things. — Anyone who directs his passion toward things (sciences, the public welfare, cultural interests, arts) takes much of the fire away from his passion for people (even when they are representatives of those things, as statesmen, philosophers, artists are the representatives of their creations).

488

Equanimity in action. — As a waterfall moves more slowly and floats more leisurely as it plunges downward, so a great man of action tends to act with more *equanimity* than his tempestuous desire prior to acting would have led us to expect.

489

Not too deep. — Those persons who grasp a thing in all its depth rarely remain true to it forever. For they have brought its depths into the light: where there is always much that is terrible to see.

490

Delusion of idealists. — All idealists imagine that the causes they serve are essentially better than everything else in the world and do not want to believe that if their cause is to flourish, it will require exactly the same foul-smelling manure as is necessary for every other human undertaking.

491

Self-observation. — Human beings are quite well defended against themselves, against any surveillance and besiegement by themselves; they are not ordinarily able to perceive anything more than their outer defenses. The real stronghold is inaccessible to them, even invisible, unless their friends and enemies turn traitor and lead them in by a secret path.

492

The proper profession. — Men rarely persevere in a profession when they do not believe or persuade themselves that it is fundamentally more important than any other. It is the same with women in regard to their lovers.

493

Nobility of character. — Nobility of character consists in large part of good-naturedness and a lack of mistrust, and thus contains precisely what greedy and successful people like to treat with superiority and scorn.

494

Goal and path. — Many people are stubborn in regard to a path once they have entered upon it, few in regard to the goal.

495

What rouses indignation in an individual lifestyle. — People are always irritated with anyone who adopts extremely individual guidelines for his life; they feel themselves degraded to the status of common beings by the exceptional treatment that person confers upon himself.

496

Privilege of greatness. — It is the privilege of greatness to produce great pleasure with the slightest of gifts.

497

Unintentionally noble. — A person behaves nobly without intending to do so if he has accustomed himself to wish for nothing from other people and to always be giving to them.

498

Condition for heroism. — If someone wants to become a hero, then the snake must already have become a dragon; otherwise he lacks a suitable foe.

499

Friend. — Shared joy, not shared suffering, is what makes a friend.

500

Making use of the ebb and flow. — We must know how to use for the purpose of knowledge the inner current that draws us toward a thing and then, in turn, the one that after a time draws us away from that thing.

501

Joy in oneself. — "Taking joy in a thing" is what we say: but in truth we are taking joy in ourselves by means of the thing.

502

The modest one. — Anyone who is modest toward people displays his arrogance toward things (city, state, society, the age, humanity) all the more strongly. That is his revenge.

503

Envy and jealousy. — Envy and jealousy are the shameful private parts of the human soul. The comparison can perhaps be extended.

504

The most refined hypocrite. — Not to speak of oneself at all is a very refined form of hypocrisy.

505

Annoyance. — Annoyance is a physical disease that is by no means done away with by subsequently eliminating the cause of the annoyance.

506

Advocate of truth. — Truth is least likely to find advocates not when it is dangerous to speak the truth, but when it is boring to do so.

507

More onerous than enemies. — Those persons who we are convinced might not treat us sympathetically in all circumstances, while for some reason (gratitude, for instance) we are obliged to maintain the appearance of unconditional sympathy toward them on our part, torment our imagination much more than our enemies do.

508

Out amid nature. — We are so glad to be out amid nature because it has no opinion about us.

509

Everyone superior in one thing. — In civilized circumstances, everyone feels himself superior to everyone else in at least *one* thing: the general goodwill toward others depends upon this, insofar as everyone is someone who can provide help under certain circumstances and may therefore allow himself to be helped without shame.

510

Reasons for consolation. — At the time of a death, we generally need reasons for consolation, not so much to ease the violence of the pain as to excuse ourselves for feeling so easily consoled.

511

Those true to their convictions. — Anyone who has a lot to do maintains his general views and opinions almost unchanged. Likewise everyone who works in the service of an idea: he will never again examine the idea itself, he has no time anymore for that; indeed, it goes against his interests to consider it discussable at all.

512

Morality and quantity. — The higher morality of one person in comparison with that of another often lies simply in the fact that his goals are quantitatively greater. The preoccupation with petty things, within a narrow circle, pulls the latter person downward.

513

Life as the yield of life. — However far human beings may reach with their knowledge, however objective they may seem to themselves to be: in the end, they still carry away nothing but their own biography.

514

Iron necessity. — Iron necessity is a thing that people perceive in the course of history to be neither iron nor necessary.

515

From experience. — The irrationality of a thing is no argument against its existence, but rather a condition for it.

516

Truth. — Nobody dies nowadays from fatal truths: there are too many antidotes.

517

Fundamental insight. — There is no preestablished harmony between the furthering of truth and the well-being of humanity.

518

Human fate. — Anyone who thinks more deeply knows that he is always in the wrong, regardless of how he may act and judge.

519

Truth as Circe. — Error has made animals into men; might truth then be capable of making man back into an animal?

520

The danger of our culture. — We belong to a time whose culture is in danger of perishing from the means to culture.

521

Greatness means: giving direction. — No river is made great and fertile by itself alone: but rather it is made so by absorbing and bearing onward so many tributaries. So it is, too, with all who are great in spirit. All that matters is that a single *one* provides the direction that the many tributaries then must follow; not whether he is at the beginning poorly or abundantly endowed.

522

Weak conscience. — People who speak of their importance for humanity have a weak conscience with regard to an ordinary, bourgeois integrity concerning the keeping of contracts and promises.

523

Wanting to be loved. — The demand to be loved is the greatest of all presumptions.

524

Contempt for humanity. — The most unambiguous sign of someone's disdain for human beings is when he takes account of everyone else only as means for *his* ends, or otherwise not at all.

525

Adherents out of contradiction. — Anyone who has enraged other people has always gained a party in his favor as well.

526

Forgetting experiences.—Anyone who thinks a great deal and thinks objectively easily forgets his own experiences, but not the thoughts that were called forth by them.

527

Holding firmly to an opinion.—Someone holds firmly to an opinion because he flatters himself that he came upon it himself, someone else because he learned it with difficulty and is proud of having grasped it: both, therefore, out of vanity.

528

Shunning the light.—A good deed shuns the light just as anxiously as an evil deed: the latter fears that pain (as punishment) would result if it were to become known, the former fears that pleasure (namely, the pure pleasure in oneself that ceases as soon as any satisfaction of vanity supervenes) would vanish if it were to become known.

529

The length of the day.—When we have a lot to put in it, a day has a hundred pockets.

530

Genius of tyrants.—If the soul is stirred by an unconquerable desire to tyrannically get one's own way and this fire is steadily maintained, even a modest talent (in politicians, artists) gradually becomes an almost irresistible natural force.

531

The life of an enemy.—Anyone who lives for the sake of battling an enemy has an interest in keeping that enemy alive.

532

More important.—We take something unexplained and obscure to be more important than something that has been explained and made clear.

533

Appraisal of services performed.—We esteem the services that someone performs for us according to the value that the other person sets upon them, not according to the value that they have for us.

534

Unhappiness.—The distinction that lies in unhappiness (as if it were a sign of shallowness, unpretentiousness, or commonness to feel happy) is so great that when someone says: "But how happy you are!" we generally protest.

535

Fantasized fear.—Fantasized fear is that evil, apish goblin who leaps on to a person's back at the very moment when he is already most heavily burdened.

536

Value of tasteless opponents.—We sometimes remain true to a cause only because its opponents are unceasingly tasteless.

537

Value of a profession.—A profession makes us thoughtless; therein lies its greatest blessing. For it is a bastion behind which we can justifiably withdraw when the common sorts of misgivings and cares assail us.

538

Talent.—The talent of many a person seems less than it is because he has always set himself tasks that are too great.

539

Youth. — Youth is unpleasant; for in youth it is not possible or not reasonable to be productive in any sense whatsoever.

540

Too great goals. — Anyone who publicly sets great goals for himself and afterward privately perceives that he is too weak for them does not generally have enough strength publicly to retract those goals, and inevitably becomes a hypocrite.

541

In the current. — Strong waters carry much stone and underbrush along with them, strong spirits many stupid and muddled heads.

542

Dangers of spiritual liberation. — Even when a person is seriously intent upon his spiritual liberation, his passions and desires are secretly hoping to discern some advantage for themselves as well.

543

Embodiment of spirit. — When someone thinks a great deal and shrewdly, not only his face, but also his body acquires an appearance of shrewdness.

544

Seeing badly and hearing badly. — Someone who sees little sees less than is there; someone who hears badly always hears something more besides.

545

Self-gratification in vanity. — A vain person wants not only to be prominent, but also to feel prominent, for which reason he disdains no means for deceiving and defrauding himself. He takes to heart not the opinion of others, but his opinion of their opinion.

546

Vain by exception.—Someone who is generally self-sufficient can become vain and susceptible to honor and praise under the exceptional circumstances of being physically ill. To the extent that he loses himself, he must try to win his way back to himself through the opinions of others, from the outside.

547

The "rich in spirit."—Someone who seeks spirit has no spirit.

548

Hint for party leaders.—If we can impel people to declare themselves for something publicly, we have usually also brought them to declare themselves for it inwardly; from then on, they want to be found consistent.

549

Contempt.—People are more sensitive to contempt from others than to their contempt for themselves.

550

Cord of gratitude.—There are slavish souls who go so far in acknowledging favors that they strangle themselves with the cord of gratitude.

551

Trick of the prophet.—In order to guess in advance how ordinary people will behave, we must assume that they will always make the least possible expenditure of intelligence to extricate themselves from an unpleasant situation.

552

The only human right.—Anyone who deviates from tradition becomes a victim of the extraordinary; anyone who remains within tradition is its slave. In either case, he will be destroyed.

553

Lower than the animal.—When a human being neighs with laughter, he exceeds all the animals in his vulgarity.

554

Partial knowledge.—Someone who speaks a little bit of a foreign language gets more enjoyment from it than someone who speaks it well. The pleasure lies with the one who has partial knowledge.

555

Dangerous helpfulness.—There are people who want to make other people's lives harder for no other reason than to offer them afterward their recipes for making life easier, for example, their Christianity.

556

Industriousness and conscientiousness.—Industriousness and conscientiousness are often antagonists because industriousness wants to take fruit from the tree while it is still sour, while conscientiousness lets it hang too long, until it falls off and is smashed.

557

Suspecting others.—People whom we cannot tolerate we try to see as suspect.

558

Lacking the right circumstances.—Many people wait their entire lives for the opportunity to be good in *their* way.

559

Lack of friends. — The lack of friends lets us conclude that envy or arrogance is present. Many a person owes his friends simply to the fortunate circumstance that he gives them no reason for envy.

560

Danger in quantity. — With one talent more, we often stand less secure than with one fewer: as a table stands better on three than on four legs.

561

A model for others. — Anyone who wants to give a good example must mix a grain of folly into his virtue: then others will imitate him and at the same time raise themselves above the person they are imitating — which people love to do.

562

Being a target. — The malicious speeches of others about us are often not really concerned with us, but are instead the expressions of an annoyance or a bad mood that arose from quite different causes.

563

Easily resigned. — We suffer little from wishes that have been denied when we have trained our imagination to detest the past.

564

In danger. — We are in the most danger of being run over when we have just gotten out of the way of some vehicle.

565

The role adapted to the voice. — Anyone who is forced to speak more loudly than he normally does (as to someone who is half deaf, or in front of a large audience) generally exaggerates the things that he has to convey.—Many people become conspirators, malicious gossips, or intriguers, simply because their voices are best suited to a whisper.

566

Love and hate.—Love and hate are not blind, but are blinded by the fire that they carry around with them.

567

Enmity turned to advantage.—People who cannot make their merit fully clear to the world try to arouse a strong enmity against themselves. They then have the comfort of thinking that this stands between their merits and an acknowledgment of them—and that many others suppose the same thing: which is very advantageous for their sense of worth.

568

Confession.—We forget our guilt when we have confessed it to another, but generally the other person does not forget it.

569

Self-satisfaction.—The golden fleece of self-satisfaction protects against blows, but not against pinpricks.

570

Shadows in the flame.—The flame is not itself as bright as those that it illuminates: so, too, the wise man.

571

Our own opinions.—The first opinion that occurs to us when we are suddenly asked about something is generally not our own, but only the conventional one appropriate to our caste, rank, lineage; our own opinions rarely swim up to the surface.

572

Origin of courage.—An ordinary person is as courageous and invulnerable as a hero if he does not see the danger, if he has no eye for it. Conversely: the hero has his one vulnerable spot on his back, in the place, that is, where he has no eyes.

573

Danger in the physician.—We must be born for our physician, otherwise we will perish by him.

574

Miraculous vanity.—Anyone who boldly prophesies the weather three times and does so successfully believes a little bit, deep down in his soul, in his prophetic gift. We give credit to miraculous and irrational things when it flatters our self-esteem.

575

Profession.—A profession is the backbone of life.

576

Danger of personal influence.—Anyone who feels that he exerts a great inner influence upon someone else must allow him completely free rein, indeed be pleased to see occasional resistance and even induce it himself: otherwise he will inevitably make an enemy for himself.

577

Giving heirs their due.—Anyone moved by selfless sentiments in founding something great takes care that he raises heirs for himself. It is the sign of a tyrannical and ignoble nature to see an opponent in every possible heir of his work and to live in a constant state of self-defense against them.

578

Partial knowledge.—Partial knowledge is more often victorious than full knowledge: it conceives things as simpler than they are and therefore makes its opinion easier to grasp and more persuasive.

579

Not suited to be a party member.—Anyone who thinks a great deal is not suited to be a party member: he too quickly thinks himself all the way through the party.

580

Bad memory.—The advantage of a bad memory is that we can enjoy the same good things for the first time several times.

581

Causing oneself pain.—Ruthlessness of thought is often the sign of a discordant inner disposition that desires numbness.

582

Martyr.—The disciple of a martyr suffers more than the martyr.

583

Residual vanity.—The vanity of many people who have no need to be vain is a habit, left over from and magnified since the time when they still had no right to believe in themselves and first had to beg for the small change of this belief from other people.

584

Punctum saliens of passion.—Anyone who is about to fly into a rage or to fall intensely in love reaches a point where his soul is filled like a vessel: and yet one drop of water must still be added, a good will for passion (which we generally term a bad will). Only this droplet is necessary, and then the vessel runs over.

585

Ill-humored thought. — People are like the charcoal kilns in the woods. Only when young people have stopped glowing and been carbonized do they, like the latter, become *useful*. As long as they are smoldering and smoking, they may be more interesting, but they are useless and all too often disagreeable. — Humanity makes pitiless use of every individual as material for heating its great machines: but what are the machines for, if all the individuals (that is, humanity) serve only to keep them going? Machines that are their own purpose — is that the *umana commedia*?

586

Of the hour hand of life. — Life consists of rare individual moments of the highest significance and countless intervals of time in which at best the shadowy images of those moments hover around us. Love, spring, every beautiful melody, mountains, the moon, the sea — only once do all those things speak fully to the heart: if in fact they ever do find their way completely into words. For many people do not have any such moments and are themselves intervals and pauses in the symphony of real life.

587

To attack or to engage. — We frequently make the mistake of becoming actively hostile to a direction or a party or an age because we happen to see only its superficial side, its stunted features, or the "defects of its virtues," which necessarily adhere to it — perhaps because these are the aspects in which we ourselves have participated the most. Then we turn our backs on them and seek an opposite direction; but it would be better to search out their good, strong sides or to cultivate them within ourselves. Admittedly, it requires a more powerful vision and a better will to promote what is becoming and is imperfect than it does to see through it in its imperfection and to disavow it.

588

Modesty. — There is a true modesty (that is, the recognition that we are not our own work); and it is quite becoming for someone of great spirit, because he is precisely the one who can grasp the idea of complete irresponsibility (even for the good that he produces). People do not hate the immodesty of a great person insofar as he is feeling his strength, but because he wants to experience his strength first by hurting others, treating them in a domineering way, and seeing how much of this they can endure. This usually shows that he actually lacks a feeling of certainty about his own strength and consequently he makes people doubt his greatness. To this extent, immodesty is very inadvisable from the point of view of shrewdness.

589

First thought of the day. — The best way to begin each day well is: upon awakening, to think about whether we cannot bring pleasure to at least one person on this day. If this could count as a substitute for the religious habit of prayer, our fellow human beings would gain an advantage from the change.

590

Arrogance as the final means of consolation. — When someone accounts for a misfortune, his intellectual deficiencies, or his illness by seeing in them his prescribed fate, his trial, or the mysterious punishment for something he previously did, he thereby makes his own existence interesting for himself and conceives himself in a more elevated way than he does his fellow human beings. The proud sinner is a familiar figure in all religious sects.

591

Vegetation of happiness.—Right beside the sorrow of the world and often upon its volcanic ground, human beings have laid out their little gardens of happiness; whether they observe life with the eye of someone who wants knowledge alone from existence, or of someone who submits and resigns himself, or of someone who rejoices in difficulties that have been overcome—everywhere they will find some happiness sprouting beside the misfortune—and indeed, the more happiness, the more volcanic the ground was—only it would be ridiculous to say that the suffering itself could be justified by this happiness.

592

The road of our ancestors.—It makes sense for someone to cultivate further in himself the *talent* on which his father or grandfather expended effort and not to turn to something completely new; otherwise, he deprives himself of the possibility of reaching perfection in any craft whatsoever. Hence the proverb says: "What road should you take?—that of your ancestors."

593

Vanity and ambition as educators.—As long as someone has not yet become an instrument of general human utility, ambition may still torment him; but if that goal has been attained and he is working with the necessity of a machine for the good of all, then let vanity arrive; it will humanize him in small ways, make him more sociable, more tolerable, more considerate, once ambition has completed the rough work (by making him useful).

594

Philosophical novices.—If someone has just partaken of the wisdom of a philosopher, he goes through the streets feeling as if he has been transformed and has become a great man; for he finds only people who do not know of this wisdom, and he therefore has a new, unfamiliar judgment to propound concerning everything: because he acknowledges a code of law, he thinks that he is now obliged to conduct himself like a judge as well.

595

To please by displeasing. — People who prefer to attract attention and thereby to displease others desire the same thing as those who want not to attract attention and to please others, only in a much higher degree and indirectly, by means of a step that seems to take them away from their goal. They want influence and power, and therefore display their superiority even in ways that make it disagreeable; for they know that someone who does finally attain power pleases others in almost everything that he does and says, and that even when he displeases them, he still seems to please. — The free spirit, too, and likewise the believer, want power because it can make them pleasing for once; if an ill fate, persecution, prison, or execution threatens them because of their doctrine, they still rejoice in the thought that their doctrine will in this way be scratched and burned into humanity; they take it as a painful, yet powerful, albeit slow-working means of attaining power nonetheless.

596

Casus belli and the like. — The prince who, having decided to wage war upon a neighbor, invents a *casus belli*, is like the father who foists a mother upon his child, one who is henceforth to be considered as such. And aren't almost all publicly proclaimed motives for our actions stepmothers of this kind?

597

Passion and rights. — Nobody speaks more passionately about his rights than someone who deep down in his soul doubts whether he has any. By drawing passion on to his side, he wants to deaden his understanding and its doubts: thus he acquires a good conscience and, along with it, success among his fellow human beings.

598

Trick of the renouncer. — Anyone who protests against marriage in the way that Catholic priests do will try to construe it in the lowest and meanest conceivable way. Likewise, anyone who rejects the honor of his contemporaries will conceive of their concept of honor as something vulgar; thus, he makes the renunciation and his struggle against it easier for himself. Moreover, someone who on the whole denies himself many things will readily allow himself to indulge in small things. It might be possible that someone who is elevated above the applause of his contemporaries still does not want to deny himself the satisfaction of small vanities.

599

Age of arrogance. — Between the twenty-sixth and the thirtieth years lies the real period of arrogance for talented people; it is the time of their first ripeness, with a strong residue of sourness. Based upon what they feel within themselves, they demand respect and humility from other people who see little or nothing of what they themselves see, and because these are not immediately forthcoming, they avenge themselves by that arrogant glance or gesture, by that tone of voice that a subtle ear and eye recognize in all the products of that age, whether they be poems, philosophies, or paintings and music. Older, more experienced people smile at this and recall with emotion this beautiful age at which we are angry at the fate of *being* so much and *seeming* so little. Later, we really do *seem* to be more — but we have lost the fine belief that we *are* very much: unless we remain the incorrigible fools of vanity for the rest of our lives.

600

Deceptive and yet solid. — As we may, in order to pass by an abyss or to cross a plank over a deep stream, require a railing — not so much to hold on to, for it would immediately collapse if we were to do that, but to give our eye an image of security —

so in our youth we require people who unknowingly serve us like that railing; it is true that they would not help us if we really were in great danger and wanted to support ourselves upon them, but they provide a comforting sensation of nearby protection (for example, fathers, teachers, friends, as all three generally are).

601

Learning to love.—We must learn to love, learn to be kind, from our youth on up; if education and chance provide us with no opportunity for practicing these feelings, then our soul will dry out and become incapable of even understanding those tender inventions of loving people. Hatred must likewise be learned and nourished, if someone wants to become a skillful hater: otherwise the germ for that, too, will gradually die out.

602

Ruins as embellishment.—Those who pass through many spiritual transformations preserve some views and habits of earlier states, which then extend like a piece of enigmatic antiquity and gray stonework into their new way of thinking and behaving: often serving to ornament the entire area.

603

Love and respect.—Love desires, fear avoids. That is the reason why someone cannot be both loved and respected by the same person, at least not at the same time. For someone who respects another acknowledges his power, that is to say, he fears it: his state is one of awe. Love, however, acknowledges no power, nothing that divides, contrasts, elevates, and subordinates. Because it provides no respect, people whose ambition is to be respected are secretly or openly averse to being loved.

604

Prejudice in favor of cold people.—People who quickly catch fire, quickly grow cold and are therefore on the whole unreliable.

Hence there is a prejudice in favor of all those who always are cold, or present themselves as such, that they are especially trustworthy, reliable people: we confuse them with those who catch fire slowly and sustain it for a long time.

605

The danger of unconventional opinions. — Occupying ourselves casually with unconventional opinions has the attraction of a sort of itch; if we give in to it, we begin to rub the place; until finally an open, painful wound results, that is: until the unconventional opinion begins to disturb and torment us in our social position and our human relationships.

606

Desire for intense pain. — When it has passed, passion leaves behind an obscure longing for it and, even as it vanishes, throws us one more seductive glance. It must in fact have provided a sort of pleasure to be scourged with its whip. More moderate sensations seem flat by contrast; we always, it seems, prefer more intense displeasure to feeble pleasure.

607

Ill humor with others and the world. — When, as so often occurs, we vent our ill humor on others while we are really feeling out of humor with ourselves, we are basically striving to cloud and delude our judgment: we want to give this ill humor a motive a posteriori in the oversights and deficiencies of others and thus to lose sight of ourselves. — Strict religious people, who judge themselves without pity, have likewise spoken the most ill of humanity: there has never lived a saint who reserved sin for himself and virtue for others: just as little as anyone who, according to Buddha's prescription, has concealed his goodness from other people and has let them see only his bad side.

608

Cause and effect confused. — We unconsciously look for the principles and dogmas that fit our temperament, so that it finally appears as if the principles and dogmas have created our character, have given it stability and reliability: whereas precisely the reverse has taken place. Our thinking and judgment are, it seems, to be made the cause of our nature after the fact: but actually it is our nature that causes us to think and judge in this way or that. — And what destines us to play this almost unconscious farce? Indolence and convenience, and not least the desire of vanity to be seen as consistent through and through, the same in nature as in thought: for this procures respect, imparts confidence and power.

609

Age and truth. — Young people love what is interesting and peculiar, regardless of how true or false it is. More mature spirits love truth for what is interesting and peculiar in it. Fully mature minds, finally, love truth even where it seems plain and simple and is boring to ordinary people because they have noticed that truth tends to speak of its highest spiritual possessions with an air of simplicity.

610

People as bad poets. — Just as in the second part of a verse bad poets seek a thought to fit their rhyme, so in the second half of their lives people tend to become more anxious about finding actions, positions, relationships that fit those of their earlier lives, so that everything harmonizes quite well on the surface: but their lives are no longer ruled and newly redirected by a strong thought, and instead, in its place, comes the intention of finding a rhyme.

611

Boredom and play. — Need forces us to work, and with its yield the need is silenced; the constant reawakening of needs habituates us to work. But in the pauses when the needs are silenced and, as it were, asleep, boredom overtakes us. What is this? It is the habit of working as such that now makes itself felt as a new, additional need; and the more strongly that someone has become accustomed to working, perhaps even the more strongly that someone has suffered from his needs, the stronger this need will be. To avoid boredom, human beings either work beyond the measure set by their other needs or they discover play, that is, work that is not meant to silence any need except the need to work as such. Anyone who is tired of play and has no new needs providing further reason to work is sometimes overtaken by the longing for a third state that is related to play as floating is to dancing, as dancing is to walking, the longing for a blissful, serene mobility: it is the artist's and philosopher's vision of happiness.

612

Lesson from pictures. — If we observe a series of pictures of ourselves, from the time of late childhood up to manhood, we find to our pleasant surprise that the man looks more like the child than he does like the youth: therefore that, in a way probably typical of this process, a temporary alienation from our basic character has intervened over which the collected, concentrated strength of the man has regained mastery. To this perception corresponds another, that all the strong influences of passions, teachers, and political events that surround us in our youth later seem to have been reduced once again to a fixed measure: certainly they continue to live and work within us, but our fundamental feelings and opinions are predominant and use these things as sources of energy, no longer as the regulators that they were in our twenties. Thus, the thoughts and feelings of the man once again appear more in accord with those of his childhood—and this inward fact expresses itself in the aforementioned outward one.

613

Tone of a certain age.—The tone in which young people speak, praise, blame, or recite is displeasing to an older person because it is too loud and at the same time muffled and unclear, like the tone in a vault that takes on a certain resonance from the emptiness; for most of what young people think does not flow out of the fullness of their own natures, but instead accords with and echoes what has been thought, spoken, praised, or blamed in their vicinity. But because sensations (of attraction and aversion) resound much more strongly in young people than the reasons for them, when they speak their sensations aloud there emerges that muffled, echoing tone that signals the absence or paucity of reasons. The tone of a more mature age is stern, abrupt, moderately loud, but, like everything clearly articulated, carries a very long way. Old age, finally, often brings a certain mildness and indulgence to the sound and sweetens it, as it were: in many cases, admittedly, it sours it as well.

614

Backward and anticipatory people.—The disagreeable character of someone who is full of mistrust, feels envy at every success of competitors and neighbors, and becomes violent and enraged toward divergent opinions shows that he belongs to an earlier stage of culture and is therefore a relic: for the way in which he interacts with people was proper and suitable for the circumstances of an age when might made right; he is a *backward* human being. A different character, one that has a rich capacity to share in the joys of others, wins friends everywhere, feels affection for all that is growing and becoming, shares the pleasure of others in all their honors and successes, and claims no privilege of being alone in recognizing truth, but is instead filled with a modest mistrust—that is an anticipatory person who is striving toward a higher human culture. The disagreeable character stems from the time when the rough foundations of human intercourse still had to be constructed, the other one lives on its highest floors, as far as possible from the wild animal that, locked up in the cellars beneath the foundations of culture, rages and howls.

615

Comfort for hypochondriacs. — When a great thinker is temporarily subjected to the self-torture of hypochondria, he may comfort himself by saying: "it is your own great strength on which this parasite feeds and grows; if that were less, you would have less to suffer." The statesman may speak in the same way when jealousy and vengefulness, in general the mood of the *bellum omnium contra omnes* with which he as representative of a nation must necessarily be strongly endowed, occasionally intrudes into his personal relationships as well and makes his life difficult.

616

Estranged from the present. — There are great advantages if at some point we estrange ourselves to a great extent from our age and are, as it were, driven from its shore back into the ocean of archaic worldviews. Gazing from there toward the coast, we survey its entire shape for the first time and have the advantage, when we approach it once again, of understanding it better as a whole than do those who have never left it.

617

Sowing and reaping from personal failings. — People like Rousseau understand how to use their weaknesses, deficiencies, and vices as manure for their talent, as it were. When he deplores the depravity and degeneration of society as a distressing consequence of culture, this is based upon personal experience, the bitterness of which gives sharpness to his general condemnation and poisons the arrows with which he shoots; he unburdens himself first as an individual and intends to look for a cure that will directly benefit society, but indirectly and by means of that benefit himself as well.

618

Being philosophically minded.—We generally strive to acquire a *single* mental posture, a *single* class of opinions, for all the situations and events in life—that is what we are most likely to call being philosophically minded. But it may have a higher value for the enrichment of knowledge if we do not make ourselves uniform in this way, but instead listen to the soft voice of different situations in life; these bring their own particular views along with them. Thus, we take an attentive interest in the life and being of many things by not treating ourselves as fixed, stable, *single* individuals.

619

In the fire of contempt.—It is a new step toward becoming independent when for the first time we dare to express views that are considered disgraceful for those who hold them; even our friends and acquaintances tend to become nervous then. The gifted nature must make its way through this fire, too; afterward it will belong much more to itself.

620

Sacrifice.—Provided there is a choice, a great sacrifice will be preferred to a small sacrifice: because we compensate ourselves for the great one with self-admiration, as we cannot possibly do for the small one.

621

Love as a trick.—Anyone who really wants to get to *know* something new (be it a person, an event, a book) does well to take up this new thing with all possible love, to quickly avert his eye from and even to forget everything in it that appears hostile, offensive, or false to him: so that, for example, we give the author of a book the greatest possible head start and, as at a race, actually yearn with a pounding heart for him to reach his goal. By proceeding in this way, we press into the heart of the new thing, to the point that gives it motion: and this is precisely what getting to know it means. If we have gotten this far, the understanding can set its restrictions afterward; that overestimation, that temporary staying of the critical pendulum, was simply a trick for enticing the soul of the thing to come forth.

622

Thinking too well and too ill of the world. — Whether we think too well or too ill of things, we always have the advantage of thereby reaping a higher pleasure: for when a preconceived opinion is too positive, we generally attribute more sweetness to things (experiences) than they actually contain. A preconceived opinion that is too negative causes a pleasant disappointment: the pleasantness in the things themselves is supplemented by the pleasantness of the surprise. — A gloomy temperament will, however, have the opposite experience in both cases.

623

Profound people. — Those whose strength lies in how deeply they are impressed by things — we generally call them profound people — are relatively collected and decisive when anything happens suddenly: for at the first moment the impression was still shallow, only later does it *become* profound. But things or people that have long been anticipated and expected stimulate such natures the most and make them almost incapable of maintaining their presence of mind when these things finally do arrive.

624

Involvement with the higher self. — Everyone has his good days when he finds his higher self; and true humanity demands that we judge someone only according to this state, and not according to his workday condition of constraint and servitude. We should, for instance, appraise and honor a painter according to the highest vision that he was able to see and to represent. But people themselves get quite differently involved with this higher self of theirs and frequently play their own parts, insofar as they later imitate over and over the self of their best moments. Many people live shyly and humbly in the presence of their ideal and would like to deny it: they are afraid of their higher self because when it speaks, its words are demanding. Moreover, it has a supernatural freedom of coming and staying away as it pleases; it is therefore frequently called a gift of the gods, whereas in reality it is everything else that is a gift of the gods (of chance): this, however, is the person himself.

625

Solitary people.—Some people are so used to being alone with themselves that they do not compare themselves at all with other people, but spin out their monologic lives in a peaceful and cheerful mood, conversing quite well with themselves, and even laughing. But if we do bring them to compare themselves with others, they tend toward a brooding underestimation of themselves: so that they must be forced to *learn* a good and just opinion of themselves from others first: and they will always be wanting to deduct and to bargain away something from this acquired opinion as well.—We must therefore grant certain people their solitude and not be so foolish, as frequently happens, as to pity them on account of it.

626

Without melody.—There are people for whom a steady inner repose and a harmonious ordering of all their capacities are so characteristic that all goal-oriented activity is repugnant to them. They resemble music that consists of nothing but long, drawn-out harmonic chords, without ever showing even the start of an articulated, active melody. All movement from without serves only to establish their boat at once in a new state of equilibrium on the lake of euphonic harmony. Modern people generally become extremely impatient when they encounter such natures, who *become* nothing, without our being able to say that they *are* nothing. But in certain moods, the sight of them arouses that uncommon question: why melody at all? Why isn't it sufficient for us when life mirrors itself peacefully upon a deep lake?—The Middle Ages were richer in such natures than our age is. How rarely do we still encounter someone who is able to live so very peacefully and cheerfully with himself, even amid the crowd, saying to himself as Goethe did: "The best thing of all is the profound stillness toward the world in which I live and grow, and where I gain what they cannot take from me with fire and sword."

627

Living and experiencing.—If we consider how some individuals know how to manage their experiences—their insignificant daily experiences—so that these become a field that bears fruit three times a year; while others—and how many they are!—though driven through the pounding waves of the most stimulating destinies and the most varied currents of ages and peoples, still remain like a cork, ever buoyant, ever on the surface: we are finally tempted to divide humanity into a minority (a minimality) of those who understand how to make a great deal out of very little and a majority of those who understand how to make very little out of a great deal; indeed, we encounter those reverse wizards who, instead of creating the world out of nothing, create a nothing out of the world.

628

Seriousness in play.—In Genoa, at the time of evening twilight, I heard from a tower a long chiming of bells: it refused to end and rang, as if insatiable for itself, above the noise of the streets and out into the evening sky and the sea air, so horrible and at the same time so childlike, so full of melancholy. Then I recalled the words of Plato and suddenly felt them in my heart: *nothing human is worth taking very seriously: nevertheless*— —

629

Of conviction and justice.—To demand that someone later, in coldness and sobriety, stand behind what he said, promised, resolved in passion—this is among the heaviest burdens that oppress humanity. Having to acknowledge for all future time the consequences of wrath, of inflamed vengefulness, of enthusiastic devotion—that can stimulate a bitterness toward these feelings that is all the greater when precisely these things are everywhere made the objects of idolatry, especially by artists. They foster an *esteem for the passions* and have always done so; admittedly, they also glorify the terrible atonement for passion that someone takes upon himself, those vengeful outbursts that have death, mutilation, voluntary banishment as consequences, and the resignation of a shattered heart. In any case, they keep curiosity about the passions awake; it is as if they wanted to say: without passions you have experienced nothing at all.—Because we have sworn to be faithful, though perhaps to a purely fictitious being such as a god, because we have given our heart to a prince, a party, a woman, a priestly order, an artist, or a thinker, in a state of blind madness that enchanted us and made that being seem worthy of every honor and every sacrifice—are we now inescapably bound? Weren't we in fact deceiving ourselves at that time? Wasn't it a hypothetical promise, made under the admittedly unspoken assumption that those beings to whom we dedicated ourselves really were what we imagined them to be? Are we obligated to be true to our errors, even after we have seen that we are doing damage to our higher self as a result of this loyalty?—No, there is no law, no obligation of this kind; we *must* be traitors, act unfaithfully, forsake our ideals again and again. We do not advance from one period of life into another without arousing and continuing to suffer from these pains of betrayal. In order to avoid these pains, wouldn't we have to guard ourselves against the upsurge of our feelings? Wouldn't the world then become too barren, too spectral for us? We should instead ask ourselves whether these pains are a *necessary* consequence of a change in convictions or whether they do not in fact depend upon an *erroneous* opinion and estimation. Why do we admire someone who remains true to his convictions and despise someone who changes them? I fear that the answer must be: because everyone presumes that only motives based upon the more vulgar sorts of advantage or personal fear can cause such a change. That is to say: we basically believe that nobody changes his opinions as long as they are advantageous for him, or at least as long as they do not do him any harm. But if this were the case, it would provide grim testimony about the *intellectual* significance of all convictions. Let us for once examine how convictions arise and consider whether they are not greatly overestimated: doing this will demonstrate that the act of *changing* our convictions has in all circumstances been measured by a false standard and that we have up to now tended to suffer too much from such a change.

630

Conviction is the belief that we possess the absolute truth about some specific point of knowledge. This belief therefore presupposes that there are absolute truths; likewise, that perfect methods have been found for attaining them; finally, that everyone who has convictions makes use of these perfect methods. All three assertions immediately prove that someone with convictions is not a person of scientific thought; he stands before us at the age of theoretical innocence and is a child, however grown-up he may be in other respects. Yet entire millennia have lived within those childish presuppositions, and from them have flowed humanity's mightiest sources of strength. Those countless human beings who sacrificed themselves for their convictions believed that they were doing it for the absolute truth. They were all wrong in that: there has probably never yet been a human being who sacrificed himself for the truth: at least the dogmatic expression of his belief will have been unscientific or half-scientific. But in reality, one wanted to be right because one thought that one *had* to be right. Letting one's belief be torn away perhaps meant putting one's eternal salvation in question. In a matter of such extreme importance, the "will" was all too audibly the prompter of the intellect. The presupposition of every believer of every persuasion was that he *could* not be refuted; if the objections proved extremely strong, it still remained possible for him to malign reason and perhaps even to plant the "*credo quia absurdum est*" as the banner of the most extreme fanaticism. It is not the conflict of opinions that has made history so violent, but the conflict of belief in opinions, that is, of convictions. Yet if all those who thought so highly of their convictions, made all kinds of sacrifices to them, and spared neither honor, nor body, nor life in their service had devoted merely half of their strength to investigating by what right they adhered to this or that conviction or the way in which they had come to it: how peaceful human history would then appear! How much more knowledge there would be! We would have been spared all the cruel scenes resulting from the persecution of every sort of heretic, for two reasons: first, because the inquisitors would have inquired above all into themselves and would have gotten beyond the presumption that they were defending the absolute truth; and then, because the heretics themselves would not have given any further credence to propositions as badly grounded as the propositions of all religious sectarians and "true believers" are, once they had investigated them.

631

From the times when people were accustomed to believing in the possession of absolute truth stems a deep *discontent* with all skeptical and relativistic positions toward any questions of knowledge whatsoever; we generally prefer to surrender unconditionally to a conviction held by people in authority (fathers, friends, teachers, princes) and feel a sort of remorseful conscience if we do not do this. This tendency is entirely comprehensible and its consequences give us no right to make vehement reproaches against the development of human reason. But the scientific spirit in human beings must gradually bring to maturity the virtue of *cautious reserve*, the wise moderation that is more familiar in the sphere of practical life than in the sphere of theoretical life and that, for example, Goethe depicted in Antonio as an object of exasperation for all Tassos, that is, for those natures that are unscientific and at the same time inactive. The person with convictions has in himself a right not to comprehend the cautious thinker, the theoretical Antonio; the scientific person, on the other hand, has no right to blame him for that; he makes allowances for him and knows moreover that in certain cases the other will cling to him, as Tasso finally does to Antonio.

632

Anyone who has not made his way through various convictions, but has instead remained attached to the belief in whose net he first became entangled, is at all events a representative of *backward* cultures precisely because of this constancy; in accordance with this lack of cultivation (which always presupposes cultivatability), he is hard, injudicious, unteachable, without gentleness, always suspicious, an unscrupulous person who seizes upon every means for making his opinion prevail because he simply cannot comprehend that there have to be any other opinions; in this regard, he may perhaps be a source of strength and even salutary in cultures that have become all too free and flaccid, yet only because he forcibly stimulates opposition to himself: for in this way, the more delicate creations of the new culture, which are forced to struggle with him, become strong themselves.

633

We are in essential respects still the same people as those in the age of the Reformation: and why should it be otherwise? But the fact that we no longer allow ourselves to use certain means for assisting our opinion to triumph distinguishes us from that time and proves that we belong to a higher culture.

Anyone today who still combats and suppresses opinions with accusations or with outbursts of rage, as people did in the Reformation, clearly betrays the fact that he would have burned his opponents if he had lived in different times and that he would have had recourse to all the expedients of the Inquisition if he had lived as an opponent of the Reformation. This Inquisition was at that time reasonable, for it signified nothing other than the general state of siege that had to be imposed upon the whole realm of the church and which, like every state of siege, gave one a right to use the most extreme measures, under the presupposition, of course (which we no longer share with those people), that one *possessed* the truth in the church and *had* to preserve it at any price and by any sacrifice for the salvation of humanity. Now, however, we no longer concede so easily to anyone that he might possess the truth: rigorous methods of inquiry have disseminated enough mistrust and caution that everyone who advocates opinions violently in his words and actions is felt to be an enemy of our present-day culture, or at least to be a backward person. In fact: the pathos that we possess the truth counts for very little today in relation to that admittedly milder and less resonant pathos of searching for the truth, which does not grow weary of relearning and examining anew.

634

Besides, the methodical search for truth is itself the result of those ages in which convictions were feuding with one another. If the individual had set no importance upon *his* "truth," that is, upon his being right, there would be no methods of inquiry at all; but in this way, with the eternal conflict among the claims of various individuals concerning absolute truth, they moved forward step by step in finding irrefutable principles by which the justice of these claims could be tested and the strife could be settled. At first, people followed authorities in making decisions; later, they criticized one another's respective ways and means for finding the ostensible truth; in between, there was a period when people drew the consequences of the opposing principle and perhaps found them to be harmful or to cause unhappiness: from which everyone was supposed to conclude that the conviction of one's opponent contained an error. *The personal struggle of thinkers* finally sharpened these methods enough so that truths really could be discovered and the aberrations of earlier methods laid bare for everyone to see.

635

On the whole, the methods of science are at least as important an outcome of inquiry as any other result: for the scientific spirit rests upon the insight into methods, and all the results of science could not avert a renewed prevalence of superstition and folly if those methods were to be lost. Clever people may *learn* as much as they please about the results of science: we can always tell from their conversation, and especially from the hypotheses it contains, that they lack the scientific spirit: they do not have the instinctive distrust for misguided ways of thinking that has sunk its roots into the soul of every scientific person as a result of lengthy training. It is sufficient for them to find any hypothesis whatsoever about something, and then they are all on fire for it and think that takes care of it. What it really means for them to have an opinion is: to be fanatical about it and henceforth to set their heart upon it as a conviction. When something is unexplained, they become ardent for the first idea to occur to them that looks like an explanation for it: from which, especially in the field of politics, the most awful consequences continually ensue. — Therefore, everyone today ought to have acquired a thorough grounding in at least *one* science: then he will know what method means and how necessary the most extreme presence of mind is. Women in particular should be given this advice; as women, they are now the helpless victims of any and all hypotheses, especially when these give an impression of being clever, charming, animating, invigorating. Indeed, upon closer examination, we perceive that the greatest part by far of all cultivated people still desires convictions and nothing but convictions from a thinker, and that only a tiny minority wants *certainty*. The former want to be forcefully carried away in order to have their own strength increased; the latter few have the objective interest that neglects personal advantages, even the aforementioned increase in strength. Everywhere that a thinker behaves and presents himself like a *genius*, looking down as if he were a higher being to whom authority is due, he is counting upon the former, greatly preponderant class. Insofar as the genius of that sort maintains the ardor of his convictions and awakens mistrust against the cautious and modest scientific sensibility, he is an enemy of truth, however much he might believe himself to be its suitor.

636

There is also, to be sure, a quite different species of genius, that of justice; and I cannot resolve myself to rate this kind lower than any other sort of philosophical, political, or artistic genius. Its style is to avoid with heartfelt indignation everything that blinds or confuses the judgment of things; it is in consequence an *opponent of convictions*, for it wants to give everything its due, whether it be something living or dead, real or imagined—and for that purpose it must perceive things clearly; hence, it places everything in the best light and goes over it with a careful eye. In the end, it will give, even to its opponent, blind or short-sighted "conviction" (as men call it:—women term it "belief"), what is due to conviction—for the sake of truth.

637

From the *passions* grow opinions; *laziness of spirit* allows these to harden into *convictions*.—But anyone who feels a *free*, restlessly living spirit can prevent this hardening by constant change; and even if he is on the whole a thinking snowball, he will generally have not opinions, but only certainties and precisely measured probabilities in his head.—But we, who are mixed beings, at one time heated through by fire, at another chilled through by spirit, should kneel down before justice as the only goddess that we acknowledge above ourselves. *The fire* in us generally makes us unjust and, to the mind of that goddess, impure; we may never touch her hand while in this state, nor does the earnest smile of her pleasure rest upon us then. We worship her as the veiled Isis of our lives; with shame we offer her our pain as penance and sacrifice whenever the fire attempts to burn and consume us. *Spirit* is what saves us from burning out entirely and turning to ashes; it lets us tear ourselves away from the sacrificial altar of justice or wraps us in asbestos. Redeemed from the fire, driven by the spirit, we then stride from opinion to opinion, through the shifting of parties, as noble *betrayers* of all the things that can ever be betrayed—and yet without any feeling of guilt.

638

The wanderer.—Anyone who has come even part of the way to the freedom of reason cannot feel himself to be anything other than a wanderer upon the earth—though not a traveler *toward* some final goal: for that does not exist. Yet he does want to observe and to keep his eyes open for everything that really is going on in the world; hence, he dare not attach his heart too firmly to any individual thing; he must have something wandering within himself that finds its pleasure in change and ephemerality. Such a person will admittedly have bad nights, when he is tired and finds the gate of the city that should have offered him rest to be closed; it may furthermore be that, as in the Orient, the desert reaches all the way up to the gate, that the predators howl, farther off at one moment, nearer the next, that a strong wind rises up, or that robbers carry off his pack animals. Then the terrible night will sink over him like a second desert upon the desert and his heart will be weary of wandering. When the morning sun does rise, glowing like a god of wrath, and when the city does open, he may see in the faces of those who dwell there even more desert, filth, deceit, insecurity than there are outside the gates—and the day may be almost worse than the night. So it may go at times for the wanderer; but then, as compensation, come the rapturous mornings of other regions and days, when already with the dawning day he sees swarms of muses dancing past him in the mist of the mountains, or later when, as he walks silently beneath the trees in the equanimity of his morning soul, nothing but good and bright things are thrown out to him from the treetops and hidden depths of the foliage, the gifts of all those free spirits who are at home amid the mountains, woods, and solitude and who, like him, are wanderers and philosophers, in their now joyful, now meditative way. Born of the mysteries of the dawning day, they reflect upon how it can have such a pure, luminous, radiantly bright face between the ringing of the tenth and twelfth hours: — they seek the *philosophy of the morning*.

Among Friends
An Epilogue

1

How lovely, in silence to be together
Lovelier still, to laugh together—
Under Heaven's silken shawl
Leaning back on moss and beeches,
Loud in friendship as our laughter
Shows the whiteness of our teeth.

If I did well, then we'd keep silence;
If I did badly—then we'd laugh
And make it ever worse and worse
Make it worse by laughing harder,
Till we climb into the grave.

Friends! Yes! Shall this be so?—
Amen! Until we meet again!

2

No excuses! No forgiveness!
Grant, you cheerful, free at heart,
To this book with its unreason
Ear and heart and refuge now!
Believe me, friends, that my unreason
Has not been a curse for me!

What I find, what I am seeking—

Can that be found in any book?
Hail in me the guild of fools!
Learn then from this foolish book,
How reason finally—"comes to reason!"

Therefore, friends, shall this be so?—
Amen! Until we meet again!

Reference Matter

Notes

Many of the aphorisms contained in *Human, All Too Human* can be found in the notebooks (*Pd*) that Nietzsche kept during the several years prior to its publication, with the earliest material dating from summer 1875. The surviving notebook material is printed in volume 12 of this edition, which also includes Nietzsche's varying organizational plans for the text and copies of portions of it made by Peter Gast and Albert Brenner. Relevant fragments are referred to in the notes by designation of their notebook and fragment number, for example 18 [1].

In September 1876, Nietzsche had Peter Gast either copy or write from dictation a preliminary compilation of fragments under the provisional title "The Plowshare" (*Sd*). The extant manuscript of this text contains both corrections and later additions in Nietzsche's own hand. While in Sorrento, Albert Brenner wrote out a second manuscript version (*Sd*) that incorporated additional later material into the text, to which Nietzsche continued to add aphorisms jotted down on loose sheets of paper (designated by Colli-Montinari as the Sorrentino papers). Nietzsche prepared a final version of the text after his return to Basel in fall 1877; this manuscript was also written out by Peter Gast, with Nietzsche's corrections to it completed by 10 January 1878 (*Pm*). The printer's proofs (*Pp*), with corrections by Nietzsche, Gast, and also Peter Widemann (*Cp*), still exist.

When Nietzsche's new publisher, E. W. Fritzsch, was preparing a revised edition of his works in 1886, the numerous unsold copies of *Human, All Too Human* were rebound and reissued as volume 1 of the new text; the newly titled volume 2 included *Mixed Opinions and Maxims* and *The Wanderer and His Shadow*. Nietzsche's own handwritten versions of the revised preface and the concluding poem for this edition also survive. Nietzsche's library contained two single-volume copies of the text, the first including *Human, All Too Human*, *Mixed Maxims and Opinions*, and *The Wanderer and His Shadow*, but without the prefaces to the second edition, the second including all three texts as published in the second edition. Both contain numerous emendations in Nietzsche's hand (*Se*), primarily to the first two chapters of the text. The revisions to the first copy are from 1885 and were made in connection with a major reworking of the text that Nietzsche was planning at that time. Many of the changes in the second copy involve a complete revision of Aphorisms 1–3 that Nietzsche wrote out on loose sheets in January 1888, likewise in preparation for an anticipated new edition of the text.

The following symbols are used throughout the notes:

[ ]	Deletion by Nietzsche
| |	Addition by Nietzsche
{ }	Addition by the translator
⟨ ⟩	Addition by the editors (Colli and Montinari)
———	Unfinished or incomplete sentence or thought

Variants are referred to by the following abbreviations:

Cp	Correction in the proofs
Fe	First edition
Le	Twenty-volume 1894 Leipzig edition of Nietzsche's works
Pd	Preliminary draft
Pm	Printer's manuscript (clean final copy of handwritten manuscript)
PmN	Change made by Nietzsche in the printer's manuscript

Pp	Page proofs
Sd	Second draft
Se	Subsequent emendation
Up	Uncorrected proofs
CW	*The Complete Works of Friedrich Nietzsche*

In Place of a Preface: Notes

3 *at all."*] This passage comes from Part 3 of Descartes' *Discourse on Method*, and was translated by Nietzsche not from Descartes' original edition in French, but from the Latin translation done by Etienne de Courcelles seven years later. For a fuller discussion, see Robert A. Rethy, "The Descartes Motto to the First Edition of *Menschliches, Allzumenschliches*," *Nietzsche-Studien* 5 (1976): 289–97.

Preface: Notes

Pd ⟨All variants are from notebooks dated fall 1885–fall 1886.⟩: This introductory book that has known how to find its readers among a wide circle of nations and peoples and must know how to perform some art that can tempt even shy and obstinate spirits. [is precisely in Germany read the most carelessly. There is nothing astonishing in this: it demands an excess of time, of clarity in the heavens and in the heart, of *otium* in the most audacious sense—nothing except those good things that are precisely what one cannot easily demand or obtain from Germans. They have a lot to do.]: yet it is precisely in Germany that this book has thus far been read and heard most carelessly: why is this so? "It is too demanding"—I have heard—"it demands subtle and indulged senses, an excess of time, of clarity in the heavens and in the heart, of *otium* in the most audacious sense—nothing but good things that in fairness [cannot be demanded or obtained from present-day Germans. They have a lot to do: what is it to them if we have thinking to do?] we Germans of today do not have and can also not provide."—Is it allowed today, when after ten years I send it for a second time on its travels — — —This means to answer reasonably: and as thanks ——— ⟨continuation; first version⟩ So what I have to say today, I will say exclusively into the ears of those good Europeans to whom this book was dedicated from the beginning and [expressly] pay no heed to the Germans, namely to the good Germans, [since] they have [better] more necessary things to do than to listen to me, there is no doubt about it! What does it matter whether I betray the fact that this book is hard to understand—that it stimulates confusion and, in short—leads astray, that it requires a preface and a warning sign. ⟨second version⟩ [—Spoken among ourselves: that answer was a great [stupidity] misunderstanding: I am permitted to say that to your ears, presupposing that you do not already know it, you [free spirits] good Europeans and free spirits to whom this book was dedicated from the beginning.] Admittedly: to say to *your* ears, you free spirits and good Europeans to whom this book was dedicated from the beginning, that courteous German reply was a stupidity. It seems that this book is hard to understand, that it stimulates confusion and leads astray? that it requires a preface and a warning sign? [it requires quite different things and presuppositions than that good German does] It is not at all a book for happy idlers, to whom that good German was inclined to deliver it: [likewise] but precisely the opposite of that.

Pd: This must be gone through by everyone in whom there is a task being embodied and "coming into the world": the secret need and necessity of this task will rule over all his separate, individual destinies like a long pregnancy, long before he himself has glimpsed and given it a fixed name. Given that it is the problem of rank ordering that I can call *my* problem: only now, at [the middle] the midday of my life, do I see how many preparations (and even masks) the problem required before it was permitted to rise up before me: and how I first had to experience the most varied and contradictory states of distress and happiness [of the soul and the adventures of many souls, losing nothing] in my soul and body, as an adventurer and circumnavigator of the soul[, as it were]—forcing my way in everywhere, without fear, almost without love, despising nothing, losing nothing, savoring everything, and testing everything to its foundation, purifying all of its accidental and [personal] transitory elements into eternal ones and sifting them [through as the transformative human being]—until I am at least permitted to say: here is [my] a new problem! I see my ladder[!— I sat upon every rung!] and I myself—I have sat upon each of its rungs!

Pd: Toward a Preface. I do not believe that anyone has ever looked into the world with as deep a suspicion as I have: and anyone who knows something of the indescribable fears of solitude, which brings that absolute [originality] difference in views [with it] to those who have been afflicted with it, will understand how I [sought shelter somewhere to recuperate and to forget myself temporarily—that I justifiably invented a relation and equality of wishes for myself. People reproach me by saying that I deceived myself about Schopenhauer as well as about Richard Wagner and quite rightly invented them according to my needs. This is true: and what then do *you* know about how much I reproached myself with this] often sought shelter somewhere to recuperate from myself, as if to forget myself temporarily in any sort of reverence or enmity or scientism—that where I was lacking what I needed I artificially compelled a relation and equality of eyes and desires[—]to appear to me and quite rightly invented them in order not to feel so isolated and alone. There is no doubt that in more youthful years I willfully deceived myself about Schopenhauer as well as about Richard Wagner and made them fit my needs. This is true and in a much worse and higher sense than anyone could conceive: but what then do *you* know about the slyness of self-recuperation that lay in this self-deception? [Will people reproach me by saying that I did not understand how to undeceive myself at the right time?] And about how I did not tolerate the veil over my eyes for a single hour more, as soon as I could once again put up with seeing clearly—with seeing myself clearly?

1: 5, 6 *Prelude to a Philosophy of the Future]* Subtitle of Nietzsche's *Beyond Good and Evil* (1886).

2: 7, 5 *acedia]* "torpor."

3: 9, 4–5 *mater saeva cupidinum]* "savage mother of the passions."

8: 13, 19 *otium]* "leisure."

8: 13, 23 *proverb]* "*Si tacuisses, philosophus mansisses.*" Had you not

Chapter 1: Notes

1: Pd: Up until now, we have been lacking a chemistry of the moral, aesthetic, and religious world. Here, too, the most precious things are made out of base, despised things. — How can something rational arise from something irrational, logic from illogic, disinterested contemplation from desiring contemplation, living for others from egoism, truth from error — the problem of the emergence from opposites. Precisely: it is no opposite, but instead only a sublimation (something ordinarily subtracted).

Revision (January 1888): *Chemistry of concepts and feelings about value.* — At almost every point, philosophical problems are once again assuming the same form for their questions as they did two thousand years ago: how can something arise from its opposite, for example, something rational from something irrational, something sentient from something dead, logic from illogic, disinterested contemplation from willful desire, living for others from selfishness, truth from error? Metaphysical philosophy has up to now helped itself get past this difficulty by simply *denying* that one emerged from the other and assuming that more highly valued things had their own origin, immediately out of the in-itself of things. A contrary philosophy, on the other hand, the youngest and most radical that has yet existed, [the] a genuine *philosophy of becoming* that simply does not believe in any "in-itself" and consequently denies any civil rights to the concept "being" as well as to the concept "appearance": this sort of antimetaphysical philosophy has made it apparent to me in individual cases (— and this will presumably be its result in every case) that this formulation of the question is false, that *those opposites* [from which previous philosophy, led astray by the folk metaphysics of language] in which previous philosophy has believed, led astray by language and by the peremptory utility of its [crude falsifications] crudeness and simplifications,

(preceding text:)
spoken, you would have remained a philosopher. Boethius, *De consolatione philosophaie*, bk. 2, 7.

do not even exist, in short, that we first of all require a *chemistry of the fundamental concepts*, that we presuppose that they have come into being and are still becoming. In order to be finished once and for all with such crude [and boorish concepts as "egotistical action," as "disinterested contemplation," as "pure reason," as] and geometrically squared oppositions as "egotistical" and "unegotistical," desire and spirituality, "living" and "dead," "truth" and "error," a microscopic psychology is just as necessary as a skill in all forms of historical perspectivist optics such as has never yet existed and was not even *permitted*. Philosophy, as I want it and understand it, has previously had *conscience* against it: the moral, religious, and aesthetic imperatives said No to the methodology of investigation that is demanded here. We must first of all have freed ourselves from these imperatives: *we must, against our own conscience, have dissected our own conscience.*... The history of concepts and of their transformation under the tyranny of the feelings about value—do you understand that? Who has enough desire and courage to pursue such investigations? [It may perhaps be part of] Now, when it may perhaps even be part of being at the pinnacle of the humanization that has been *attained* for a human being to feel resistance against the history of his beginnings and to want not to turn his eyes toward any sort of *pudenda origo*: wouldn't we have to be almost inhuman to want to [turn our eyes in] look, seek, discover in the opposite direction?—

pudenda origo] "shameful origin."

15, 10 *egoism]* *Se*: selfishness

15, 12–15 *by denying...Historical philosophy]* *Se*: simply *denied* that one emerged from the other and assumed that more highly valued things had their own origin, immediately out of the in-itself of things. The philosophy of becoming

15, 25–16, 10 *appears to...inclination?]* *Pm*: reveals its presence only to the keenest observation. All that we need is a chemistry of the religious, moral, aesthetic representations: along with the insight that in this area the most magnificent colors have been extracted from base materials.

2: *Se*: All philosophers have the common failing that they start with present-day human beings and suppose that they will reach the goal of knowing all about human beings by investigating and analyzing them. Involuntarily, they allow "man" to hover before their eyes as an *aeterna veritas*, something that remains the same through all the turmoil of becoming, a secure measure for things. Finally, however, all that the philosopher asserts about "humanity" is basically nothing more than testimony about the human being of a *restricted* stretch of time—and perhaps about a still more restricted corner of [time] [space] the earth. A lack of historical sensibility was up until now the original failing of all philosophers: even today, they inadvertently take the most recent shape of the European human being, as he emerged and emerges under the imprint and pressure of specific political and economic events, as the fixed form from which we must proceed—whereas everything *essential* in human development occurred during primeval times, long before those four thousand years with which we are more or less acquainted; during these years, humanity may well not have changed essentially. The philosopher judges in the opposite way: he perceives "instincts" in present-day humanity and immediately assumes that everything instinctive belongs to the unchangeable facts of humanity and must therefore provide a key to understanding existence generally; all teleology is built upon speaking of the human being of the last four millennia as something *eternal*, toward which all the things of the world have from their beginning naturally been directed. But everything has come to be; there are *no eternal facts*: there are therefore no eternal truths either.—From now on, therefore, history is necessary for philosophers, and along with history the virtue of the historian: modesty.

Revision (January 1888): *The original failing of philosophers.*—Up until now, all philosophers have suffered from the same malady— they thought unhistorically, antihistorically. They started with the human beings that [chance] their time and surroundings offered them, [above all with themselves] preferably even with themselves and with themselves alone; they believed that they could already reach their [a] goal, a knowledge of "human beings," through self-analysis. Their own feelings about value (or those of their caste, race, religion, health) counted for them as an unconditional measure of value; nothing was more alien and more offensive to them than that self-renunciation of the genuinely *scientific* conscience: which, as such, enjoys its freedom in a benevolent contempt for the person, for every person, for every personal perspective. These philosophers were above all persons; each of them even felt in himself, "I am the person himself," the *aeterna Veritas* of human beings, as it were, the "human being in itself" [; as I know from myself]. From this unhistorical optic that they used against one another, the greatest number of their errors can be derived—above all, the fundamental error of everywhere seeking what endures, everywhere presupposing something enduring, everywhere treating alteration, change, contradiction with contempt. [The philosopher as the goal of things, teleology] Even under the pressure of a culture *dominated* by [in the middle of] history (—as German culture was at the turn of the century), the typical philosopher will still present [presents] himself at least as the goal of all becoming, toward which all things from the beginning have been directed: this [is] was the spectacle that Hegel offered to the astonished Europe of his time.

16, 16 *aeterna veritas]* "eternal truth."

16, 20 *original failing]* Nietzsche's German coinage, *Erbfehler*, plays off the German term *Erbsünde*, "original sin," to convey both a religious sense and the more literal sense of "inherited" or "congenital."

16, 32–34 *assumes...generally]* Pm: on that basis draws conclusions concerning the nature of the world (as Schopenhauer did)

17, 1–6 *four millennia...modesty.]* Pm: three millennia as an eternal being. Everything has come to be; *there are no eternal facts.*— Hence *historical philosophizing* is necessary.

3: Revision (January 1888): It is the characteristic sign of a stronger and prouder taste, no matter how easily it may seem the opposite of that, to esteem the small, unpretentious, cautious truths found by rigorous methods more highly than those [blissful, intoxicating untruths in which the faith of artistic ages seeks its happiness and its intoxication] remote, shimmering, enshrouding generalities toward which the need of religious or artistic ages gropes. People whose intellectual training has either remained backward or, for good reasons, must be held back (—[that is] the case with women) have something like scorn for those small certainties on their lips; a physiological discovery says *nothing* to an artist, for instance: reason enough for him to think little of it. Such backward people, who occasionally presume to play the part of judges (—the three [artist-actors] backward individuals in the great style whom our age can exhibit have all three done this: Victor Hugo for France, Carlyle for England, Wagner for Germany) point with irony toward — — —

17, 14–17 *modest...there.*] *Up*: beautiful, splendid, intoxicating, perhaps even enrapturing do those stand here, so modest, simple, sober, apparently even discouraging do these stand there.

18, 9–10 *a spirited glance*] *Se*: a spirited inward glance

4: *Pd*: Ethics and art remain on the surface of things; they deceive, because they enrapture. People are as proud here as is the case in astrology.

18, 14 *and aesthetic*] *Se*: aesthetic, and logical

8: 20, 2 *Pneumatic explanation*] This phrase refers to a form of exegesis in which the holy spirit rather than philological analysis is presumed to disclose the meaning of the words.

11: *Pd*: The people who shaped language did not believe that they were giving names to things, but that they were expressing complete knowledge about them: it was the first stage of scientific communication.

21, 26–27 *aeternae veritates*] "eternal truths."

13: *Pd*: For a *dream*, as also for loud sounds, etc., an immediate explanation will be found.

23, 26–27 *The immediate...fantasy.*] *Up*: Dreams are *causae post effectum*, indeed, erroneously assumed *causae*.

causae post effectum] "causes after the effect."

24, 3–8 *In my...truth.*] *Pd*: One hypothesis is sufficient: *God* as truth. As people draw conclusions while dreaming, so humanity perhaps drew conclusions for many millennia.

15: 25, 32 *philosophers in general have]* *Pm*: Schopenhauer

16: 26, 19–30 *about…possibility]* *Se*: from that effect to this cause, to the unconditioned that tends always to be regarded as the sufficient ground for the world of appearances. On the other hand, after having distinctly set forth the concept of the metaphysical as what is unconditioned, *consequently also unconditioning*, we must conversely deny every connection between the unconditioned (the metaphysical world) and the world known to us: so that in the actual appearance the thing in itself does *not* appear to us at all, and every deduction drawn from the latter to the former is to be rejected. The first side ignores the fact

27, 6 *has made appearances]* *Se*: has, on the basis of human needs, of human affects, made "appearances"

28, 1 *Homeric laugh]* A loud, ringing laugh, from the Homeric phrase *asbestos gelos*, "unquenchable laughter." *Iliad*, bk. 1, 599.

17: 28, 17 *irresponsibility]* *Se*: personal unburdening

18: *Pd*: Metaphysics, which deals with the fundamental errors of human beings, but as if they were fundamental truths.

18: 28, 27 *substance."]* Afrikan Spir, *Denken und Wirklichkeit: Versuch einer Erneuerung der kritischen Philosophie* (Leipzig, 1877), 2, 177.

29, 3 *belief.]* *Sd*: belief. [Now what are its lowest forms? Those in which it is visible how that belief grew out of sensation?—An only slightly organized being has a sensation; another one follows it regularly, for instance, if it sees someone squeezing, it feels a pain. In the moment of squeezing, it reproductively creates the sensation of pain: both sensations grow together, and the result is a sensation of fear with its consequences of flight and avoidance.]

29, 5–6 *prior…judgment]* *Sd*: other ones is precisely that belief in the connection of a thing to us in pleasure or pain: belief is "anticipatory feeling"

19: 30, 29 *nature]* Immanuel Kant, *Prolegomena*, sec. 36, trans. Lewis White Beck (Indianapolis: Bobbs-Merrill, 1950), 67. Trans. modified. In Kant's text, the phrase "a priori" stands in parentheses after "laws."

20: Cf. 22 [28].

Sd: The first stage of cultivation has been reached when human beings get beyond superstitious and religious concepts and fears and no longer believe, for example, in dear little angels, as the cultivated ladies of Rome did: if someone is at this stage of liberation, then a *reverse movement* is necessary; he must grasp and recognize the historical justification as well as the psychological one for such conceptions, how poetry rests upon them and how he would rob himself of the greatest results that humanity has thus far produced without such a reverse movement. — With respect to philosophical metaphysics, I am perhaps the first one who has attained the negative goal here and then gone back: whereas even the most enlightened people get only as far as liberation from metaphysics and look back upon it with superiority. Here too, however, as in the hippodrome, we should bend back around the end of the track.

22: 32, 12 *"monumentum aere perennius"]* "a monument more lasting than bronze," a phrase that Horace uses to refer to his own poetry. Horace, *Odes* 3, 30, 1.

32, 33 *works.] Pm*: works [(for example, through prophylaxis against certain diseases everywhere on earth)].

33, 4 *lifetime.] Pm*: lifetime. [This mistrust, this restlessness manifests itself conspicuously in architecture, clothing.]

23: *Sd*: The less that people are constrained, the greater the inner movement of motives becomes, and the greater in turn the outward restlessness. Interminglings of people occur when they no longer feel themselves so strictly tied to a particular place. Just as all styles of art are reproduced one beside the other, so, too, are all the stages and forms of morality, of custom. — Such an age has the sense that various customs can be *compared*, something that was not possible before, when their dominance was localized; likewise with the styles of art. An increase in aesthetic feeling will finally decide among so many forms and allow most of them to die off, perhaps to the benefit of the Greek ones. Likewise, a selection of the higher morality! Destruction of the lower moralities! It is the age of comparison!

26: *Pd*: there perhaps lies the greatest advantage that we gain from

Schopenhauer, that he forces us back into older, powerful views of things, to which no path would otherwise so easily lead us.

35, 28 *metaphysics]* *Pm*: metaphysics [(and after him, Hartmann's witchery in the broad daylight of Berlin)]

27: 36, 16 *philosophy]* *Sd*: philosophy, as Ph. Mainländer does for Schopenhauer's philosophy,

36, 31–37, 2 *In order...science.]* *Pm*: *Art* can be very useful in relieving an overburdened heart *without* at the same time strengthening those conceptions; art serves as a transitional means toward that sort of liberating philosophy. And in general, to employ a Goethean phrase with a slight variation: "Whoever possesses science and art does not need religion." Goethe, *Zahme Xenien* 3, 119, where the phrase actually reads, "Whoever possesses science and art / also has religion."

31: 39, 3 *thinker]* *Pd*: thinker who would like to make all people into thinkers

33: 40, 15 *pure]* *Se*: rich; *Le*: richer

34: *Sd*: My philosophy turns into tragedy. Truth becomes hostile to life, to better things. The question remains: whether we *could* consciously remain in untruth? For there is no longer any Thou Shalt. Morality is as thoroughly destroyed as religion. Knowledge can allow only pleasure and displeasure to persist as motives: how will they come to terms with truth? They, too, rest upon errors (at least as attraction and aversion). All of human life is sunk deeply into untruth: we cannot pull it forth; we would take away not only our past, but also our present motives (honor, being good, etc.). Preparation for a tragic philosophy would be its name; in truth, there would remain a much simpler life, more purified of affects (the old motives would continue to be active due only to habit, which is hard to overcome, and gradually grow weaker and weaker). We would live among human beings and with ourselves as in nature, without praise or reproaches, rejoicing in everything as soon as we no longer fear it—*a play*!

42, 2 *destruction]* *Se*: dissolution, disintegration, self-destruction

42, 15 *emphasis]* *Emphasis* in the German text, possibly used with the rhetorical sense of meaning more than one actually says, or with reference to the further Greek meaning of "mere appearance."

Chapter 2: Notes

35: Se: On the moralistic superficiality in Germany.—That reflection upon what is human, all too human is among the means by which we can lighten the burden of life, that the practice of this art lends us presence of mind in difficult situations and amusement in tedious surroundings, that we can even gather maxims from the thorniest and least gratifying stretches of our own lives and thus make ourselves feel somewhat better: people believed that, knew that—in earlier centuries. Why has this century forgotten it, when at least in Germany the moralistic poverty makes itself known by many signs? Yes, one might doubt [can ask] whether Germany has in general ever "moralized" yet. Attend to the judgment of public events and personalities: consider the success that ridiculously narrow, old-maidish books have (for example, Vilmar's literary history, or Janssen), but above all, admit that the art of and also the pleasure in psychological dissection and combination is lacking in all ranks of German society, where people speak about human beings, to be sure, but not at all *about humanity*. Yet why do people allow the richest and most innocuous material for amusement to escape them? Why do they no longer read the great masters of the psychological maxim any more?—for, said without any exaggeration: cultivated people in Germany who have read La Rochefoucauld and his spiritual and artistic relatives, up through the last great moralist, Stendhal, can rarely be found; and much more rarely anyone who knows them and does not belittle them. But probably even this uncommon reader will take much less pleasure in them than the form adopted by those artists ought to give him; for even the subtlest mind is not capable of properly appreciating the art of polishing maxims if he has not himself been brought up for it and competed at it—like me: forgive me the pretension of being an exception among the Germans. Without such practical instruction, we take this creating and forming to be easier than it is; we do not have a sharp enough feel for what is successful and attractive. Hence, the German readers of maxims get a relatively paltry satisfaction from them, hardly any pleasure in tasting them, so that they respond just like people generally do in looking at cameos: they praise them because they cannot love them, and are quick to admire, but even quicker to run away.

43, 4 *Advantages...observation]* Pm: *Right of psychological observation.* [Introduction.] Preface ⟨Aphorisms 35–38 were still being thought of as a preface in Pm.⟩

43, 13–14 *and...Europe]* Up: and Russia

43, 25 *Europe]* Pm: Germany

43, 25–26 *his...relatives]* Sd: Vauvenargues, Champfort, and Stendhal

36: Cf. 23 [41].

44, 35–45, 3 *veut"]* "What the world calls virtue is generally only a phantom formed by our passions, to which we give an honest name in order to do with impunity what we please." La Rochefoucauld, *Réflexions: Sentences et maximes morales,* 606.

45, 5 *Observations]* Paul Rée, *Psychologische Beobachtungen* (Berlin, 1875).

45, 11 *beings.]* Se: beings. Yet finally it is still true: ⟨lines 4–12 of Aphorism 37, "countless...seriousness," were to be appended at this point as conclusion for this aphorism.⟩

37: Se: However the balance between the pro and con may be drawn here: given the present state of philosophy, the reanimation of moral observation has become necessary, and humanity cannot continue to be spared the gruesome sight of the psychological dissecting table and its knives and forceps. The older philosophy has always had paltry excuses for evading the investigation of the origin and history of human valuations. With what consequences: that has now made itself quite clearly visible after many examples have demonstrated how the errors of the greatest philosophers generally have their starting point in a false explanation of particular human actions and sensations, how a false ethics is constructed on the basis of an erroneous analysis of the so-called unegotistical actions, for example, which in turn leads one to make use of religion and mythological confusion, and finally the shadows of these dismal spirits fall even upon physics and our entire worldview. ⟨in the right margin:⟩ Gradually *seq*. But if it is certain that moral superficiality [in psychological observation] has laid the most dangerous snares for human judgment and inference up to now and will continue to do so, what is now required is a persistent laboring that does not tire of piling stone upon stone, pebble upon pebble, what is required is the moderate courage not to be ashamed of such humble work and to defy all contempt for it.

46, 16 *coldest*] *Pm*: coldest [contemporary]

46, 20 *person."*] Paul Rée, *Der Ursprung der moralischen Empfindungen* (Chemnitz, 1877), sec. 8.

46, 20–28 *hardened…have.*] *Pd*: steeled and sharpened by the most comprehensive historical knowledge, the kind that our age has been the first to be able to procure—this proposition is the ax that gets laid to the root of the "metaphysical need." What will remain after thus setting aside metaphysics is a row of strictly scientific problems, with which, however, nobody will ever again quiet spiritual needs.

38: 47, 4 *willed it.*] *Pm*: willed it. [If here at the end, after these sorts of preliminary remarks concerning the right to psychological observation in general, an essential question in regard to precisely this book still remains: I am not the one who can answer it. The foreword is the author's right, but the reader's is—the afterword.

47, 9 *do they find*] *Pp, Fe*: can they find

39: Cf. 19 [36], 19 [39].

47, 21 *intelligible freedom*] This phrase was already used in antiquity by Plato and others in reference to a world of ideas that could only be apprehended by the mind and that served as a pattern for the things of the world of appearance. Kant's reformulation of this concept emphasized that these "noumena," although independent of experience and the senses and therefore not knowable for human understanding, served a regulative function for practical reason by providing the ultimate goals of and impulse toward moral behavior.

NOTES TO PAGES 47-54 325

47, 25–27 *their...consequences*] *Se*: the beneficial or harmful consequences (that they have for the community)

48, 2 *soil.*] *Pd*: soil, so that it necessarily bears the color and type of its origin.

48, 10 *sensations is*] *Se*: valuations is at the same time

48, 16–19 *as in...necessity*] *Se*: as in the opinion of this philosopher it does in fact proceed—but that human beings themselves were by the same necessity precisely the people that they are

48, 24–25 *esse*] "being"; *operari*] "action."

48, 31–35 *where...freedom.*] *Se*: where, without regard to the genuine folly of the last preceding assertion, the false inference is made that from the fact of uneasiness, the justification and the rational authorization for this uneasiness is deduced; from that false deduction, Schopenhauer first arrives at his fanciful conclusion about a so-called intelligible freedom. (Plato and Kant are equally culpable in the emergence of this mythic creature.)

49, 13–14 *of the consequences.*] *Pd*: of wholly losing their eyesight, hence of the [presumed] consequences. But philosophy should attend not to the consequences of truth, but only to the truth itself.

49, 14 *consequences.*] *Sd*: 20 [2] follows at this point.

40: 49, 16 *Ueber-Thier*] This is one of the earliest occurrences in Nietzsche's writing of a noun constructed with the prefix *Ueber*, here joined with "animal" to characterize human beings as beyond, yet retaining unerasable traces of, their animal origins.

41: 49, 29 *the motives*] *Se*: the new [motives]

42: 50, 19 *not*] *Se*: *not*

43: 51, 2–3 *But...rolls.*] *Sd*: But these organs have developed further, have themselves become more delicate, have been brought into connection with other ones that continually supply a counteremotion to cruelty.

44: 51, 14 *Swift*] This comment was actually made by Alexander Pope.

46: 52, 29–32 *offense...him*] *Pd*: offense than we do—then perhaps the disciples of a martyr suffer more than the martyr.

50: 54, 14 *Plato's*] Plato, *The Republic*, bk. 3, 387–88.

54, 14 *soul*] La Rochefoucauld, 4.

55,18 pudendum] "object of shame."

55,21 faire."] "Know, too, that there is nothing more common than doing ill for the pleasure of doing it." Prosper Mérimée, *Lettres à une inconnue* (Paris, 1874), I, 8.

51: 55, 33 inherits] Pm, Fe: practices ⟨reading error by Gast⟩

54: 57, 14 others] Jonathan Swift, *Humoristische Werke* (Stuttgart, 1844), 2: 188.

57: 59, 27 individuum] "indivisible"; *dividuum]* "divisible."

64: at end of Sd: Self-defense is in order against such backward people, that is, a way of helping oneself that also grew only in earlier cultures: but we are led back into them if someone is too coarse and backward to understand a more refined spirit: the best mode of self-defense is clearly expressed contempt: a cold, scornful word directed at the irate person, a smile and gesturing hands as a reaction to a cold, malicious glance.

67: 62, 25 sancta simplicitas] "holy simplicity."

69: 63, 29 as well.] Matthew 5:45.

71: 64, 23 agony.] Pd: agony—thus Hesiod understood hope: this old Boeotian, however, was not understood by the philologists. Who today is a Boeotian?

80: 67, 4–6 respectable...life.] Pd: respectable, that should be self-evident. But Christianity has falsified people's feelings concerning this: we must learn how to feel naturally.

81: 67, 25 Xerxes] Herodotus, bk. 7, 38–39.

87: 68, 24 Luke 18:14] "For every one who exalts himself will be humbled, but he who humbles himself will be exalted."

91: 70, 2 moralité larmoyante] "morality of tears."

92: 70, 11 ambassadors] Thucydides, bk. 5, 87–111.

93: 71, 20–21 valet"] "Each person has as much right as he has power"; *creditur"]* "as the power he is believed to have." This phrase occurs throughout Spinoza's *Tractatus Theologico-Politicus* and is cited by Schopenhauer in *Parerga and Paralipomena*, trans. E. F. J. Payne (Oxford, Clarendon Press, 1974), 2, sec. 124, 242. R. H. M. Elwes translates the phrase in his edition of the *Tractatus* (London, 1895) as "the rights of an individual extend to the utmost limits of his power as it has been conditioned" (ch. 16, 200). As this chapter of Spinoza's text makes clear, "right" is used to signal the nature and limits of moral responsibility. Thus, "he who does not yet know reason, or has not yet acquired the habit of virtue, acts solely according to the laws of his desire with as sovereign a right as he who orders his life entirely by the laws of reason" (201).

96: Se: To be moral, to follow custom, to be virtuous, means showing obedience to long-established law or tradition. Whether we submit to it with difficulty or readily does not matter for a long time; it is enough that we do so. We eventually [today] call someone "good" who, as if by nature, after long inheritance, hence easily and readily, does what is customary, whatever this may be (takes revenge, for instance, if taking revenge belongs to good moral behavior, as among the ancient Greeks). He is called good because he is good "for something"; but since benevolence, sympathy, concern for others, moderation, and the like were always felt to be "good for something," to be useful amid the shifting of customs, we later refer especially to the benevolent, helpful person as "good"—originally there were other, more important types of usefulness — — — Evil means being "not moral" (immoral), acting against custom, resisting tradition, however reasonable or stupid it may be; but in all the moral codes of various times, harming the community (and the "neighbor" contained within it) has been particularly felt to be the genuinely immoral, so that now the word "evil" makes us think first of harming our neighbor and our community intentionally. The fundamental opposition that human beings have used for differentiating moral and immoral, good and evil, is not the "egotistical" and the "unegotistical," but instead: attachment to a tradition or law and dissociation from it. How the tradition originated does not matter here; it was in any case without regard to good and evil or any immanent categorical imperative, but above all for the purpose of preserving a community, a familial association... ⟨remainder identical to printed text, except that "morality of piety" is underlined in *Se*⟩.

99: 76, 17 *greater] Se:* stronger

100: 76, 35 *adytum]* The innermost part of a temple; the secret shrine from where oracles were delivered.

101: 77, 17 *Judge not.]* "Judge not, that you not be judged." Matthew 7:1.

77, 22 *Genevan]* PmN: noble

77, 32 *have learned]* Se: have been habituated

103: 79, 13 *Schopenhauer says?]* On Ethics, Parerga, 2, sec. 114, 214

79, 24–34 *Solely...second]* Pm: Only utility, that is, concern for the consequences, for some eventual displeasure, can originally forbid such actions. Sympathy is not an original, but instead a late phenomenon. Moreover, it is not pure pain, [for it has two elements of] but instead a pleasure in emotion and,

104: 80, 10–11 *we...self-preservation]* Pm: (for example, in the lie of necessity, as Schopenhauer describes it). But where is there anything immoral?

80, 21–22 *thus...toy]* Pm: thus, it is not immoral, for instance, for a child to be cruel to animals, as an Italian would be.

80, 31–81, 8 *But what...intellect]* Pm: On the other hand, human beings are sympathetic as a result of having flirted with strong sensations, whence the art of tragedy, the pleasure in executions.

105: 81, 30–34 *disappear...vanity.]* Sd: be suppressed.—In the relationship between worker and employer, "salary" is a false concept: it is here a matter of the contractual exchange of products, according to whether the one has more need of this, the other of that kind of product: thus, the worker has more need of money, housing, food, the employer of someone else's bodily or intellectual energies.

106: 82, 16 *mechanism.]* Sd: mechanism, [a false conception that frequently works as a motive, for example, when we praise, reward, punish, take revenge, and so on.]

107: Pd: The total irresponsibility of a human being for his behavior and his nature is the bitterest drop that the man of knowledge must swallow: although we might at first like to believe the exact opposite. All our evaluations, distinctions, and aversions are thereby devalued and falsified: our deepest feeling, which we offer up to endurance and heroism, is nothing more than an error; we are allowed neither to praise nor to blame, just as we neither praise nor blame nature. Just as we love [or do not love] but do not praise a good work of art, because it cannot help being what it is, just as we stand before a plant, so we must stand before the actions of human beings, before our own actions. We can admire the strength, beauty, and fullness [and so on] of them, but cannot find any merit therein. The chemical process has just as little [much] merit as the laborious struggle of a father who must decide whether to sacrifice his daughter or to defile his mouth with a lie (as the great W. Scott depicts it in the dungeon of Edinburgh) or the sacrifice of 8 sons, which the aged teacher of a chieftan makes for the latter's fame (splendidly told in the beautiful maiden of Perth). First of all, these actions contain an error as their motives, in the former case that there is a God who forbids lying, in the latter case that the fame of a chieftain counts for more than the life of 8 sons. And second, our feeling is connected to that false conception previously mentioned, as if these figures could even have acted or even have decided differently. — If we perceive that all motives of honor and shame must be left aside because we honor or blame only "free" actions and not natural processes, we do not in our sorrow know how it is that people really ought to continue to live: if not according to motives of utility, which are in turn those of pleasure and displeasure. — But to appraise truth itself higher than untruth — [why? This is already morality.] how do we come to do such a thing in regard to that very sentence? Is this a concern of utility or of morality?

Chapter 3: Notes

- *108: Pd*: One can either eliminate a misfortune or alter our state of mind concerning this misfortune (a different effect) therapeutics influence of a toothache on our sensibility — art
- Added above *Sd*: decrease of energy when religion and art appear (in Plato's favor)
- *109: Sd*: How can we exchange the false assumption that there is a God who wants what is good, who is the watcher and witness of every action and of every moment, who loves us and wants

the best for us in every affliction—how can we exchange this for truths that are just as salutary and beneficial? Such truths do not exist; philosophy can at best set untruths against them. Yet the tragedy is that we cannot believe those untruths if we have the strict method of truth in our hearts, but on the other hand, the development of humanity has made us so delicate and irritable that we need remedies and consolation.

86, 3 *priests*] *Se*: *homines religiosi* "religious men."

86, 17 *truth.*] *Se*: truth, or more precisely: from seeing through error.

86, 20 *life."*] *Manfred*, 1.1.10-12. Byron's text has "deepest" rather than "deepst" in line 11.

86, 27 *jacentes"*] Horace, *Odes*, bk. 2, 11, lines 11-14. "Why then to endless cares excite / Thy wearied mind's unequal powers?/ No, rather free from toil and care, / Beneath the pine or plane-tree spread." Translation by H. E. Butler (Boston, 1932).

87, 4 *conscience.*] "conscience! There therefore remains: — — —

110: Cf. 19 [100].

87, 16 *sensu allegorico*] "through the allegorical sense."

88, 4 *truth.*] Schopenhauer, "On Religion," *Parerga*, vol. 2.

89, 3 *consensus gentium...hominum*] "a consensus of all human races ...of all men."

89, 5 *consensus omnium sapientium*] "a consensus of all those who know."

89, 11 *fitting!"*] Goethe, "Kophtisches Lied," lines 3-7.

89, 13-14 *to be folly.*] *Se*: to be only folly.

111: This fragment is a reworking of section 2 of Nietzsche's lectures of 1875-76, "Der Gottesdienst der Griechen," *Vorlesungaufzeichnungen*, in *Werke*, ed. Fritz Bornmann, 366-69.

89, 31 *moira*] "fate."

90, 3 *Lubbock*] John Lubbock's study in historical anthropology appeared in a German translation by A. Passow, with an introduction by R. Virchow in 1875 (Jena) as *Die Entstehung der Civilisation und der Urzustand des Menschengeschlechtes, erläutert durch das innere und äußere Leben der Wilden*; acquired by Nietzsche on 28 July 1875.

90, 17 *his subjectivity*] *Se*: the music and the noise of his soul

112: at end of *Sd*: on Archilochus Sappho

113: *Pd*: Morning churchbells in the Berne Alps—in honor of a crucified Jew who claimed to be the son of God.

Pd: Is it believable that something like that is still believed?

Pd: Son of God—belief without proof is already a piece of antiquity.

114: Cf. 5 [150].

94, 14 *symmachia]* "alliance."

118: 96, 3 *disciples.]* *Pd*: Religions should never prevail, but always only be coming into being.

119: Cf. 19 [56].

123: Cf. 19 [63].

125: Cf. 5 [196].

131: 99, 22 *Madonnas"]* Schopenhauer, *The World as Will and Representation*, vol. 1, bk. 4, sec. 71.

133: 102, 14 *us"]* Lichtenberg, "Bemerkungen," *Vermischte Schriften* (Göttingen, 1867), sec. 1, 83.

102, 16 *trompé."]* "If we think we love our mistress out of love for her, we are very much mistaken." La Rochefoucauld, *Réflexions*, maxim 374, 77.

137: title in *Sd*: *On explaining cynicism*

Pd: Defiance of oneself (Schopenhauer and asceticism). To express views that are harmful to oneself, disavow earlier ones, call down upon oneself the disdain of others. A very high degree of passion for power and domination that rises up against one's own base fearfulness, mountain climber.

105, 31 *spernere se sperni]* "to answer disdain with disdain." Hildebert of Lavardius, *Carmina Miscellanea*, 124.

138: title in *Sd*: *Moral greatness from affect*

139: 107, 23–28 *The saint…reflection.]* *Sd*: Therefore: everywhere that the will is not exceptionally strong and free, its complete subjection is desirable. Otherwise, there is wavering, lack of clarity, a partial release from moral customs; the happiness of morality does not accompany such a man.—But the higher thing is to be one's own law.

140: Cf. 23 [113].

141: 108, 27–31 *But in order…more]* *Sd*: Instead of being thankful that certain bodily functions necessary to good health are connected to pleasure, they stigmatized them and used the word "pleasure" with a contemptuous meaning;

109, 1 *truth.*] *Sd*: truth. [In this, humanity must return to the harmless view of the Greeks, whose gloomiest philosopher, Empedocles, sees in Aphrodite—two human beings who take pleasure in each other—the best, happiest, and most hopeful phenomenon on earth and reveals absolutely none of that monkish, half-lustful horror with which Schopenhauer views these things.—Plato, admittedly, slandered all the senses, first and foremost the eyes and ears; and after all, even among the Greeks there are exceptions who exhibit unreason and unnaturalness.]

109, 1-7 *Of course...born.*] *Pd*: A thought that in superlative Christianity is once more knotted together—into the most entangled paradox that I know. Thus, procreation and birth are the fault of the child that has just been conceived and born (not that of the father, the mother).

109, 7 *born."*] Pedro Calderón de la Barca, *La Vida es Sueno*, 1: 2, quoted by Schopenhauer, *World*, vol. 1, sec. 63.

109, 9 *itself*] *Sd*: itself, [as it is for Schopenhauer,]

109, 16 *spirit*] Empedocles, *On Nature*, 35.

110, 30 *animated.*] *Sd*: animated: [(Christianity is the creation of an overripe period of culture: as such, it works upon fresh, barbaric peoples like poison and corruption) while the spirit of antiquity wanted a particular kind of emotion, that of joy at every level, the Christian spirit sought for the *emotion* of pain (from which the yearning for a licentious feeling of pleasure incidentally and occasionally grew).]

142: 112, 9-14 *Novalis...tendency.*] *Sd*: His artistic skill lies in spinning out of himself a sequence of inner states that every other man likewise knows and experiences, though the latter does so under the contingency of external influences, the former from purely internal motives, from the coupling together of faulty knowledge, good intentions, and ruined health.—This insight should not hinder us from conceding that the ascetic and the saint, with regard to their result if not their elements, belong among the most splendid and fruitful forces in humanity—within a certain space of time, in which religious madness displaced all sense for truth.

112, 12–14 *tendency."]* Novalis, *Schriften*, ed. R. Samuel and P. Kluckhohn (Leipzig, 1928), 3: 294, cited by Nietzsche from the Tieck-Schlegel edition of 1815, 2: 250.

143: 112, 26–27 *pneumatic interpretation of the Bible]* See note to Aphorism 8.

Chapter 4: Notes

145: Cf. 22 [36].

114, 9–10 *Paestum]* Called Posidonia by the Greeks, this city in Lucania is the site of the ruins of two renowned Doric temples.

147: 115, 25–30 *he has...limitation]* Sd: he has remained a child or an adolescent, at an early age his aesthetic drive overcame him, and he can only represent things homogeneous with that period.

148: Cf. 5 [162].

149: 116, 20–22 *What...error.]* Sd: The beauty of the Gulf of Naples by evening light, seen from Posilipp, is this sort of beauty [and the adagios of Beethoven].

151: crossed out at the beginning of *Sd*: One principal device used by the idealizing poet is a sort of impure thinking. Meter in particular assists him in this.

153: 117, 32–118, 3 *If...test.]* Sd: Every spiritual gain is tied up with losses, therefore long development {is necessary} and beginning with the naive conceptions of religion! That is best taught — — —

154: Cf. 5 [115], 5 [121].

118, 11 *Simonides]* Theon, *Progymnasmata*, 33. Walz 1: 215.

158: 120, 14–15 *Every...art.]* Pd: Degeneration follows every manifestation of greatness, even among the Greeks. At every moment, the impetus toward a terrible outcome seems to be present.

120, 19 *them.]* Pd: them, just as Rome finally lay amid desolation.

160: at the upper edge of the *Sd*: They are related to real characters as the shoe in the painter's picture is to the real shoe. And the painter's knowledge of shoes stands in general in the same relation to the knowledge that the shoemaker has of them. Cf. 22 [77].

161: 122, 19 *orator]* Hegesias of Magnesias.

162: 123, 10–11 *stars"]* Nietzsche is citing (somewhat inaccurately) from Goethe's poem "Between Both Worlds." The first line actually reads "William! Star of the loveliest height." The subsequent quotation comes from Goethe's poem "Comfort in Tears."

163: *Pd*: What is talent, natural gifts! All modern men have it; the greatest artists have sometimes been only slightly gifted. But character, the earnestness of the artisan are lacking: one wants to paint something perfect immediately. First 100 outlines for short stories, then more science, nature, excerpts, notebooks full of thoughts, and so on. And like Scott, wait for years. Always to be telling stories (anecdotes), collecting characters.

164: 126, 3 *work.]* *Sd*: work. Even the concept "genius" has a religious origin: we should believe neither in a god nor in any associated idea of genius any more.

126, 23 *humanity.]* Plato, *Phaedrus*, 244a.

165: crossed out at the end of the *Sd*: as Goethe, for example, so many times. Schiller would not have been in the position to make something as bad as the "Aroused."

Nietzsche is referring here to a play by Goethe, begun in 1793 but completed only in 1816 after its initial publication in fragmentary form in 1814.

171: Cf. 22 [82].

129, 25 *in majorem artis gloriam]* "for the greater glory of art."

172: Cf. 22 [82].

173: 130, 14 *corriger la fortune]* "correcting fate."

173: 130, 18 *sonata]* Beethoven's Piano Sonata no. 29, opus 106, the *Hammerklavier*.

184: *Pd*: It is not the best of a book that is untranslatable, but instead only (the intellectual limits of what is individual in it) what is unfree in the individual.

188: Cf. 19 [22].

192: Cf. 19 [32].

NOTES TO PAGES 134-45

194: 134, 27-30 *whom...insanity.]* *Pm*: and on account of the overstimulation of their nervous systems, really not completely responsible for their actions.

195: 135, 2-5 *It stands...higher]* *Pm*: All words are used in exaggerated ways; we have dug the furrow as deeply as possible, for example, art, custom, property, and so on. The highest

196: *Pd*: One often finds among middling writers, among the manufacturers of sensationalist novels (Miss Braddon), the greatest psychological certainty, perhaps along with an incapacity to provide reasons for the actions. "How would you act?"—just as the greatest pianist has perhaps reflected very little upon the technical conditions and the special virtues and vices of every finger (dactylic ethics) (utility, educability of the fingers).

203: 138, 6 *barbaric,]* *Pm*: barbarism [especially given such bad teachers:]

138, 21 *practice.]* *Sd*: practice. Putting Greek in place of Latin is another sort of barbarism: if it is only a case of getting to know great works, it is all right, but people of that age are not mature enough; one must first have sailed through the reefs of our culture in order to sail into that harbor with pleasure. Thus, premature acquaintance only spoils the more profound effect. But everything is a lie among teachers and students; during all of their lives, neither one nor the other reaches the point of having a genuine feeling for anything ancient, nor even for Goethe; they do not even rightly know what tastes good and have always simply been ashamed of deviating from others in their sensibility.

205: Cf. 22 [64].

206: 139, 8 *tiptoe...joy.]* *Sd*: tiptoe. Wieland, for example, understood how to brew such a drink out of marvelous free-spiritedness and ribaldry.

208: beneath the aphorism title in *Sd*: Afterlife of the Greeks

212: Cf. 19 [99], 21 [75].

141, 18 *superstitious]* *Pm*: superstitious? [Or sexual satisfaction less infatuated?]

217: 145, 7-12 *In...understanding.]* *Pd*: Just as Böcklin, for example, in a way makes the eye more intellectual and goes far beyond pleasure in colors; the ugly side of the world has been conquered by the aesthetic understanding.

219: 146, 16 *Council of Trent]* The Catholic council held intermittently from 1545 to 1563 in Trent, on the Alpine borders of Germany and Italy, as a response to the Protestant secession. Although it produced numerous reforms within the Catholic Church, it rejected any compromise with Protestant positions on doctrinal matters.

146, 20 *character.]* *Sd*: character[; hence a restored Protestantism].

146, 28 *Polyhymnia.]* One of the nine Greek muses; the muse of the sublime hymn.

146, 34 *life.]* *Sd*: life. [If the thought of a rebirth of the ancient world now surfaces once again, we will long for a more inspired ancient world than did the fifteenth century.]

147, 1 *Murillo]* *Sd, Pm, Up, Cw*: Carracci

147, 3–5 *if our...doubt it.]* *Sd*: if Beethoven's music were to move stones, it would do this in a way more like Bernini than like antiquity.

147, 8–11 *the juxtaposition...Renaissance.]* *Sd*: ecstasy and naiveté juxtaposed. We all, insofar as we are not yet modern, are a bit Berninian.

220: 147, 23 *Gothic cathedrals]* *Sd*: Wagner's art

221: 148, 8 *finally]* *Pm*: finally, due to Wagner,

148, 29 *Mahomet]* Voltaire's play appeared in 1741.

149, 21 *longer?]* *Sd*: longer? [We are already clearly being pushed more and more toward the worship of primitive poetic conditions.] Can a poetry that has gone wild, that revels in the cult of power, of color, of effects, maintain respect for art? Won't it, because of its intent to intoxicate, have to bring a feeling of disgust in its wake? Won't science with its pitiless whip of logic always inevitably triumph in a place where debauchery and disgust have degraded the concept of art?

150, 12 *opinion."]* Lord Byron, in a letter to John Murray of 15 September 1817. The actual quotation reads "With regard to poetry in general I am convinced the more i think of it—that he and *all* of us—Scott—Southey—Wordsworth—Moore—Campbell—

I—are all in the wrong—one as much as another—that we are upon a wrong revolutionary poetical system—or systems—not worth a damn in itself—& from which none but Rogers and Crabbe are free—and that the present & next generations will finally be of this opinion." *Byron's Letters and Journals*, ed. Leslie A. Marchand (Cambridge, Mass.: Harvard University Press, 1976) 5: 265.

150, 14 *writers."*] Lord Byron, in a letter to John Murray, 14 July 1821. The actual quotation reads "You will find all this very *un*like Shakespeare—and so much the better in one sense—for I look upon him to be the *worst* of models—though the most extraordinary of writers." *Byron's Letters and Journals*, 8: 152.

222: 151, 34 *good."*] This is the final verse of Goethe's poem "The Bridegroom."

152, 7–12 *Just as...one.*] *Pd*: Music is the measure of the wealth of feeling that has actually been acquired; the many concepts and false judgments that helped us get there are forgotten; the intensity and variety of feeling remains and demands its satisfaction. Music purges it partially.

223: 152, 23–34 *Greece...see it.*] *Pm*: Greece. We view the artist himself as a relic and honor him as something primeval and venerable on which the happiness of earlier times depended; what is best in us has perhaps been inherited from the sensations of earlier times, which we can scarcely approach in an immediate way any more.

Chapter 5: Notes

224: Cf. 12 [22]

153, 4 *Refinement...degeneration.*] *Pd*: Value of wounding

153, 6–8 *have a sense...beliefs.*] *Pd*: live with a sense of community and with other sympathetic affections.

154, 19 *free*] *Pp, Fe*: fine

154, 36 *freedom."*] Machiavelli, *The Prince*.

154, 31–155, 4 *As for...resist that.*] added in *Pm*; *Sd* continues with 20 [11].

225: 155, 30–35 *Moreover...faith.*] *Pd*: The only question is whether

226: 156, 5–10 *an Englishman...England...Englishness...an Englishman*] *Pd*: "a German...Germany...Germanness...a German

227: 156, 24 *pudendum*] "object of shame."

230: 158, 32 *esprit fort*] "a strong spirit."

231: *Pd*: The free spirit emerges like the genius. Three forms of this emergence. Then application to the free spirit.

159, 15–19 *I have...talents.*] *Pd*: When someone also has to perform the functions of the eye with the ear, his eye becomes sharper. The loss or defect of one characteristic frequently causes some talent to develop brilliantly.

233: Cf. 5 [191], 5 [194].

234: Cf. 5 [185].

235: Cf. 5[188].

161, 13–14 *again and again?*] *Sd*: again and again? The highest judgment about the value of life would perhaps then be the result of that moment in which the tension between opposites in chaos, between will and intellect, would be the strongest, specifically as a struggle within the being of a single individual.

162, 1–5 *The state...thwarted.*] *Pd*: Both, taken together, give us the *fatum tristissimum*.

fatum tristissimum] "the saddest of fates."

236: at the top of *Sd*: Transition of the Greeks from the tragic into the temperate zone: Sophists. ⟨The same phrase appears as the title in *Pm*.⟩

237: 164, 7 *the Enlightenment*] *Sd*: science

241: at the end of *Sd*: ⟨Prom(etheus) and his vulture⟩

242: 166, 23 *integrated*] *Pm* and *Fe*: initiated

243: 167, 5–6 *diplomat's smoothness*] *Pm*: matchmaker's smoothness

167, 9 *lawyer in understanding*] *Se*: attorney in divining

246: *Pd*: Furrowed hollows later meadows—metaphor for wildness.

248: 169, 28–30 *Ah...appartenons.*] Ah, my dear Sulzer, you do not know well enough this cursed race to which we belong.

250: 171, 9–17 *They are...demeanor?*] *Pd*: They are not brave, free men, but instead curious, decrepit courtiers of the aged, indeed senile, culture.

251: 172, 4–6 *If this requirement...near-certainty.] Pm*: Otherwise, development will proceed differently, if it is not consciously directed.

172, 11–14 *humanity...once again?] Pm*: Sterne once said something in *Tristram* about this whole process.

252: Pd: Why is knowledge pleasureable?—1) Because we become conscious of our strength 2) are victorious over others 3) in general raise ourselves above everyone else by knowing better on a single point. Host of secondary reasons. The methods of knowledge have been won by conflict.

Noted by Nietzsche in *Sd*: citation on the motives of scholars from me

172, 30 *my paraenetic essay] Pp*: Friedrich Nietzsche in his paraenesis {*Human, All Too Human* was originally supposed to appear under a pseudonym}.

172, 35 *together"]* "Schopenhauer as Educator," *CW*, 2: 230. {Nietzsche slightly alters the original here.}

173, 2 *stimuli"]* "Schopenhauer as Educator," *CW*, 2: 225.

256: 174, 19 *time.] Pm*: time. [This must be required of all human beings; then things will proceed more logically in politics and morality.]

257: 174, 22–23 *gray and tedious] Pm*: despotic and obtrusive

174, 23–26 *to be sure...In almost] Pm*: the youth embraces his love differently than does the man. Likewise, in almost

174, 31–32 *historical disciplines] Pm*: disciplines of philology

258: 175, 3 *Perseus]* Benvenuto Cellini, *The Autobiography of Benevenuto Cellini*, trans. John Addington Symonds (New York: Garden City Publishing, 1932), 2, sec. 58, 424–25.

259: Pd: Somewhat in the way that now the higher education of women was founded in marriage (for in loving the mortal gives of his best).

175, 13 *oration]* Cf. Thucydides, 2: 45.

175, 24–25 *best."]* "denn liebend giebt der Sterbliche vom Besten." Friedrich Hölderlin, "The Death of Empedocles," 2: 4. Nietzsche's citation comes from Friedrich Hölderlin, *Kurze Biographie und Proben aus seinen Werken* (Leipzig, 1859).

175, 27–32 *the aspect...the sole] Sd*: τεκνοποιία ἡδονή {bearing children, pleasure} —nothing more, no spiritual intercourse, no genuine affairs of love. And then the ἀγών {contest}, which likewise excluded women. The religious cults were the sole

261: 176, 28 *gloom?] Pm:* gloom? [how could they stand this gloom?]

176, 34 *its paths...it] Pm:* the thinker; at that time one

177, 36 *tortoise.] Pm:* tortoise[: always slowly forward.]

178, 8 *Achilles]* Nietzsche is referring to one of Zeno of Elea's paradoxes, which argued that if the tortoise had a head start on Achilles in a race, Achilles would never catch up; for while Achilles covered the initial distance separating them, the tortoise will have advanced further, and so on indefinitely.

178, 8 *the tortoise...Achilles] Pm:* the stone and stupidity

178, 13–15 *in one night...destroyed.] Pm:* overnight the [philosophizing] Greeks fell fatally ill.

178, 21–22 *themselves...announcing them.] Pm:* brought to fulfillment; the scissors always cut in between.

178, 26 *transmitted to us; all] Pm:* transmitted to us, hard to read; thus, all

178, 27–29 *whoever...purest type] Pm:* I sense a wealth of the most singular and beautiful types, the best of which the Greeks later forgot.

178, 33 *depictions of them.] Pm:* depictions of them[; he lacks in an almost enigmatic way the sense for great and polyphonic natures.]

178, 35–36 *hordes...schools.] Pm:* tribes of Stoics and Epicureans.

179, 29–30 *ochlocratic]* "rule of the mob."

262: Cf. 5 [146].

180, 13 *or science] Sd:* and Aristotle

263: 180, 19 *becomes what he is]* A favorite quotation of Nietzsche's, from Pindar's Pythian Ode 2, 72; used as the subtitle to *Ecce Homo*.

264: 180, 30–33 *it is...knowledge.] Sd:* it is not the woman who gleams, shines, and stimulates, but instead the often plain, unpretentious truth whom he woos.

265: Pd: von Bär reason in school

181, 17 *man"]* Goethe, *Faust*, Part 1, lines 1851–52.

266: Pd: Value of the abstract talk of teachers in the *Gymnasium*.

181, 31 *Gymnasium]* The German *Gymnasium* is a secondary school with a highly rigorous course of study designed to prepare students for the university.

267: Pd: The absurd learning of many languages! We fill the memory with words and sounds.

183, 9 *language!]* *Pm* and *Fe*: language?

269: Pd: We can stand ahead of our time in our views, yet only so far ahead that we anticipate the vulgar views of the next decade, hence merely adhere to public opinion before it is public (for example, Hillebrand).

271: 184, 16 *judgments"]* Schopenhauer, *Ethics*, 114.

184, 17–21 *attained...principle]* *Sd*: become predominant. Drawing conclusions that are false is the rule, as for example in the way that mythology equates cows and clouds.

272: Cf. 16 [28], 23 [145].

185, 4 *Goethe for example]* *Sd*: Luther Goethe Wagner

185, 5 *four]* *Pm*: six

185, 9–28 *People...years.]* *Sd*: We pass ever more quickly through the usual phases of past culture. We begin as religious persons, whose greatest liveliness lies perhaps at the age of 10, then pass over into attenuated forms (pantheism) while we are approaching science, get completely beyond God immortality and the like, but lapse into a metaphysical philosophy; this, too, loses credibility for us, art seems to impart the most to us (metaphysics as disposition) but the scientific sense becomes ever more rigorous and now we arrive at natural science and history etc.—all within 30 years.

273: Pd: Anyone who presently begins with religion metaphysics art goes backward a ways and to that extent loses strength and time. But he has thereby gained a springboard for a greater leap forward and quickly reaches the front again.

274: Cf. 21 [68].

276: heading above *Sd*: Plato as a cultural power

278: 188, 33–34 *between...maintain]* *Pm*: in regard to culture can be maintained only with difficulty

279: 189, 19–21 *Everyone...trick.]* *Sd*: Everyone who idealizes things must understand how to see out of his own eyes as well as out of the eyes of some specific other person.

282: Pd: Unfashionable: our time suffers from the absence of great

342   NOTES TO PAGES 190–94

moralists—Montaigne Plutarch are not read—the *vita contemplativa* generally not respected. Cloisters abolished, rage for work—disdain, even hatred for divergent views even among scholars, "madness"—tremendous acceleration of life, hence seeing and judging partially or falsely as during a train ride—disdain for free spirits by scholars ("thoroughness," "division of labor")

Pd: absence of moralists—Montaigne Larochef(oucauld) no longer read—the *vita contemplativa* disdained—cloisters abolished—lack of the reflective life—disdain for divergent views—hatred even among scholars.—tremendous acceleration of life.—Hence seeing and judging partially or falsely—disdain for free spirits by scholars (for example, Lichtenberg's)

190, 12 *vita contemplativa*] "a life devoted to contemplation or meditation."

283: Cf. 16[38], 16[40].

191, 5 *species being*] *Gattungswesen* is a term of central importance for Feuerbach and Marx, defined at length by Feuerbach in Chapter 1 of *The Essence of Christianity* (1841).

284: 191, 22 *otium*] "leisure."

191, 21–27 *Scholars...sloths?*—] *Pd*: In an age that has forgotten what leisure or *otium* is, a word in favor of idleness may also be permitted.

285: Cf. 17 [53], 17 [54], 17 [55].

192, 7 *element.*] *Sd*: element: [(at which we might most easily succeed by mixing Asian and Russian-peasant blood with European and American).]

286 Cf. 16 [42], 16 [43].

192, 19 *well.*] *Sd, Pd*: well. (Moreover, things are divided into those concerning which knowledge and those concerning which opinions are possible; we can speak only of the latter category of things here.)

287: 192, 26, *Censor vitae*] "The censor of life."

288: at end of *Pd*: It is a struggle against the necessity that ostensibly encompasses human beings.

289: 193, 13–14 *mind...him.*] *Pd*: mind. The sick person is often healthier in his soul than the healthy person.

292: 194, 25 *step and a steady*] *Sd*: step, good courage, and a steady

194, 29 *knowledge.*] *Sd*: knowledge. [The sciences are encamped

around you and look toward you: they wait lined up in rows for
you to become their leader.]

194, 34 religious] Sd: religious[, through music,]

195, 10–11 on the one hand—on the other.] Sd: relativism

195, 19–32 the experiments...refreshment.] Sd: happiness unhappiness injustice love friendship dissolve into your goal without remainder. Collect the honey of knowledge from diverse afflictions disturbances illnesses: whether you stand alone, are hated, misunderstood, disdained: the clouds of misfortune hanging over you are the udders from which you will squeeze your milk.

196, 4–5 anger...sound.] Sd: anger: you have recognized it: and called to it—and it was good.

Chapter 6: Notes

294: Pd: Many people behave like copies of people greater than themselves and many people are better pleased with these copies than with the originals—just as with pictures.

295: Cf. 19 [12].

301: Pd: The surest means for reassuring people who are extremely embarrassed is to praise them.

304: Pd: compelling intimacy

306: Sd: The physician is either a genius or an actor; the most dangerous physicians are those who imitate the ingenious physician in an ingenious way.

Pd: The physician is either a genius or an actor; the most dangerous physicians are the actors who imitate the genius well enough to be confused with him and perhaps deceive even him.

309: 199, 25 *offences.]* Pd: offences: they burden us with them.

310: 199, 28–29 *thoughts...immoral.]* Pd: tormenting thoughts in their heads is: to make them wait for a long time. Christianity has made people immoral, because it promised them the final judgment and up to now has kept them waiting for it.

312: Pd: Giving to someone whom we have injured the opportunity for a witticism in order to put him in good humor or even to give him personal satisfaction in regard to us is a diplomat's trick.

324: Pd: Society in Basel. Nobody thanks the clever person for the sacrifice he makes when he visits a social circle where cleverness is lacking (where it is not polite to be clever).

331: at the end of *Pp*: Everyone is at home on a different star.

335: Cf. 17 [14].

337: *Pd*: We are mistaken about the degree to which we believe ourselves to be hated or feared, out of vanity—important.

341: 205, 18 *an even greater rage] Pm, Fe*: an even greater ill-humor. ⟨misreading by Gast⟩

346: 206, 29 *engendered] Pm, Fe*: aroused

349: *Sd*: When we contradict an opinion, we generally lay out our own opinion wrongly, or at least differently than we would otherwise have laid it out.

351: *Pd*: Why I have pangs of conscience after social gatherings: 1 2 3 4 5 reasons.

352: *Pd*: We are misjudged; the annoyance does not cease when we reflect upon it. Even worse when we are judged correctly.

354: *Pd*: Φίλτατοι—relatives!

Φίλτατοι "most beloved or dearest ones."

360: Cf. 5 [184].

367: 212, 14 *sans gêne]* "without embarrassment or constraint."

368: 212, 31 *called a ladder] Fe: called* a ladder; other manuscript and proof stages: called a ladder

369: *Pd*: In conversation with someone, we are happiest when we have the opportunity to let our spirit and charm shine: two people who know human nature and are conversing with each other could toss a *fine opportunity* for some witticism back and forth, because each graciously allows the other to have it in order to gain for himself the advantage of the other person's good favor.

371: *Pd*: Why are inclination and aversion so infectious? Because refraining from pro and con is so hard and agreement so pleasant.

372: *Pd*: Irony a pedagogical technique of the teacher (Socrates). Precondition: that it be taken seriously for a time as modesty and suddenly expose the *other person's presumption*. Otherwise it is silly fooling around.—Sarcasm is the quality of snappish dogs in the human spirit: to which is added the human element of malicious laughter.—We ruin ourselves if we cultivate our skill in this.

At top of *Sd*: Plato

373: Pd: Presumption in affection, in friendly advice, in admission of errors, in pity for others. This evil drop spoils everything {—} "to seem more important than we are"—a miscalculation of presumption underlies this. We atone for the momentary success by a sort of revenge that is taken by those who have suffered from our presumption. Nothing is to be warned against more strongly. We can grind our greatest merit completely into the dust. People make us pay most dearly for humiliating them. Even a proud demeanor makes sense only where we are certain not to be taken as presumptuous (friends, wives).

Pd: Presumption in signs of respect, in benevolent familiarity.

374: Pd: Dialogue (letter), otherwise among many people everyone: "this is what I am, this is what I say, now make of it whatever you please!"

375: Pd: Waiting for recognition from the future only makes sense if humanity were to remain unchanged.—So it would only mean: eventually being understood in our historical isolation.

217, 6 *thesis] Pm, Fe*: affair ⟨misreading by Gast⟩

376: at the end of *Pd*: 12 March 1877

Chapter 7: Notes

378: 219, 11 *wife, because] Sd*: wife; first, because the instinct for friendship is very strong in him, and next, because

379: Pd: Children have to rediscover the unresolved dissonances between their parents afterward in themselves and to suffer from them.

219, 14–16 *resonate...sufferings.] Pd*: will reappear in their child; the history of his inner sufferings can be deduced from this.

380: Pd: Men love women according to the image of woman drawn from their mother that they carry inside themselves.

381: Cf. 19 [13].

382: Cf. 18 [40].

383: 220, 13–15 *A mother...himself.] Sd*: Fathers more rarely.

388: Cf. 16 [31].

389: 221, 3 *mother.]* Plato describes Aphrodite in the *Symposium* 203b–d as the offspring of *poros* (resource) and *penia* (penury, need).

392: Cf. 16 [17].

221, 13–14 *some...appears.] Sd*: the maternal element is included, not, however, the paternal element.

393: Cf. 18 [38].

394: 221, 20–24 *downward...medicine.] Pd*: downward. But many men require an association that pulls them downward. And the risk of neurosis!

221, 22–24 *Men...medicine.] Up*: Men or women who are too spiritual in nature require an association that pulls them downward.

397: 222, 10–11 *slowly....still.] Pd*: slowly; every love continues to grow.

401: 222, 27–29 *alone....as well.] Pd*: alone and would like to put him under lock and key; at most, their vanity concedes that his importance should also be evident to other people.

Pd: alone and would like to put him under lock and key. That is what is disgusting about it.

404: Pd: The courtesan is **more honest** than the girl who wants to rely solely upon her youthful charms to maintain her for life: they are prompted in their cunning by the shrewdest mothers.

405: Cf. 17 [13].

406: 223, 26 *we should...ourselves] Pd*: I would...myself

408: 224, 8 *a scholar] Pd*: Paul de Lagarde

See *Uber die gegenwärtige lage des deutschen reichs. ein bericht* (Göttingen, 1875), 44–45.

224, 9–10 *the cultivated...resemble] Sd*: we resemble (I mean the cultivated men of contemporary Germany resemble)

224, 11 *Faust]* Mephistopheles, Wagner, Faust, and Gretchen are the central characters in Goethe's *Faust*.

224, 12–13 *to continue...proposition] Pp*: this is the consequence of that remark

411: Pd: Women have understanding and little $\mathring{\eta}\theta os$ and spirit. Men have spirit and therefore get further with their understanding.

412: Pd: Drones in the beehive of humanity

225, 20 *Hesiod*] *Theogony*, 585–602.

416: *Pd*: precisely because of their injustice, we must have the greatest suspicion about their emancipation.

227, 7–8 *For...science is?*] *Sd*: I have never yet met a woman who really knew what science is.

417: 227, 18–19 *Delphic cauldron and laurel wreath*] These were the traditional emblems of the Greek shrine of Apollo at Delphi, where priests delivered oracles.

227, 21–24 *Yet if...four, then*] *Pd*: A reason can always be found afterward for why some person was to be avoided or sought out or why some cause or party was to be esteemed or opposed, so that

418: 227, 33–228, 3 *Exceptions...marriage.*] *Sd*: (Moreto the magistrate)

A reference to Augustin Moreto y Cabaña's *El valiente justiciero*, one of the texts read by Nietzsche's group in Sorrento.

421: Cf. 17 [29].

422: 229, 10 *father*] *Pm*: mother

423: *Pd*: Parents do not know children: the grossest errors in judgment 1) ?too much experience? 2) we do not reflect upon what lies nearest at hand

229, 17 *grossest*] *Pm*, *Fe*: greatest ⟨misreading by Gast⟩

425: *Pd* written on the reverse side of the birth announcement of Fernand Ott, born in Paris, 27 October 1877, son of Alfred and Louise Ott.

230, 32 *storm and stress*] An allusion to the eighteenth-century German *Sturm und Drang* literary period.

426: Aphorisms 426–37 were added by Nietzsche himself subsequently as an addition to the *Pm* and sent to the printer with the note: "Continuation and conclusion of the chapter, 'Woman and Child.'"

Pd: Those who think are like the prophetic birds of the ancients, speaking the truth, flying alone

427: *Pd*: Against contentment—the free spirit must tear apart the *spider's web* of his external existence again and again

232, 5 *dragon's teeth*] A reference to the Greek myth of Cadmus sowing the dragon's teeth from which armed warriors sprang up.

428: *Pd*: all too close relations of one friend with another, bestiality must manifest itself when people are freed from restraint—as engravings are not to be handled with bare hands—eventually we have a miserable piece of paper in our hands

430: *Pd*: women as the lightning rods of public disfavor

431: *Pd*: the conciliation of women

433: 234, 8 *peace.]* Plato, *Apology*, 30e.

436: 235, 2 *ceterum censeo]* "Moreover, I am of the opinion." Marcus Cato is purported to have concluded all his speeches before the Roman Senate with the phrase, "Moreover, I am of the opinion that Carthage should be destroyed." Plutarch, *Lives*, trans. John Dryden (New York: Modern Library), 431.

437: 235, 23 *said.]* Plato, *Phaedo*, 116b, 117c-e.

Chapter 8: Notes

438: 236, 11 *perdu."]* "When the rabble gets involved in reasoning, all is lost." Letter from Voltaire to Danilaville, 1 April 1766.

439: 238, 4-5 *wishes can be seen.]* *Pm*: wishes.—[In Germany we are still very far from this state.]

440: *Pd*: We should understand nobility of blood to mean the inherited art of commanding and of proud obedience.

441: 238, 24-26 *amazing...truth]* *Pm*: powerful effects will no longer be attainable. But it itself rests upon absolute authority, upon the belief in definitive truth, and is religious

442: 239, 17 *patria]* "fatherland."

444: 239, 33 *evil.]* *Sd*: evil. Here: it is optimism ⟨Nietzsche originally wanted to have Aphorism 477 follow at this point.⟩

446: *Pd*: Socialism is not at all a problem of rights ("how far should we give into its demands"), but rather a question of power (how far **can** we yield to its demands?) "steam" is not a right—A right takes shape here for the first time on the basis of clarity about how *great* the force is—In the meantime, education of the masses in a prudent egoism so that treaties are possible

447: 241, 14-20 *Because...person.]* *Pd*: Anyone who has money and influence installs the opinion that he wants to have there by itself.—Anyone who knows human beings and wants to attain his own goals through them is in any case on a bad road and —— —

450: 242, 29–243, 10 *Before...development.] Sd*: Anyone who cannot break free of this division will still have the old slavish sensibility toward the master in all his other relationships; it is a model relationship that is instinctively carried over into marriage, into one's attitude toward domestic servants, workers, party associates, the pupils of a teacher.

451: 243, 13 *class] Pm*: caste

453: 244, 27 *le désordre organisé"]* "organized disorder." Prosper Mérimée, *Lettres à une inconnue*, 2: 372.

244, 29 *war.] Sd*: war. [This attitude may be useful for the welfare of a state: it is inimical and harmful to the welfare of culture in general. — Hence the existence of individual states (which necessarily stand in a relation of uninterrupted *bellum omnium contra omnes* to one another) is in general a hindrance to culture.]

bellum omnium contra omnes: the war of all against all. Thomas Hobbes, *Leviathan* (1651), part 1, chapter 13, described the state of nature as, "such a warre, as is of every man, against every man."

454: 244, 32 *those...society] Pd*: socialists

455: 245, 10–11 *what...requires.] Sd*: state and morality [as Pericles says in his funeral oration]. Thucydides, bk. 2, 44.

245, 20 *lifetime.] Sd*: lifetime. [It is ridiculous when a society of people who have nothing abolishes the right of inheritance. People without children should not be allowed to exercise all political rights.]

457: *Pd*: Slaves and prostitutes are not badly off at all; what impels us to abolition?

246, 6 *slavery] Pm*: slavery [(likewise the elimination of prostitution)]

246, 9 *slaves] Pm*: slaves [(and prostitutes)]

461: 248, 13–16 *Wherever...are.] Pm*: That individual human beings tower so exceptionally far above the others is the result of the most despicable neglect of the people and of their cultivation: because the general level is so low, those individuals stand so high.

462: *Pd*: the exigencies of life are to be assigned to the one who suffers the least from them, that is, in relation to one's insensibility. Hard labor.

463: 249, 12 *Ecrasez l'infame!"]* "Crush the infamous thing!" Vol-

465: Cf. 24 [6].

468: *Pd*: Innocent corruption in scholarly bodies.

470: 250, 17 *Almost...politician] Pd*: Political parties

471: 250, 30 *forefathers] Pm, Fe*: antiquity ⟨reading error by Gast⟩

472: 252, 5–10 *This...here.] Pd*: Thus arises what we call enlightened despots (the despot, that is, necessarily enlightens himself).

254, 12–14 *most...another)] Sd*: remaining parts of governmental functions (something such as the necessary representation of the people in relations with others)

254, 16–17 *private...individual)] Sd*: individual (or at least the private person)

255, 14 *without...abhorrence] Up: sine ira et studio* "Without anger or self-involvement." This was Tacitus's description of the objectivity he sought in his *Annals*.

254, 23–255, 23 *To briefly...repelled!]* This section of the aphorism was sent to the publisher subsequent to delivery of the manuscript with the following note in Gast's writing. "The following lines belong to the long aphorism, 'State and religion' (in the chapter 'A Glance at the State'). You will, dear Mr. Schmeitzner, find the point of connection; this material follows immediately upon that and is therefore a continuation of that number.

473: 255, 26 *decrepit] Sd*: decrepit enlightened

255, 35 *tyrants]* For Plato's own account of his visit to and relations with Dionysus and Dion, rulers of Syracuse, see his Seventh Letter.

474: Cf. 5 [197], 5 [200].

257, 3 *panegyric]* Thucydides, bk. 2, 35–46.

475: 258, 11–12 *conserving...engendering] Se*: conserving (or establishing) nations, but instead of engendering and breeding

258, 23–24 *noblest...purest] Se*: most loving...justest

258, 27 *scholars] Sd*: philosophers

258, 25–259, 2 *world....Greeks'.] Pm*: world and whose freethinkers, physicians, and philosophers, moreover, during the darkest centuries of the Middle Ages preserved unbroken the ring of European culture through which we are bound to Greek and Roman antiquity — a service and gift without parallel!

259, 2 at bottom of *Pp*: The hen does not discuss the eggs — it just sits on them.

477: *Pd*: It is optimism to expect much more from a humanity that wages no wars. Wild egoism, hatred of other peoples, the *bellum omnium contra omnes* is as necessary as the sea and the weather to bring the spring, summer, and autumn of humanity.

259, 20 *mystical fancy*] *Pm*: optimism

259, 25-26 *shared...enemy*] *Sd*: shared ardor of fraternity

260, 6 *war, adopt*] *Up*: war, as far as it rests with them, adopt

260, 15 *wars—*] *Pm*: wars [(presumably the socialist ones)]—

260, 15-17 *wars...existence.*] *Sd*: wars in order not to die of weakness and to turn into barbarians.

478: 260, 20 *in the south*] *Sd*: here ⟨that is, in Sorrento⟩

480: 261, 28 *national*] *Pm*: national[-liberal]

262, 6 *that*] *Pm*: that national-liberal

481: 262, 21 *two...billions*] *Pp*: 2184 million; *Se*: five billion

263, 14-15 *more...countries*] *Pm*: compulsory favoring of outward prosperity

482: 263, 20 *laziness*] A reference to the subtitle of Mandeville's *The Fable of the Bees, or Private Vices, Publick Benefits* (1714), quoted by Nietzsche in "Schopenhauer as Educator," *CW*, 2: 172.

Chapter 9: Notes

488: *Pd*: Waterfall slowly falling, a great man, a tempestuous youthful drive

491: 265, 19-23 *themselves...path.*] *Pd*: their own surveillance: they detect the outer defenses — fr⟨iends⟩ and enemies betray the stronghold.

495: *Pd*: Almost all of our fellow human beings will characterize any very individual guidelines for life as impractical: as they would in fact be for them.

496: Cf. 23 [92].

498: Cf. 24 [8].

499: Cf. 19 [9].

Pd: Shared joy makes a friend, sympathy a companion in suffering. {Nietzsche here coins a term, *Mitfreude*, that highlights the contrast he wants to make with the standard German term for sympathy, *Mitleid*, which like the Greek root of the English word, literally means "shared suffering."}

501: 267, 7 *oneself]* Nietzsche's title carries two possible meanings, for *Freude an sich* might mean either "joy in oneself" or, in parallel to the philosophical use of *an sich*, "joy in itself."

503: *Pd* continues: Nor are there any gestures revealing them: the body silences these.

509: 268, 15–17 *can...shame.] Sd:* can provide help and show himself as superior.

512: *Pd:* the higher morality lies in the quantity of the goals

517: Cf. 23 [82].

269, 22 *preestablished harmony]* A term coined by Leibniz to describe the harmonious relations that hold the parts of a compound whole, such as the monads that he contended constitute the most basic elements of the world, together, a state that for him provided evidence for the agency of God in constructing those relations.

520: 270, 6 *in danger...culture.] Pd:* perishing by the means to culture, or cannot even come to be.

525: 270, 28 *Adherents...Anyone] Pd:* The advantage in the enmity of others:—anyone

270, 28 *enraged] Pd:* enraged and infuriated

528: 271, 12–16 *fears that...known.] Pd:* fears the pain of punishment, the former the loss of inner happiness as a result of the satisfaction of vanity, for vanity is the acid that eats away a good deed after it has been done, as if it had never been done.

532: Cf. 19 [108].

272, 2–3 *obscure] Pm, Pp:* clear ⟨reading error by Gast⟩; *Fe:* unclear

543: 273, 19 *Embodiment of spirit.] Pm:* Physical effect of spiritual activity.

273, 21 *shrewdness.] Pd* continues: But aren't scholars known for being awkward and clumsy?—Then the proposition must be false.

NOTES TO PAGES 273–80   353

545: Cf. 20 [6]

546: Pd: Someone who is generally self-sufficient feels in moments of vanity as if an illness has befallen him; he is annoyed with himself for this, but not ashamed of himself. — In fact, he is especially susceptible to honor and praise when he is physically ill.

547: Pd: We always show ourselves to be without spirit when we seek spirit [as the true musician flees music, rather than running after it].

549: Pd: Nothing makes people feel their lives so burdensome as contempt, and indeed, they are more sensitive to contempt from others than to their contempt for themselves. ⟨*Pd* continues with Aphorism 117⟩

550: Cf. 22 [99]

553: Pd: I know of no [more animalistic] more offensive remainder of orginal bestiality than loud and neighing laughter.

554: 275, 9 *Partial knowledge.] Pm:* Pleasure in partial knowledge.

275, 11 *well…pleasure] Pd:* well. For the former feels how much different he is from all those who do not understand it; the latter, by contrast, observes that he cannot compare himself with those who do speak it extremely well. — Thus it is elsewhere as well; the pleasure

555: 275, 16–17 *recipes…Christianity.] Pd:* highest recipes for the art of living.

556: 275, 22 *conscientiousness] Pd:* the intellect

558: Cf. 19 [37].

559: 276, 4–5 *the fortunate…envy.] Pd:* a fortunate gift for keeping his envy and arrogance concealed.

563: Pd: People with a detesting imagination toward what lies behind.

568: Cf. 18 [56].

577: 278, 25–26 *great…It] Pd:* noble among human beings takes care that he has noble heirs; it

278, 27–28 *to live…them.] Pd:* to make a desert around himself.

581: Cf. 18 [6].

583: Cf. 19 [45].

584: 279, 26 *punctum saliens]* "salient point."

585: Pd: It is like with the kilns in the woods: only when we have stopped glowing and been carbonized do we become useful. As long as it is smoldering and smoking — — —

280, 12–13 *umana commedia*] "human comedy."

280, 12–13 *umana commedia*] *Sd*: *humana comoedia* ⟨Clearly revised to emphasize the parallel with Dante's *Divina commedia*.⟩

586: *Pd*: Individual experiences, i.e., spring or a melody, have their full significance only once in life — everything else is repetition, often only a shadowy image.

587: 280, 28 *defects of its virtues"*] From George Sand, "Everyone has the defects of his virtues."

281, 2 *disavow it.*] *Sd* concludes: [Thus I am completely right in my critique of the cultivated Philistines and the historical disease: but it would be better to promote the modern world because of this, not leave it in the lurch.]

588: 281, 4 *Modesty.—There*] *Sd*: Anyone who humbles himself wants to be exalted — that is the [way of the world] meaning of ordinary modesty. Nevertheless, there ⟨Cf. Aphorism 87⟩

589: 281, 19–21 *If…change.*] *Pd*: At the same time a substitute for the religious habit of prayer, from which our fellow human beings would profit.

590: 281, 25 *illness*] *Pm*: vice

591: 282, 2–4 *Right…happiness*] *Sd*: The sorrow in the world has caused human beings to suck a sort of happiness from it;

592: 282, 17–18 *Hence…ancestors.*] *Sd*: Young men should reflect upon this!

593: 282, 22–24 *may still…arrive;*] *Pd*: will still torment him: if he has attained this goal, then vanity torments him:

595: Cf. 16 [25].

596: Cf. 19 [54].

283, 22 *casus belli*] "reason for war."

598: 284, 3 *Catholic priests do*] *Up*: the Catholic church does

284, 3–4 *Catholic…way.*] *Pd*: the Catholic clergy does will have almost exclusively the lowest and meanest possible conception of it in their heads.

599: *Pd*: Between 26 and 30 years of age, the first ripeness wants to express itself as arrogance. Many people maintain the expression of arrogance. We always recognize it, smile at it; it is part of youth (also of genius). There is nothing that older people are more acute in noting!

600: *Pd*: Fathers teachers considered as railings (even if they do not hold fast, they comfort our sight.

284, 33 *give our eye]* *Pm, Fe*: awaken in our eye ⟨reading error by Gast⟩

601: *Pd*: We must learn to love from our youth on up. *Hatred* can be rooted out, if it is not practiced.

603: 285, 26 *awe]* Nietzsche is playing upon the German terms *Ehre*, which means respect or honor, *Furcht*, which means fear, and *Ehrfurcht*, which combines both (and which he here writes *Ehr-furcht*), meaning reverence or awe.

605: *Pd*: We feel *an itch from free opinions* that stimulates us to rub it until an open, painful wound results.

606: 286, 13–14 *behind]* *Pm*: behind [like its trailing train]

286, 14–16 *for it…whip.]* *Pd*: for it; being tormented with fiery, biting whips must in fact have brought pleasure.

607: 286, 28 *others:]* *Pm*: others [and looks only for the latter]:

286, 30 *side.]* *Sd* at end: [By contrast, Christ says (Matth.), "let your good works be seen by the people."] {"Let your light so shine before men, that they may see your good works and give glory to your Father who is in heaven." Matthew 5:16}

608: 287, 5 *stability and]* *Pm, Fe*: stable ⟨reading error by Gast⟩

609: *Pd*: The simple character of goodness—felt to be boring. Youth desire what is unusual—

287, 17–18 *Fully mature]* *Pm*: Mature

287, 19–21 *people…simplicity.]* *Pd*: people. It requires much spirit to love the simple truth; but because people perceive this, they so often simulate this love for the works of the Greeks.

612: *Pd*: Photographs of childhood and of the man alike. So, too, our thought enters a phase that rewrites our childhood nature, and strong influences are reduced to a fixed measure.

615: 290, 13 *bellum omnium contra omnes]* "the war of all against all." See note to Aphorism 453.

616: *Pd*: There are great advantages in being driven away from the shore.

617: at top of *Sd*: [Aristophanes]

290, 26 *reaping]* *Up*: planting; *Cp*: plowing

621: 291, 27–29 *Anyone...thing]* *Pd*: We do well to take up something new

291, 29–292, 7 *to quickly...forth.]* *Pd*: to overlook what is hostile and offensive in it and to give the writer a head start and to withhold our criticism for once. Then we come to the heart of the new thing, whether a person or a book. Afterward the understanding can set its restrictions upon this overestimation: with it, we have drawn forth the soul from the body of the thing.

624: 292, 31 *higher self]* *Pd*: ideal

293, 6–11 *shyly...gods]* *Pd*: shyly before it and humbly. Many fear it as the most demanding moments. We cannot rely on it; a gift of the gods, so it seems,

626: *Pd*: There are people with the indolence of harmony: no melody wants to take shape, and instead all movement brings with it only a different state of harmony. Natures of the Middle Ages. They make us impatient, bored: but in certain moods all of life mirrors itself as if upon in a deep lake: with the question: why and for what end melody?—

294, 12 *sword."]* A quote from Goethe's diary, 13 May 1780.

627: Aphorisms 627 and 638 were sent to Schmeitzner after the others, accompanied by the following note in Gast's handwriting: "NB: the final pages of the entire book manuscript are quarto pages; these two numbers here are to be inserted before those quarto pages and numbered accordingly." These quarto pages contained the present aphorisms 629–37 and 628 (entitled at that point, *Epilogue*); at the last moment, Nietzsche switched Aphorisms 628 and 638.

628: *Pd*: Chiming of bells at evening in Genoa—melancholy, horrible, childlike. Plato: nothing mortal is worth taking very seriously.

Pd: *Nor are any human things*. I heard at evening in Genoa a chiming of bells from a church tower: there was something so melancholy, horrible, childlike in it, that I felt what Plato said: "nor are any human things worth taking very seriously."

294, 28 *Seriousness in play.]* *Cp*: *Play and seriousness.*; *Up*: *Epilogue*; *Sd*: *Nevertheless*

294, 34 *seriously"]* Plato, *Republic*, 10, 604b–c.

629: *Pd*: We admire someone who suffers and dies for his convictions, we despise someone who forsakes them; from fear of disadvantage, shame or from stubbornness, we stick to them. — Conviction is knowledge replaced by impulses of the will.

295, 5–7 *for all...devotion]* *Sd*: the consequences of wrath or of the sexual drive

295, 18 *heart]* *Up*: oath

295, 27 *our higher self]* *Up*: ourselves and others

295, 29–30 *our ideals...again.]* *Up*: the ideals of our youth.

295, 32–35 *In order...us?]* *Sd*: It would be sad if, in order to avoid these pains, we wanted henceforth to guard ourselves against the upsurge of our feelings. ⟨revised from:⟩ "We gradually come to guard ourselves against the upsurge of our feelings; we also judge the disloyalty of others toward us mildly, for it is necessary. If we must at some time be traitors, then at least noble traitors.

296, 6–7 *the more...fear]* *Up*: personal advantage or apprehension

296, 11 *convictions.]* *Sd*: convictions. [—A conviction is a piece of impure knowledge that proceeds from the impulses of the will.]

630: 296, 18–28 *Conviction...strength.]* *Sd*: Because a *strong feeling* makes us perceive the object to which it relates quite forcefully, we make the mistake of believing that it *proves* the truth of a fact: whereas it only proves itself or some *imagined* reason. A strong feeling proves the strength of a representation, not the truth of what it represents.

296, 30–297, 6 *absolute...for him]* *Sd*: "truth": they were all wrong in that, there has probably never yet been a human being who sacrificed himself for the "truth"; at least the dogmatic expression of his belief was unscientific or half-scientific. One does not want to let anything tear one's beliefs away, i.e., instead of *pro ratione voluntas*, we want to be right: which is why the disputations of heretics of all kinds do not proceed with scientific rigor; they do not have any of the coldness and skepticism of the theoretical person, for they believe that their salvation depends upon this, they are struggling for the foundation of their salvation and do not believe that they *could* be refuted: if the objections are extremely strong, it still remains possible for them *pro ratione voluntas]* "a will for reason."

297, 7 *credo quia absurdum est*] "I believe it because it is absurd." A statement falsely attributed to St. Augustine.

297, 9–10 *belief...convictions.*] *Sd*: so many almost unteachable parties and individuals with closed ears who are always screaming the same things.

631: 297, 31–32 *conviction...princes)*] *Sd*: metaphysics, even though it be the metaphysics of materialism,

298, 5–6 *Tassos*] Antonio and Tasso are characters from Goethe's play, *Torquato Tasso* (1790).

298, 7 *person with convictions*] *Sd*: artist

298, 12 *Antonio.*] *Sd*: Antonio. Above all, he perceives that the person with convictions is *useful*.

633: *Pd*: Anyone who today would suppress his opponent would under different circumstances have burned him.

Title in *Sd*: *Mistrust of the pathetic and violent advocates of "truth."*

299, 22, *anew.*] *Sd*: anew. What irony lies in the fact that Goethe in his *Farbenlehre*, that Schopenhauer with all his metaphysical views, were wrong and that their pride in these things was in any case unjustified! It teaches humility, or at least caution; besides which, if nobody is responsible for his actions, hence not for his good achievements either, he cannot claim any praise for them, nor can he even demand that we be pleased with him. He must wait and guard against making reproaches against other people—who always behave innocently.

634: 299, 24–25 *Besides...another.*] *Sd*: The belief in the value of truth is much older than the certainty of the methods for finding truth; "I am right to think this way" denotes the moral element in this and means "I have a right to do so," but rights are not always reasons.

299, 27–28 *methods of inquiry*] *Sd*: truth

635: 300, 12 *Clever*] *Pm*: Cultivated

300, 21–22 *to be...to set*] *Se*: right away to be fanatical about it and finally to set

300, 21–26 *about it...ensue.*] *Sd*: about it. Thus religions once worked: from this stems habituation. In the head of an unscientific person, unexplained things stand side by side with those that *are explained*: but here the scantiest and crudest things suffice.

300, 33–301, 11 *Indeed...suitor.]* *Sd*: One class of people desires convictions from a thinker, the other desires certainty, the ones want to be forcefully carried away in order to have their own strength increased (rhetoric), the others have an objective interest that neglects personal advantages (even that of an increase in strength). Everywhere that an author behaves like a genius, looking down as if he were a higher being, authority is being demanded and an appeal is being made to those natures who desire convictions, strong impulses of the will in particular directions.

637: 301, 32 *at one time heated]* *Up*: half heated

302, 4–6 *with...us.]* *Up*: in burning, igniting, and suffering, we bring her our sacrifice.; *Cp*: in burning or in inciting the combustion of others, we bring her our sacrifice.

638: 302, 14–16 *has...not]* *Se*: wants to get even part of the way to the freedom of reason cannot for a long time feel himself to be anything other than a wanderer upon the earth—and not even

Translator's Afterword

> The foreword is the author's right, but the reader's is —
> the afterword.
>
> — *Human, All Too Human*, Aphorism 38, variant

When *Human, All Too Human* appeared in April 1878, Friedrich Nietzsche was a 33-year-old professor of classical philology at the University of Basel in Switzerland, entering what would prove to be the final year of his academic career. That Nietzsche had managed during the preceding two years to prepare the text for publication was in itself a remarkable feat, for throughout this period he suffered from recurrent, frequently incapacitating physical ailments. His primary symptoms included intense headaches accompanied by eye pain so severe that it made reading or writing impossible, a state further aggravated by spells of nausea and vomiting. With the various doctors whom he had consulted unable to diagnose or treat these problems effectively, Nietzsche found himself frequently confined for days at a time to a darkened room, trying to avoid any intensification of his symptoms.

These difficulties in health had plagued Nietzsche almost since his arrival in Basel in April 1869, but became increasingly severe late in 1875, when he was forced for the first time to withdraw from some of his pedagogical functions. When his condition failed to improve, he applied for and received a year's leave for the period from October 1876 through September 1877, and it was largely during this year that *Human, All Too Human* was conceived and written. Although Nietzsche returned to Basel for the fall 1877 semester, he only partially resumed his teaching even at that point. By May 1879, urged by the university to reach a definitive decision in regard to his status, Nietzsche submitted his resignation. In accepting that resignation the following month, the university governing body and Basel civic authorities showed their appreciation for his work and their sympathy for his situation by granting Nietzsche a medical pension, initially for a six-year period, with a stipend that amounted to two-thirds of his most recent salary.

Nietzsche spent the year's leave of 1876–77 mostly in two places, Sorrento, Italy, and Rosenlauibad, a health resort in the mountains outside of Berne. The prospect of living in Sorrento had first been suggested to Nietzsche by Malwida von Meysenbug, a friend whom he had met in 1872 through their mutual connection with the Wagner circle, whose concern for Nietzsche's health led her to propose an extended stay in the milder climate of Italy. The two of them were joined there, at Nietzsche's suggestion, by his close friend of the time, the psychologist and philosopher Paul Rée, and by a young student, Albert Brenner, who spent some of his time assisting Nietzsche in organizing and copying his manuscript material. The stay in Sorrento allowed Nietzsche to work in a tranquil and largely uninterrupted way; the daily routine left each member of the household at liberty during the early part of the day, with afternoons often devoted to lengthy walks and evenings to communal reading. The six months there, then, were spent in intimate daily contact with a small circle of friends whose influence can be traced in both direct and indirect ways in the concerns of *Human, All Too Human*. By contrast, the subsequent summer months in Rosenlauibad, where Nietzsche continued intensively expanding and reorganizing his notebook material, were lived much more entirely on his own.

Ecce Homo provides highly dramatized testimony about the importance of the fundamental changes in lifestyle that Nietzsche was forced to adopt during this period. Freed from the time pressures of his pedagogical obligations ("Bücherwürmerei," "bookworminess," as he termed it) and removed from the cultural polemics that had absorbed a good deal of his attention during the preceding years, Nietzsche had ample space for reflection and self-assessment for the first time since taking up his professorial position at the age of 25. "Illness likewise gave me the right to completely reverse all my habits; it allowed, it commanded me to forget; it conferred upon me the necessity of lying quietly, of being idle, of waiting and being patient.... But that is what it means to think!"[1] Looking back upon his past from a point after the completion of his major works, he felt that the consequence of these externally imposed alterations in his lifestyle was a return to himself, to his own essential identity. "With this book, I freed myself from what did not belong to my nature."[2]

Human, All Too Human is thus a book born of illness, a book born of geographical and intellectual detachment, and a book that reflexively emphasizes the interpretive significance of such biographical context. In style as well as substance, *Human, All Too Human* was a medicinal text for Nietzsche, his antidote to the prevalent tendencies of contemporary German and European culture. Nietzsche himself would later read (and doubtless already read) his illness symptomatically, in allegorical or philological terms—as a sign of his own intellectual infection by perspectives that he had thought stood opposed to a chauvinistic German nationalism, but that he had begun to recognize might all too readily be appropriated by that same nationalist ethos and ideology. We might quite justifiably label those perspectives with the names that most deeply marked Nietzsche's early intellectual trajectory and writings—Schopenhauer and Wagner. But *Ecce Homo* describes the target of *Human, All Too Human* in terms at once simpler and more encompassing: "What does not constitute a part of me is idealism: the title states, 'where *you* see ideal things, *I* see—human, alas, only all too human ones.'"[3] Nietzsche's antagonists in this text extend

1. *Ecce Homo*, 326.
2. Ibid., 322.
3. Ibid.

far beyond the specific tendencies present in Schopenhauer's aestheticizing philosophical pessimism or Wagner's Christianizing musical mythology, both of which share the enthusiastic and ultimately religious antirationalism of late, decadent Romanticism. What sets *Human, All Too Human* most emphatically apart from Nietzsche's preceding works is the scope of the project it undertakes: a critique not simply of the dominant or rising intellectual and cultural tendencies of his own era, but of the epistemological, psychological, and religious foundations of European culture that had provided such fertile soil for these tendencies. Even as it takes its distance from the antirationalism of Wagner and Schopenhauer, *Human, All Too Human* takes an equally critical look at Enlightenment rationalism as well, especially for its historicist faith in the inevitable progress of human civilization as directed by an ever more fully assertive human reason.[4]

Yet this general turn against the intellectual traditions that had nurtured him was doubtless most sharply signaled by Nietzsche's break with his personal past, which is to say, with the idealist tendencies of European culture that Nietzsche saw culminating in the music of Richard Wagner. Nietzsche's markedly filial relation to Richard and Cosima Wagner had been the most intense single influence upon him almost from the moment of his arrival in Basel. Personal and intellectual at the same time, the relationship was fostered by frequent visits when the Wagners were living in nearby Tribschen and continued with frequent letters and visits even when they moved to Bayreuth in 1872. In retrospect, Nietzsche himself asserted that *Human, All Too Human* marked a sudden and definitive deflection from the intellectual trajectory that he had been following

---

4. On the intimate interdependence of these two strands in Nietzsche's thought, see Peter Heller's splendid and detailed analysis of the first section of *Human, All Too Human*, *"Von den ersten und letzten Dingen"* (Berlin: Walter de Gruyter, 1972), particularly his overview of the dialectical structure of *The Birth of Tragedy*, xii–xvi.

for some seven years, a veering away from the Wagnerian influence that *Ecce Homo* dates to his troubled departure from the inaugural Bayreuth festival of fall 1876. This first in the series of annual celebrations of Wagnerian music demonstrated how fully Wagner's cultural position had shifted from being a scandalous, anti-establishment musical outsider to the very center around which German national culture would revolve. Accompanied by a panoply of extravagant social events, it ran from August 13 through August 30 of that year, with Nietzsche in attendance for most of the festival period.

Ecce Homo characterizes his overall reaction to the scene as a sudden awakening from Wagnerian intoxication, an abrupt recognition of Nietzsche's deeply personal alienation from all that was going on around him, a conscious rejection of Wagnerian music manifested in his flight during the festival to the isolation of a nearby village, Klingenbrunn. Yet his actual itinerary was more complex, and his departure seems to have been as much a result of his ongoing physical distress as a sign of intellectual disenchantment. Nietzsche had in fact already been present for much of the rehearsal period prior to the festival, from July 23 through August 4, and had found himself increasingly unsettled by the way that Wagner's music had become subordinate to dramatic spectacle, indeed, to the social spectacle that surrounded the festival. Wagner had, in short, become fashionable, and altogether too Germanic for Nietzsche's taste. Yet Nietzsche returned from Klingenbrunn for the festival itself, leaving only on August 26 in order to return to Basel and prepare for his trip to Sorrento. Nor did this departure involve an overt or absolute rupture with Richard and Cosima Wagner; their personal ties did in fact grow increasingly attenuated over the next few years, but were not abruptly dissolved at this or any other single moment. Nietzsche's stay in Sorrento overlapped with the Wagners' vacation there, and the two groups spent at least several evenings together on seemingly harmonious terms. Well into 1877, Nietzsche was lamenting to Malwida von Meysenbug his nostalgia for the extended conversations he had been used to having with the Wagners.[5]

So it is not surprising that *Human, All Too Human* offers not so much an absolute or a personal rejection of Wagnerian idealism as a historically conditioned recognition of the limits of the perspectives represented by such figures as Wagner and Schopenhauer. Although textual variants indicate a number of comments where Nietzsche did have Wagner specifically in mind, the criticism contained in *Human, All Too Human* is notable for its impersonal analysis of the artist and the philosopher as types, acknowledging the powerful appeal and even the necessity of the activities in which they engage while at the same time dispassionately exposing both their public and their inward deceptions. In intellectual if not personal terms, though, Nietzsche's general chronology is an accurate one; the crystallization of *Human, All Too Human* into manuscript form did largely coincide with the period when Nietzsche began to distance himself from the phenomenon that Wagner had become. Although certain aphorisms can be traced to notes written as early as the summer of 1875, the bulk of the textual material was produced during the months that followed Nietzsche's departure from Bayreuth, and it was only after his departure that Nietzsche began to conceive of his rapidly expanding journal entries as an entirely new and self-contained project.

Yet the ultimate form that this material would take remained for some time undetermined. For several months, Nietzsche continued to contemplate writing a fifth essay in his series of *Unfashionable Observations*, to which he gave the provisional title, "The Free Spirit," an idea whose centrality can be traced throughout his journals of this period.[6] He even announced completion of a piece, presumably this one, to his sister in a letter of 16 October 1877. But a more elaborate plan was simul-

5. Letter to Malwida von Meysenbug, 1 July 1877.

6. Notebook entries from summer 1876, 16 [10–12, 15] contain multiple plans for a whole series of additions to *Unfashionable Observations*, which Nietzsche was clearly contemplating continuing over the next several years.

taneously taking shape as the notebook material kept growing significantly in quantity. Before his departure from Basel, Nietzsche had had Heinrich Köselitz, a onetime student of his who had previously assisted him in his editorial work, write out a clean manuscript copy of his accumulated notes. This text, amounting to some one hundred quarto pages, was given the provisional title "Die Pflugschar," "The Plowshare." Its envisioned organization already included several chapter titles that were carried over into *Human, All Too Human*, and it is in Nietzsche's notes of September 1876 that the phrase "human, all too human" first appears.[7] While in Sorrento, Nietzsche dictated a second clean copy to Albert Brenner, even as he was in the process of adding new material to the manuscript. The final organization of the material took place upon his return to Basel in fall 1877. Nietzsche once again had Köselitz write out a clean manuscript copy of the final text, which was then corrected by Nietzsche, a process that lasted into January 1878. The manuscript was sent off in sections to Nietzsche's publisher in Chemnitz, Ernst Schmeitzner, with the first printed copies available for distribution to Nietzsche's friends in April 1878.

The new directions in Nietzsche's thoughts at this time were influenced most emphatically by Paul Rée—if not as much as many of Nietzsche's friends suspected or feared, at least more than Nietzsche's later comments directly acknowledged. A German student of moral philosophy, Rée was five years Nietzsche's junior, but already a well-known author in his own right. He had heard Nietzsche lecture in Basel in 1873 and had met him socially through a mutual friend at that time, but he came to Nietzsche's renewed attention in the fall of 1875, when Nietzsche read Rée's anonymously published *Psychological Observations* and wrote an enthusiastic letter of praise to its author. "A moralist possessing the very sharpest vision," Rée was a ma-

---

7. For the chapter headings of "The Plowshare," see 17 [105]; "Human and All Too Human" appears as a heading at 18 [13].

terial determinist and psychological utilitarian, thus an ideal interlocutor for the anti-idealist reorientation that was taking place in Nietzsche's own thinking.[8] They quickly developed a close friendship, leading Nietzsche to introduce Rée into the Bayreuth Wagnerian circle (with less than complete success, not simply on account of Rée's philosophical beliefs, but due to his Jewish background) and then later to invite him to join the group in Sorrento.

The interests shared by Rée and Nietzsche largely determined the communal reading that filled the evenings in Sorrento and provided the intellectual background for their respective writing projects. Rée was at this time completing work on his dissertation, published by Schmeitzner in 1877 under the title *The Origin of Moral Sensations*. The texts that were read aloud, most often by Rée, included a wide range of literary and scholarly works—classical Greek texts by such authors as Thucydides and Plato, Albert Spir's *Denken und Wirklichkeit*, historical works by Burckhardt, Ranke, and others, and the New Testament. But the most significant materials with respect to Nietzsche's own immediate purposes were works from the French moralist tradition, texts by Montaigne, La Rochefoucauld, Vauvenargues, La Bruyère, and Stendhal. Many of the aphorisms from *Human, All Too Human* attest to the importance of this tradition, most notably Aphorisms 35–38, which provide a historically self-conscious justification for the methods and concerns of the project as a whole. Nietzsche's affinity with that tradition was directly indicated by the original title page as well, with its dedication to the memory of Voltaire on the centenary of his death. The moralists' mingling of Enlightenment rationalism with the cynical psychologizing of the French salon, and their insistence that one or another form of self-interest could be found behind all the "nobler" motives of human beings, are echoed again and again in Nietzsche's text. *Human, All Too Human* is nothing if not a work of ethical and ideological de-

---

8. From a letter to Erwin Rhode of December 1875.

mystification, a self-conscious extension of the philosophe tradition. Yet there is at the same time a certain paradoxical accuracy in Erich Heller's claim that Voltaire, for instance, "served merely as the stick with which to chastise Wagner."[9]

Nietzsche's own turn on this moralist legacy was distinctive and decisive. Both the language and the intellectual perspectives of the French moralists were deeply shaped by their own metaphysical assumptions about the eternal sameness of human nature, which led naturally to their satirical and ultimately conservative skepticism about the motives behind human behavior. Even as Nietzsche drew upon their concerns and adopted features of their style, he began working out a historical perspective on psychological causality that was to revolutionize the study of moral philosophy and be determinative for all of his own later work. *Human, All Too Human* opens out in two historical directions simultaneously, first of all toward the past, by placing its psychological observations within a historical trajectory that reaches back to and beyond the start of civilization. It delineates distinctive and incommensurable stages in the development of human consciousness, whose sedimented influences remain visible in the psychological habits of the contemporary European mind. But *Human, All Too Human* reaches simultaneously toward a future evoked by the metaphoric vision of the "free spirit," the embodiment of an ideal—if not idealist—creative potentiality in which one can already discern the outlines of the *Übermensch*.

Nietzsche's genealogical method is made especially prominent by a key organizational choice that he made as he was shaping his text for publication. He shifted "On the History of Moral Sensations," the chapter that most explicitly links him to the French moralists, into second position, preceding it by a new initial chapter that contains a critique of the practitioners of metaphysics, that is, all those legislators of human values

---

9. From Heller's introduction to R. J. Hollingdale's translation of *Human, All Too Human* (Cambridge, Eng.: Cambridge University Press, 1986), xi.

whose lack of historical sense has kept them from perceiving the complex and fluctuating nature of human beings. Nietzsche's critique of philosophy generally, and the critique of his own earlier writings that this editorial change implies, takes as its starting point this rebuke of philosophers and logicians for having "overlooked the possibility that the painting—what we human beings now call life and experience—has gradually *come to be*, indeed, is still wholly *becoming*, and therefore should not be considered as a fixed quantity from which we are allowed to draw or even simply to reject any conclusion about the creator" (Aphorism 16). As a later aphorism (208) asserts, the only permanence in human affairs, the only "real *immortality* that exists," is "that of movement." Hence "a lack of historical sensibility is the original failing [or sin] of all philosophers" (Aphorism 2) and the disclosure of this lack provides the crucial first step of the critique that *Human, All Too Human* undertakes. The same holds true for aesthetic matters as well; Nietzsche decisively rejects the idea that art can serve as an alternative source of absolute values, that it should be conceived as "an image of something *everlasting*," for "in our conception, the artist can give his image validity only for a certain time, because humanity as a whole has come to be and is changeable, and even the individual human being is neither fixed nor enduring" (Aphorism 222). Chapters 1 through 4 of *Human, All Too Human* take up and demolish in turn each of the cultural perspectives that has served throughout human history as a refuge for metaphysical idealism—philosophy, morality, religion, and art. To this largely continuous critical commentary Nietzsche appends the more discrete, more traditionally aphoristic remarks on culture, on social relations, on gender, on politics, and on psychology that fill the remaining five chapters of the text.

Nietzsche himself would surely have acknowledged that this historical and relativizing extension of the French moralist tradition is itself historically conditioned, the product of a shift in viewpoint that one can trace back to Herder or to German Romanticism, then follow through Hegel and German idealism. Yet in the third of his *Unfashionable Observations*, "On the Utility and Liability of History for Life," Nietzsche had already sought to distinguish his historical perspective from the pervasive historicist sensibility that dominated German intellectual life, the consequences of which he saw as increasingly debilitating. Here again, however, Nietzsche turned the methods and ideas that he adopted from such predecessors against the premises that they had used those methods and ideas to shield. He radicalizes the historicist perspective of German philosophy and exposes its rationalist and organicist prejudices by pushing the idea of historical causality to its most extreme formulation: the claim that human concepts and values can and often do arise from their opposites. The absoluteness of the moral distinctions upon which we typically ground our judgments and our behavior is, as the very first aphorism of *Human, All Too Human* contends, a linguistic delusion and a logical mistake. "There are no opposites, except in the habitual exaggeration of popular or metaphysical views." To the extent that metaphysics, art, and religion deny this, trying to create systems founded upon such presumed contraries, they turn themselves into fraudulent myths.

They are fraudulent—but not for that reason any less necessary for certain purposes or in certain circumstances. Aphorism 16 develops the corollary of this initial point, a premise as essential in Nietzsche's perspective as his demystification of inherited beliefs. Such metaphysical views are more than errors, more than simply incorrect, because they have served to invest the world with the values that make human lives worth living. "Because we have for millennia looked upon the world with moral, aesthetic, and religious demands, with blind inclination, passion, or fear, and have actually reveled in the bad habits of illogical thinking, this world has gradually *become* so wonderfully bright, terrible, profoundly meaningful, soulful, and has taken on color—but we have been the colorists." Even though ethical values must be seen as relative and contextual, they should not be presumed to be arbitrary with respect to their worth at any given historical moment for human society. Mythical though they may be, they correspond to a human truth, which is to say, to the all too human needs of specific developmental phases. Even if we were, for instance, to "give up art," we "would not thereby forfeit the capacity we have learned from it: just as we have given up religion, but not the heightening of sensibility and the exaltation acquired from it" (Aphorism 222).

It is here, with Nietzsche at the threshold of his mature philosophy, that *Human, All Too Human* has special value for us as his readers. It discloses to us Nietzsche in another guise alongside the critical, skeptical role with which he has so frequently been identified by contemporary philosophers and critics (by his advocates and his detractors alike), the Nietzsche who argues in Aphorism 20 that a "*reverse movement*" back from the point of skepticism is as necessary as the most radical skepticism itself. "One should, of course, look out over the final rung of the ladder, but not wish to stand upon it. Even the most enlightened people get only far enough to free themselves from metaphysics and to look back on it with superiority: while here, too, as in the hippodrome, it is still necessary to bend back around the end of the track." Turning back in this fashion means, on the one hand, acquiring the historical self-consciousness of which this aphorism speaks — not just condemnatory, not just tolerant, but actively implicated in and interested by the past that one observes. Thus, anyone who seeks to free himself from metaphysical prejudices must still "grasp the historical justification as well as the psychological one for such conceptions" and "must recognize how the greatest advancements of humanity came from them and how he would rob himself of the best results that humanity has thus far produced without such a reverse movement."

But turning back also means acknowledging the value of our self-deceptions and thus envisioning the positive, creative potentiality of the free spirit, the change in sensibility that elevates one above melancholy or embittered rumination upon the past. The freedom of this free spirit rests upon his affirmation of the method that marks for Nietzsche the necessary acquisition of the scientific spirit. In Aphorism 256, *Human, All Too Human* circles back to the text from which Nietzsche took the epigraph for his first edition, Descartes' *Discourse on the Method of Rightly Conducting Reason*. "The value of having for some time rigorously pursued a *rigorous science* does not rest directly upon the results of this pursuit: for they will be a tiny, vanishing drop in relation to the sea of what is worth knowing. But there does result an increase in energy, in deductive capacity, in tenacity of perseverance; one has learned how to attain a *purpose purposefully*."[10] With its emphasis on method rather than results, *Human, All Too Human* cautions against any Hegelian conflation of our values with the meaning of history, against any presumption that the course of human history has been shaped by an omnipotent reason, and against the belief that what may have been productive or necessary at some particular historical moment is therefore good or even defensible in any absolute ethical sense. So the cautionary note in the final, playful reversal of Aphorism 1 adds a vital tone to Nietzsche's chord. "Humanity loves to put from its mind questions concerning origins and beginnings: wouldn't we have to be almost dehumanized to find in ourselves traces of the opposite inclination?"

With more than a century lying between us and *Human, All Too Human*, it has become enormously difficult to measure the scandal of this text, to feel the tremendous shock that reading it could produce, even in Nietzsche's advocates and friends. Its ideas were profoundly provocative and even offensive to many of those who had been most interested in Nietzsche's early literary career. Although *Human, All Too Human* was read with enthusiasm by a few of Nietzsche's closest friends, such as Burckhardt and Rée, even a longtime friend such as Erwin

---

10. On the relation of *Human, All Too Human* to Descartes, see Robert Rethy, "The Descartes Motto to the First Edition of *Menschliches, Allzumenschliches*," *Nietzsche-Studien* 5 (1976): 289–97.

Rohde saw Rée's influence as having had a pernicious effect upon Nietzsche's thinking. The Wagners' response is indicative of the intensity of reaction, or impassioned avoidance, that it provoked. Richard Wagner refused to read it; Cosima Wagner simply glanced through it before dismissing it, attributing its critical skepticism to the influence of Rée and his Semitic beliefs. Chapter 4's dissection of the soul of the artist would doubtless have offended them the most, with its portrayal of the artist as a child opposed to science, its contention that artistic genius was more a matter of hard work than a divine gift, and its blunt characterization of artists as "the glorifiers of the religious and philosophical errors of humanity" (Aphorism 220). Even the more sympathetic eyes of Malwida von Meysenbug, midwife to the text in a certain sense and present for much of its gestation, saw *Human, All Too Human* as essentially a stylistic phase, one among many that she quite presciently anticipated Nietzsche would go through in his philosophy, but altogether atypical for someone "not born to analysis like Rée."[11]

The most striking feature of *Human, All Too Human*'s immediate reception, though, is that it was read by so very few people at all. By June 1879, Nietzsche's publisher had to report to him that only 120 of the 1,000 printed copies had been sold. Its fame and influence grew only retrospectively, under the impact of Nietzsche's later works. Nor has the situation changed much in the intervening years; this text remains the least well-known, least critically digested of Nietzsche's major works. This neglect may stem in part from the fact that *Human, All Too Human* seems all too continuous with Nietzsche's later work, anticipating ideas and themes that critics have found more fully developed in those later texts, thus giving them a justification for treating it as significant primarily in terms of Nietzsche's intellectual development, rather than as supplementing in any essential way the subsequent works.

But the neglect of this text almost certainly has a great deal

---

11. Letter of June 1878 to Nietzsche.

to do with its second scandalous feature, the seemingly "un-Nietzschean" style that pervades it. It is telling that the longest extended discussion of Voltaire contained in a text dedicated to his memory focuses on the French writer's stylistic self-discipline. Aphorism 221 praises his "moderation" and his "Greek aesthetic conscientiousness," justifying even the "strict constraint" of French neoclassical drama as a necessary artistic schooling, and Aphorism 195 argues that severe rhetorical self-restraint is particularly necessary now, when centuries of linguistic inflation and emotive exaggeration have debased the language that we use. "Rigorous deliberation, terseness, coldness, plainness, intentionally sustained to their very limits, the restraint of feeling and taciturnity in general—that alone can help." It was this cool and detached style as much as the philosophical content that seemed to shock Nietzsche's initial readers. Nietzsche's friend Erwin Rohde had earlier critiqued the excesses of style that he felt marred *Unfashionable Observations*, contributing perhaps to the stylistic restraint that characterizes much of *Human, All Too Human*.[12] When confronted with this new text, however, Rohde seemed to feel that Nietzsche had gone too far in the opposite direction. He described its effect upon him in a striking bodily metaphor, as an almost visceral reaction similar to "being hunted from a *calidarium* into an ice-cold *frigidarium*," a painful experience in which he felt he could no longer recognize the author.[13]

Nietzsche himself anticipated this ambivalent reaction and accurately assessed its cause. Yet even he felt a certain alienation in contemplating what he had produced. A discarded preface from 1877 describes his feelings as those of an author confronting his own text with surprise and being forced to ask "Is that I? Is that not I?" as if he were looking into the eyes

12. See Rohde's letter of 24 March 1874.

13. Letter of 16 June 1878 to Nietzsche. *Calidarium* and *frigidarium* literally mean "hot place" and "cold place," respectively; the terms refer to the warm pool and cooling pool (or room) of a Roman bathhouse.

of a child he knows to be his and yet finds at one moment to be uncanny, at the next essentially harmless.[14] The source of this puzzling estrangement, according to that preface, lies not just in what the free spirit says, but in the curiously dispassionate voice in which he speaks. "The modern free spirit is not, like his ancestors, born out of conflict, but instead out of the *peace of the dissolution* into which he sees all the spiritual powers of the old, constrained world having passed." *Human, All Too Human* has to seem a curious detour for those impressed by the enthusiastic rhetorical flights and the polemical flair of Nietzsche's earlier (or later) works. There are, to be sure, moments of stylistic ascent here as well, most often at the end of specific chapters, with their evocative glances toward the future. But more than any other of Nietzsche's texts, *Human, All Too Human* maintains a plain, straightforward style and a coldness of tone that seem never to have seduced many readers. A curious exercise in self-control, it can scarcely be made to fit into the image that most readers have of Nietzsche as a writer. As *Ecce Homo* describes the intellectual process here, "one error after another is calmly laid upon ice; the ideal is not refuted — it is frozen to death." The "belligerent postures" and "pathos" of Nietzsche's own early prose seem to him, from this interim vantage point, to themselves be part of — idealism.[15]

This stylistic self-discipline affects in important ways not just the language of the text, but its form as well. *Human, All Too Human* marks a crucially important stylistic shift for Nietzsche to the aphorism, a stylistic breakthrough in his work where the influence of the French moralists can again be ascertained. Even in his earliest works, Nietzsche's mode of thought tends toward the sort of intellectual flexibility that the aphorism enables. Thus, the shifts and turns of Nietzsche's prose in *Unfashionable Observations* are altogether characteristic of his writing: his language adopts different guises and his discourse argues

---

14. Notebook entry of fall 1877, 25 [2].
15. *Ecce Homo*, 323.

opposed positions in a way that can make the argumentative thread of his own thinking quite difficult to ascertain. That stylistic habit may well have been intensified by the particular constraints imposed by Nietzsche's physical condition during this period, since he had for various extended periods found himself forced to dictate to Köselitz material that he was himself unable to write down. As Curt Paul Janz has noted, this arrangement led Nietzsche to compose in a manner similar to the way that he had improvised music, working over pieces of prose again and again in his mind until he had the opportunity to have Köselitz write them out.[16] Yet that compositional necessity was transformed into a stylistic choice through Nietzsche's engagement with La Rochefoucauld and other masters of the aphorism, whose stylistic polish, verbal sharpness, and ironic turns Nietzsche greatly admired, as Aphorism 35 makes clear.

As with the moralists' ideas and methodology, however, Nietzsche made the aphoristic form very much his own. The greater part of *Human, All Too Human* does not really present maxims in the French style, each honed to ironic sharpness, each largely self-contained or connected only in loose thematic ways to others, but presents extended prose passages that often read more like mini-essays. Although certain sections, especially in Chapters 6, 7, and 9, more closely approximate his French models, Nietzsche's aphorisms typically carry a continuous line of thought from one section to the next, pursuing some particular idea through various perspectives in a logically coherent and rigorous way. Although he often deploys the condensed formulations favored by his French predecessors, these aphoristic nodes typically serve as a starting point for reflection rather than as a detached distillation of it. Aphorism 104 provides a good instance of Nietzsche's oscillation between terseness and commentary. He takes up aphorisms by Lichtenberg and La Rochefoucauld not in order to outdo their sty-

---

16. Curt Paul Janz, *Friedrich Nietzsche* (Munich: Carl Hanser Verlag, 1978), 1: 713–14.

listic flourish, but to explicate the psychological logic behind their spare observation that even the most altruistic behavior has an egotistical motive somewhere behind it. As much in these matters of form as in its philosophical concerns, *Human, All Too Human* shows the continued influence upon Nietzsche's thought of Schopenhauer, whose *Parerga and Paralipomena* is the single text most often cited by Nietzsche in this work. The subtitle for its second volume, *Stray Yet Systematically Arranged Thoughts on a Variety of Subjects*, provides a perfect description for Nietzsche's text as well, and the stylistic flexibility deriving from an "aphoristic" mode that ranges from a single sentence to more than ten pages in length allows Schopenhauer to blend the philosophical wit of the French moralists with his own more sustained and more explicitly systematic philosophical analysis.

Equally crucial for Nietzsche is the fact that the aphorism form allows that analysis to proceed in a distinctively interruptive mode, turning back on itself from section to section and abruptly shifting direction as Nietzsche moves to incorporate new considerations into his analysis.[17] Hence, the sequence of individual aphorisms and the shaping of those turns were matters of major importance for Nietzsche. His concern for the organizational structure of the whole can be seen in the multiple, often quite varied plans for arranging the aphorisms that his notebooks contain. Given Nietzsche's own attention to this matter, maintaining the internal form of the aphorisms, which provide no further subdivision by paragraphing, even in those aphorisms that run several pages in length, is crucial to the integrity of Nietzsche's text. The aphorism enacts at the level of form a quite specific reflective procedure; it presents concentrated bursts of thought set one against the other by the space for reflection that exists between them.

---

17. The complexity of these movements becomes evident in the detailed mapping of the first chapter that Peter Heller provides.

When reviewing *Human, All Too Human* for republication in 1886, Nietzsche made a number of significant changes—the most significant being the combination of two later works, *The Wanderer and His Shadow* and *Mixed Opinions and Maxims*, into what became Part 2 of this text (and which will appear as volume 4 of the *Collected Works*). He added a new preface and a concluding poem, thus framing the text with his own words rather than with those of others. At the same time, he deleted the quotation from Descartes, the dedication to Voltaire, and the introductory statement about the text's origin that had originally served to position this work. He also revised the first three aphorisms extensively, as the variants found in the notes indicate. Yet the fact that those subsequent revisions are more stylistic than substantive may provide the best evidence for how fully *Human, All Too Human* anticipates Nietzsche's later thought. The terms may be a bit more finely tuned, the critique a bit more sharply pointed, the names more specific. But the changes serve mostly to emphasize the continuity of his perspectives across that decade and to underscore how persistent was the reorientation in his life and thought to which *Human, All Too Human* testifies.

Index of Persons

In this index an "f" after a number indicates a separate reference on the next page, and an "ff" indicates separate references on the next two pages. A continuous discussion over two or more pages is indicated by a span of page numbers, e.g., "57–59." *Passim* is used for a cluster of references in close but not consecutive sequence.

Achilles, Greek hero and central figure of Homer's *Iliad*, 140, 178, 340

Aeschylus (ca. 525–456 B.C.), Greek tragedian, 97, 121, 129, 177

Anaximander (ca. 610–547 B.C.), Greek pre-Socratic philosopher, 177

Aphrodite, Greek goddess of love, 109, 332, 346

Archilochus (ca. 8th–7th c. B.C.), Greek satiric poet, 331

Aristophanes (444–380 B.C.), Greek comic dramatist, 97, 355

Aristotle (384–322 B.C.), Greek philosopher and scientist, 141, 178, 180, 340

Aspasia (ca. 5th c. B.C.), Greek courtesan, 230

Augustine, Saint (354–430), Christian bishop and philosopher, 358

Baer, Karl Ernst von (1792–1876), German naturalist, 181, 340

Bach, Johann Sebastian (1685–1750), German baroque composer, 146

Beethoven, Ludwig van (1770–1827), German Romantic composer, 117f, 130, 333f, 336

Bernini, Lorenzo (1598–1680), Italian baroque artist and architect, 122, 336

Bismarck, Otto von (1815–98), Prussian chancellor 1871–90, 242

Böcklin, Arnold (1827–1901), German landscape painter, 335

Boethius, Anicius Manlius Severinus (ca. 470–525), Roman philosopher and consul, 314

Braddon, Mary Elizabeth (1837–1915), British sentimental novelist, 335

INDEX OF PERSONS

Buddha (ca. 5th c. B.C.), 286

Byron, Lord, George Gordon (1788–1824), English Romantic poet, 86, 150, 229, 330, 336f

Caesar, Julius (100–44 B.C.), Roman general and statesman, 125

Calderón de la Barca, Pedro (1600–1681), 109, 332

Calvin, John (1509–64), French Reformation theologian, 77

Carlyle, Thomas (1795–1881), Scottish historian, essayist, and critic, 318

Cato, Marcus Porcius (234–149 B.C.), Roman statesman and orator, 348

Cellini, Benvenuto (1500–1571), Italian sculptor and goldsmith, 175, 339

Chamfort, Sébastien Roch Nicolas de (1740–94), French moral philosopher, 323

Circe, sorceress in Homer's *Odyssey*, 270

Dante Alighieri (1265–1321), Italian epic poet, 354

Demeter, Greek goddess of agriculture, 93

Democritus (ca. 460–361 B.C.), Greek natural philosopher, 25, 178

Demosthenes (ca. 384–322 B.C.), Greek orator and statesman, 135, 177

Descartes, René (1596–1650), French philosopher and mathematician, 311

Diogenes of Sinope (ca. 412–323 B.C.), Greek Cynical philosopher, 246

Dion (4th c. B.C.), Greek confidant of Dionysus, later tyrant of Syracuse, 350

Dionysus, Greek god of wine and fertility, 93

Dionysus (430–367 B.C.), Greek tyrant and ruler of Syracuse, 350

Empedocles (ca. 490–430 B.C.), Greek philosopher and poet, 109, 177, 332

Epictetus (ca. 1st c. A.D.), Stoic philosopher, 190

Epicurus (342–270 B.C.), Greek natural and moral philosopher, 63

Erasmus, Desiderius (1466–1536), Dutch Christian humanist, 36

Eris, Greek goddess of strife, 129

Euripides (485–407 B.C.), Greek tragedian, 129

Feuerbach, Ludwig (1804–72), German philosopher, 342

Frederick the Great (1740–86), king of Prussia, 169

Goethe, Johann Wolfgang von (1749–1832), German classical poet, novelist, playwright, and natural philosopher, 89f, 97, 123, 148–51, 181, 185, 189, 294, 298, 321, 330, 334, 337, 340f, 346, 356, 358

Hartmann, Eduard von (1842–1906), German metaphysical philosopher, 321

Hegel, Georg Wilhelm Friedrich

(1770–1831), German idealist philosopher, 317

Hegesias, of Magnesia (4th c. B.C.), Greek biographer of Alexander the Great, 334

Herodotus (5th c. B.C.), Greek historian, 326

Hesiod (8th c. B.C.), Greek epic poet, 225, 326, 347

Hildebert, of Lavardius (1056–1133), Archbishop of Tours, 331

Hillebrand, Karl (1829–84), German writer and journalist, 341

Hobbes, Thomas (1588–1679), British materialist philosopher, 349

Hölderlin, Johann Christian Friedrich (1770–1843), German classical poet, 175, 339

Homer (ca. 9th or 8th c. B.C.), Greek epic poet, 28, 51, 97, 118, 121, 140, 180, 319

Horace (65–8 B.C.), Latin lyric poet and satirist, 86, 320, 330

Hugo, Victor (1802–85), French Romantic novelist, 318

Hus, John (1369–1415), Czech priest, reformer and martyr, 164

Isis, Egyptian goddess of the earth and moon, 254, 302

Janssen, Pierre Jules (1824–1907), French astronomer and physician, 322

Jesus Christ, 53, 93, 113, 161–62, 258, 355

Kant, Immanuel (1724–1804), German Enlightenment philosopher, 30f, 34, 319, 324f

Lagarde, Paul de (1827–91), German orientalist and philosopher, 346

La Rochefoucauld, Duc de (1613–80), French moral philosopher, 43–45, 54–55, 102, 322f, 325, 331, 342

Leibniz, Gottfried Wilhelm (1646–1716), German philosopher, 352

Lessing, Gotthold Ephraim (1729–81), German dramatist and critic, 148

Lichtenberg, Georg Christoph (1742–99), German physicist and satirical writer, 102, 331, 342

Lubbock, Sir John (1834–1913), English naturalist and philosopher, 90, 330

Luther, Martin (1483–1546), German Augustinian friar who initiated the Reformation, 35, 163–64, 341

Machiavelli, Niccolò (1469–1527), Italian diplomat, philosopher, and writer, 154, 337

Mainländer, Philipp, pseudonym of Philipp Batz (1841–76), German philosopher, 321

Mandeville, Bernard de (1670–1733), British (Dutch-born) prose writer and philosopher, 351

Mérimée, Prosper (1803–70), French Romantic writer, 55, 244, 326, 349

Mirabeau, Honoré Gabriel

Riqueti, Comte de (1749-91), French statesman, 244

Montaigne, Michel Eyquem de (1533-92), French moral philosopher and essayist, 131, 342

Moreto y Cabaña, Don Agustin (1618-69), Spanish dramatist, 347

Napoleon Bonaparte (1769-1821), French general and emperor, 126, 252

Novalis, pen name of Friedrich von Hardenberg (1772-1801), German Romantic poet, 112, 332f

Palestrina, Giovanni Pierluigi (1525-94), Italian composer, 146

Pandora, Greek mythological figure of the first woman, 64

Parmenides (5th c. B.C.), Greek Eleatic philosopher, 177

Pascal, Blaise (1623-62), French mathematician, physicist, and religious philosopher, 190

Penelope, wife of Odysseus in the *Iliad*, 172

Pericles (495-429 B.C.), Greek statesman and orator, 175, 230, 257, 349

Perseus, Greek hero and slayer of Medusa, 175, 339

Petrarch, Francesco (1304-74), Italian humanist and lyric poet, 36

Pindar (ca. 518-446 B.C.), Greek lyric poet, 177, 340

Plato (ca. 428-348 B.C.), Greek philosopher, 54, 78, 126, 141, 177-78, 255f, 294, 324f, 329, 332, 334, 341-50 *passim*, 356

Plutarch (ca. 46-119), Greek biographer and historian, 44, 190, 342, 348

Polyhymnia, Greek muse, 146, 336

Pope, Alexander (1688-1744), British neoclassical poet and critic, 325

Prometheus, Greek titan, 338

Pythagoras (ca. 580-500 B.C.), Greek philosopher and mathematician, 177

Raphael (1483-1520), Italian painter and architect, 99, 123, 147

Rée, Paul (1849-1901), German moral philosopher, 323f

Rousseau, Jean-Jacques (1712-78), French novelist and political philosopher, 148, 248-49, 290

Sand, George, pen name of Aurore Dupin (1804-76), French Romantic novelist, 354

Sappho (ca. 6th c. B.C.), Greek lyric poet, 331

Schiller, Friedrich von (1759-1805), German classical poet, dramatist, and critic, 131, 148-49, 334

Schleiermacher, Friedrich (1768-1834), German Romantic philosopher and theologian, 100

Schopenhauer, Arthur (1788-1860), German philosopher, 6, 31, 35-36, 48, 57, 75, 79, 87, 162, 164, 172, 184, 313, 319-32 *passim*, 339, 341, 358

INDEX OF PERSONS

Scott, Sir Walter (1771–1832), British historical novelist, 329, 334

Seneca (4 B.C.–A.D. 65), Roman philosopher and tragedian, 190

Servetus, Michael (1511–53), Spanish anti-Calvinist, 77

Shakespeare, William (ca. 1564–1616), English poet and dramatist, 60, 97, 123, 131, 148–50, 337

Simonides (ca. 556–467 B.C.), Greek lyric poet, 118

Socrates (470–399 B.C.), Greek philosopher, 78, 97, 178, 210, 233, 235

Solon (ca. 639–559 B.C.), Greek statesman and legislator, 177

Sophocles (496–406 B.C.), Greek tragedian, 60

Spinoza, Baruch de (1632–77), Dutch-Jewish philosopher, 119, 258, 326

Spir, Afrikan (1837–90), German philosopher, 319

Stendhal, pen name of Henri Beyle (1783–1842), French Romantic novelist, 322f

Sterne, Laurence (1713–68), English satirical novelist, 339

Swift, Jonathan (1667–1745), Anglo-Irish satirist and political writer, 51, 57, 325f

Tacitus (ca. 56–120 B.C.), Roman historian, 350

Thales (ca. 636–546 B.C.), Greek pre-Socratic philosopher, 178

Theon, Aelius, Greek sophist and rhetorician, 333

Thucydides (ca. 471–401 B.C.), Greek historian, 70, 177, 326, 339, 349f

Vauvenargues, Luc de Clapier (1715–47), French moral philosopher, 368

Vilmar, August Friedrich Christian (1800–1868), German theologian and literary historian, 322

Voltaire, François-Marie Arouet de (1694–1778), French Enlightenment philosopher and writer, 36, 148, 165, 236, 249, 336, 348ff

Wagner, Richard (1813–83), German operatic composer, dramatist, and theorist, 6, 313, 318, 336, 341

Wieland, Christoph Martin (1733–1813), German poet and novelist, 335

Xanthippe (5th c. B.C.), wife of Socrates, 233–34

Xerxes (5th c. B.C.), Persian king, 67, 326

Zeno of Elea (ca. 495–430 B.C.), Greek Eleatic philosopher, 340

Zeus, supreme god of the ancient Greeks, 64

The Complete Works of Friedrich Nietzsche

IN TWENTY VOLUMES

1. The Birth of Tragedy/Early Writings
2. Unfashionable Observations I–IV
3. Human, All Too Human I
4. Human, All Too Human II
5. Dawn
6. The Gay Science
7. Thus Spoke Zarathustra
8. Beyond Good and Evil/
On the Genealogy of Morals
9. The Wagner Case/Twilight of the Idols/
The Antichrist/Ecce Homo/Dionysus
Dithyrambs/Nietzsche Contra Wagner
10. Unpublished Fragments:
From the Period of *The Birth of Tragedy*
11. Unpublished Fragments:
From the Period of *Unfashionable Observations*
12. Unpublished Fragments:
From the Period of *Human, All Too Human*
13. Unpublished Fragments:
From the Period of *Dawn*
14. Unpublished Fragments:
From the Period of *The Gay Science*
15. Unpublished Fragments:
From the Period of *Thus Spoke Zarathustra*
16. Unpublished Fragments:
From the Period of *Thus Spoke Zarathustra*
17. Unpublished Fragments:
From the Period of *Beyond Good and Evil*
18. Unpublished Fragments:
From the Period of *On the Genealogy of Morals*
19. Unpublished Fragments:
From the Period of the Late Writings
20. Unpublished Fragments:
From the Period of the Late Writings

Library of Congress
Cataloging-in-Publication Data

Nietzsche, Friedrich Wilhelm, 1844–1900.
[Menschliches, Allzumenschliches. English]
Human, all too human / Friedrich Nietzsche ;
translated, with an afterword, by Gary Handwerk.
p.   cm. — (The complete works of Friedrich
Nietzsche ; v. 3)
Includes bibliographical references and index.
ISBN 0-8047-2665-5 (cloth : alk. paper)
ISBN 0-8047-4171-9 (pbk : alk. paper)
1. Human beings.   I. Handwerk, Gary J.,
1954–   .   II. Title.   III. Series: Nietzsche,
Friedrich Wilhelm, 1844–1900. Works. English.
1997 ; v. 3.
B3313.M52N5413   1997
128—dc20   96-31901   CIP

⊚ This book is printed on acid-free paper
Original printing 1997